Guided By Angel Numbers

Olga Gerogianni

GUIDED BY ANGEL NUMBERS

Contents

Channelled messages from my Spirit Guides for my book, through free writing.

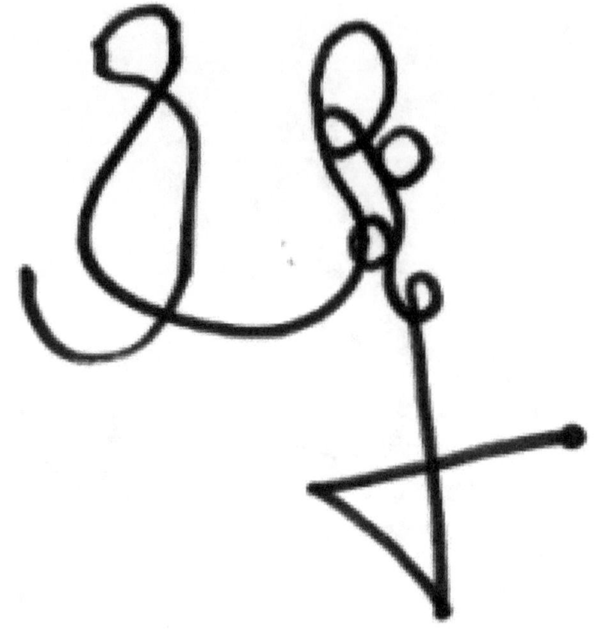

Guess who is the Mantis!
Dedicated to my Spirit Guides
Ela and Zinx

Contents

"I hope this book not only deepens your love for numbers but also reveals their true significance—from the structure of our Universe to the guidance we receive daily. Angel numbers are more than symbols; they are messengers guiding us on our paths, whispering that we are never alone. Trust your intuition, for it is the language of your soul, and know that you are always supported. May this book be the catalyst for the change you've been seeking, leading you closer to your authentic self and the life you're destined to live."

1

Understanding the Angel Numbers

I'm so thrilled to share this book with you! Writing it has been a significant part of my spiritual journey. During this time, I've connected with my higher self and fully embraced who I am and my life's mission. But don't worry. I'll share all the details as we embark on this magical journey with Angel Numbers together, hoping that you will also add more pieces to the puzzle of your spiritual awakening journey.

I can sense your excitement!

You're probably reading this book because Angel Numbers have made their presence felt in your life in a way that's both undeniable and profound. You might be wondering, "What's happening?" Let me assure you, you're not alone in this. And I mean that in two ways. Firstly, there are so many others out there who are experiencing these incredible encounters just like you. Secondly, and more importantly, you're never truly alone.

As the name implies, Angel Numbers originate from a higher plane. Whenever you encounter these sequences of numbers, it feels as if a watchful presence is trying to communicate with you. Although they are called 'Angel Numbers', suggesting a celestial source, we will explore their deeper meanings and origins further in this book. The Messengers of the Angel Numbers are always with us, guiding and supporting us on our journey. So, let's dive into this adventure together and discover the beautiful messages these numbers have for us!

In this book, we're diving into the fascinating world of Angel Numbers. These aren't just random digits; they're special sequences that somehow find their way into our lives, often when we least expect them.

For example:

You're enjoying your morning coffee, casually glancing at the clock, and bam! It's 11:11. It's not just the time that catches your eye – it's the symmetry, the uniqueness of this sequence. It almost feels like time pauses for a moment, urging you to notice these numbers.

But wait, there's more! As you're driving to work, trying not to be any later than you already are, something peculiar happens. Out of the blue, your gaze lands on a car's registration plate, and guess what? It's the same number sequence! '1111' again! You can't help but wonder, "Am I going crazy?" This is totally new for you. I mean, you've looked at clocks and car plates countless times before, but never like this. It's as if these numbers are following you, calling out to you in a way that's impossible to ignore.

1.1 Defining Angel Numbers: What They Are and Their Significance

Angel Numbers represent a unique phenomenon during our spiritual awakening journey. These are number sequences that are formed by repeated numbers, usually with three or four digits. For example, 222 or 22:22. When they appear, they instantly capture our attention in a way that's hard to ignore. They aren't related to the usual figures we encounter, such as birthdays or anniversaries. While they might occasionally align with specific dates or moments in our lives, Angel Numbers are something different.

Angel Numbers possess certain distinct characteristics that make them stand out in our everyday lives. These characteristics are essential in understanding how these numbers work and their significance in our spiritual journey.

1. **Frequency of Appearance**

   One of the most striking characteristics of Angel Numbers is how frequently they appear. You may notice the same sequence of numbers showing up repeatedly in your life, often in different combinations that blend together. Whether it's on a clock, a license plate, or a receipt, these numbers consistently emerge. This repeated occurrence is not mere coincidence; it is a deliberate pattern designed to capture your attention.

2. **Attention-Grabbing Nature**

   Angel Numbers are designed to stand out. They typically appear in a three- or four-digit sequence, which instantly draws your attention away from the mundane and toward the spiritual. These aren't just random numbers; they're patterned in such a way that they're hard to ignore, especially once you start noticing them. Additionally, when Angel Numbers appear, they have a unique way of making time feel as if it has paused, further accentuating their significance and demanding our attention.

3. **Timing of Their Appearance**

   The moments when these numbers appear are just as important as the numbers themselves. They often show up during pivotal periods in our lives, or when we're grappling with specific issues, problems, or seeking answers to our deepest questions. The timing of their appearance is a gentle nudge from the universe, signalling that these numbers hold answers or guidance pertinent to what we're experiencing at that moment.

In essence, Angel Numbers are more than mere coincidences. They're a synchronistic way of receiving guidance and assurance from the universe, tailored specifically to our personal journey and spiritual growth. As I often say to my clients:

Angel Numbers are a communication system created in a simple yet universally accepted way, to guide us.

Picture this: You're at a critical juncture in your life where everything seems to be falling apart. You're desperate for a solution, yet you feel utterly powerless. Internally, you're constantly asking yourself what the escape route could be. Carrying these thoughts, you step out of your house to go about your daily routine. You're going about your day, and suddenly, you notice 444 on a billboard, then the same number sequence on a receipt, and later on a clock. It's like these numbers are following you, but not in a spooky way – more like a gentle nudge from the universe. They've been part of the scenery of your life all along. It could even be your neighbour's house number, which you see every day, but for an unknown reason, that specific moment stands out to you, as you saw the 444 many times in recent days, in different ways. It's as if these numbers are demanding your attention.

The key to understanding Angel Numbers lies in their repetitive and synchronistic appearance. They often show up during times of contemplation and when you're seeking answers or guidance. It's like they're trying to tell you something, offer comfort, or point you in a direction you hadn't considered.

Every Angel Number sequence vibrates with its own energy and meaning. They aren't just random numbers; they are messages from a higher realm – a way for the universe to communicate with you. For example, seeing 222 might be a reminder to seek balance, while 555 could signify imminent changes.

To truly grasp the essence of Angel Numbers, it's essential to stay aware and open. Notice patterns, pay attention to how you feel when you see these numbers, and consider what thoughts or questions were in your mind at that moment. This chapter will delve deeper into these mystical sequences, helping you decode their spiritual significance and integrate their wisdom into your life's journey.

1.2 Angel Numbers and Numerology

Angel Numbers are often mistakenly thought to be interpreted solely through the methods of numerology. Sacred geometry and numerology are ancient systems that reveal how numbers and shapes create patterns in both nature and consciousness. These principles suggest that numbers are not just mathematical constructs but also universal codes, interwoven with life's design *(Lawlor, 1982)*. While we do apply numerological meanings to understand the energies of these numbers, the approach to decoding Angel Numbers is distinct.

In traditional numerology, numbers are frequently combined to form new numbers, such as summing the digits of a birth date to identify one's Life Path Number. For example, if your birthdate is 23rd May 1980, you would calculate it as follows: $2+3+5+1+9+8+0 = 28$, then $2+8 = 10$, and finally $1+0 = 1$. Your Life Path Number would be 1, which is believed to reveal significant aspects of your personal attributes and life journey.

However, this method does not apply to Angel Numbers. Angel Numbers are presented exactly as they should be; we receive their messages in full through the sequences that appear to us. In decoding them, we use the symbolism of each individual number as in numerology, but without altering them through addition or other mathematical operations. This makes the message clearer and more direct. What we are called to decode is precisely the message conveyed by the given sequence of Angel Numbers, without any need for further mathematical manipulation.

For example, when you see the sequence 222 repeatedly, it is presented exactly as it needs to be without any reduction or combination. This number is often interpreted as a sign of balance, faith, and encouragement. It suggests that you are in a phase of life where you need to keep faith and continue along your path despite any difficulties. This number might appear during times of doubt or uncertainty, indicating that you should persevere and maintain harmony in your relationships and endeavours. The message from 222 is direct and clear, focusing on stability and reassurance without needing to dissect or alter the number through additional calculations.

1.3 The Matrix

To fully engage with the realm of Angel Numbers, it's imperative to first navigate through the concept of the Matrix, a notion that has profoundly impacted our understanding of reality. The Matrix, as vividly portrayed in the acclaimed film series, unveils a dystopian reality where the world as humans perceive it is nothing but a simulated environment crafted by supremely intelligent machines. This simulated reality, where humans exist oblivious to their actual conditions, living lives they believe to be authentic, raises profound philosophical inquiries about the nature of reality, consciousness, and the authenticity of our experiences. Within this simulation, individuals lead their lives as avatars, completely unaware that their perceptions and senses are meticulously controlled and manipulated.

This concept of the Matrix serves as a compelling metaphor for the limitations and illusions that shape our perceived reality, challenging us to question the authenticity of our experiences and the world that surrounds us. By drawing parallels to philosophical and scientific discussions around simulation theory, the narrative suggests that our existence might closely resemble that of the Matrix—a complex digital construct under the surveillance of higher forms of intelligence. This framework implies that what we consider our free will and individuality might just be elements of a larger, intricate design where we, akin to avatars, navigate through a scripted existence, blind to our role in a broader scheme.

When we connect this understanding of the Matrix to Angel Numbers, the narrative deepens, revealing a more intricate relationship between our perceived reality and the mystical. Angel Numbers emerge as subtle beacons within this vast simulation, guiding us towards an awakening and the realisation of our true selves, beyond the avatars we embody. They appear as gentle nudges from the universe—or perhaps from the architects of our reality—intended to help us pierce through the illusion, recognise our authentic paths, and uncover the deeper layers of our existence.

The allure of Angel Numbers becomes increasingly evident as we peel back the layers of our reality. These numbers manifest at pivotal moments, imbued with messages tailored specifically for us, prompting a series of profound questions: Who sends these numbers our way? How are they so precisely crafted to capture our attention? What messages do they bear? And why are we chosen as the recipients? This inquiry invites us to consider a broader perspective of our existence, one that extends far beyond the confines of the physical world we know.

In exploring the concept of the Matrix, as illuminated by insights from my Spirit Guides, an alternate view of our existence unfolds—one not characterised by confinement but as a vibrant, dynamic space shaped by our decisions. This perspective suggests that our free will plays a significant role in moulding the world around us, akin to being participants in a video game where the narrative evolves based on our choices.

Consider the creation of a video game. A team of developers and engineers collaborates, each lending their expertise to different aspects of the game. Among them are specialists focused on ensuring that the actions within the game maintain its equilibrium. Players enter this world, controlling characters that seemingly act independently, making choices that feel entirely their own. Yet, these characters operate under the illusion of freedom, occasionally sensing a connection to something larger than themselves, hinting at a more profound reality.

These characters are endowed with extraordinary abilities, enabling them to alter their environment, similar to how audiences can influence the direction of interactive movies. Their decisions, thoughts, and actions have significant repercussions on the game's universe, influencing not only their own experiences but also those of other characters within the game.

Now, imagine being one of the engineers responsible for the seamless operation of this game. Your task is to communicate with the characters subtly, guiding them without breaking their immersion. Revealing too much could compromise their perception of reality and diminish their engagement with the game. Your initial attempts at communication might involve subtle repetitions in the game's environment, like a consistently appearing bird, to introduce the concept of "coincidences." These efforts aim to guide the characters, encouraging them to recognise these signs as meaningful directions.

As the characters become more aware, you introduce numerical sequences as a new method of communication, observing whether they recognise and respond to these signals. However, not every character is ready to fully comprehend their reality while still enjoying the game. Therefore, your approach must be carefully calibrated, offering just enough insight to foster understanding and engagement without disclosing too much too soon.

This video game analogy helps us comprehend how Spirit Guides might communicate with us within the framework of our reality. They utilise numbers as subtle indicators to shepherd us through our awakening process. These Angel Numbers are meticulously crafted to lead us towards enlightenment at a pace that suits us, ensuring we are not overwhelmed by the revelations they entail.

By contemplating our existence within such a dynamic Matrix, where our free will is pivotal, we begin to appreciate the significance and beauty of Angel Numbers. These numbers are not mere random sequences; they are messages specifically designed for each of us, sent at the right moments to guide, reassure, and occasionally challenge us to evolve. They form part of a sophisticated communication system, devised to help us navigate our life's journey more consciously and in alignment with our deeper purpose.

In essence, the Matrix, when viewed from this enlightened perspective, represents not a barrier but a realm filled with opportunities for growth and understanding. Angel Numbers act as our personal guideposts, decoding the deeper meanings of our experiences and the world around us. As we become more attuned to these messages, we unlock a deeper understanding of our place in the universe and the interconnectedness of all things, demonstrating that our existence, when viewed through this enlightened lens, is a journey of discovery and self-realisation far beyond the confines of any simulated reality.

1.4: Hacking the Matrix with Numbers – The Power of 0010110

As we explore the concept of the Matrix, we start to recognize how deeply the numerical sequences that we encounter are woven into the fabric of our reality. Beyond Angel Numbers, there are certain codes—referred to as "Matrix Hack Numbers"—that are said to disrupt the illusions of the simulated world we exist within. When understood and applied correctly, these codes can 'hack' into the underlying structure of reality, revealing hidden truths and influencing the outcomes of our experiences. Among the most notable of these codes is the sequence 0010110, often referred to as the "Binary Code of Awakening."

The concept of hacking the Matrix stems from the understanding that our reality, as perceived, might be akin to a simulation. Within this framework, numbers like 0010110 are more than random digits; they serve as keys or commands within the system that governs our world. Just as a programmer can alter the functioning of a software by entering a specific sequence of code, individuals can potentially alter their perception and experience of reality by tapping into these numbers.

0010110: The Binary Code of Awakening

The number 0010110 has gained prominence among those who seek to break free from the limitations of the Matrix and awaken to a deeper, more expansive understanding of existence. Often described as the code for spiritual awakening, it is believed that repeating or meditating on this number sequence can trigger a shift in consciousness, helping individuals step outside the bounds of illusion and see the truth of their existence.

But what does 0010110 truly mean, and why is it so significant?

In the realm of numerology, 0 represents potential and infinity, while 1 signifies new beginnings and creation. Together, these numbers create a dynamic interplay between the formless void (0) and the act of creation (1). The sequence 0010110 is thought to act as a gateway between these two states—helping individuals transition from the illusions of the simulated world into a state of awareness, where they can tap into their own power as creators of their reality.

The appearance of 0010110 is often described as a sign that a significant shift is occurring within the individual. It signals that the person is on the verge of breaking free from the programmed patterns of their existence and is ready to step into a new level of awareness. This awakening can take many forms, including enhanced intuition, deeper spiritual insight, or a sudden realization of one's purpose and potential in life.

Practical Uses of 0010110

Many people who resonate with the concept of Matrix hacking use 0010110 as a tool in their daily lives. It can be recited as a mantra, written down in journals, or visualized during meditation. The idea is to imprint the energy of this code into your subconscious, allowing it to work on a deeper level to alter your perception and connection to the universe.

- *Meditation:* Sit quietly and focus on the number 0010110. Visualize it in your mind, and feel the energy it brings. Many believe that meditating on this number can open new pathways in your consciousness, helping you see beyond the surface of reality.

- *Affirmation*: Repeating 0010110 as a personal mantra can align your thoughts with the deeper truths of existence. Saying it aloud or silently to yourself can serve as a reminder that you are not bound by the limitations of the Matrix.
- *Daily Intention*: Begin your day by writing 0010110 on a piece of paper or setting it as a reminder on your phone. Use it as an intention to remain aware and conscious throughout your day, questioning the nature of your reality and staying connected to your higher self.

The Deeper Meaning Behind Matrix Hack Numbers

Numbers like 0010110 are not simply seen as symbols; they are understood to be vibrational frequencies that carry the power to influence both the material and spiritual worlds. They bridge the gap between these dimensions, offering insights and transformations to those who are ready to awaken from the simulation.

The application of Matrix Hack Numbers like 0010110 points to a profound realization—that reality, as we know it, is malleable. It is shaped by our thoughts, beliefs, and the codes that govern it. By tapping into these codes, we gain the power to shape our lives consciously, moving beyond the pre-programmed scripts and limitations that may have previously defined us.

In this way, 0010110 acts as both a key and a signal—a key to unlocking deeper levels of awareness and a signal that the time for awakening has arrived. It reminds us that the Matrix, while seemingly rigid and inescapable, is not the ultimate truth. We are far more than the avatars we inhabit. We are conscious beings with the ability to transcend and transform the reality we experience.

1.5: The Power of Grabovoi Numbers

As we continue to explore the realm of numerical codes and their influence on reality, another powerful system emerges—the use of *Grabovoi Numbers*. Created by the Russian mathematician Grigori

Grabovoi, these numerical sequences are designed to manifest specific outcomes, heal ailments, and restore harmony to different aspects of life, *(Grabovoi, 2003)*. The belief behind Grabovoi Numbers is that numbers carry vibrational energies, and by tapping into these frequencies, individuals can align themselves with the desired outcome—whether it be physical healing, financial abundance, or emotional well-being.

Even though they are rarely encountered as angel numbers, I find them fascinating as a numerical concept.

Grabovoi Numbers function as a type of numerical "programming" for reality. Just as a computer responds to a command, the universe responds to these sequences when they are used with intention and focus. By writing down, repeating, or meditating on specific Grabovoi Numbers, you can align yourself with the frequency of what you want to manifest in your life.

Understanding How Grabovoi Numbers Work

Grabovoi's approach is rooted in the belief that everything in the universe has a mathematical code that defines its structure and existence. By accessing these codes, we can affect changes at the energetic and vibrational levels, bringing about healing and transformation. Each sequence of numbers corresponds to a specific intention or desire, ranging from healing illnesses to attracting financial success.

The power of Grabovoi Numbers lies in their precision. Each number in the sequence is carefully chosen to resonate with the frequency of the outcome you wish to manifest. Whether you're seeking to heal a chronic illness, attract wealth, or improve your relationships, there's a specific Grabovoi Number that corresponds to that goal.

Practical Application of Grabovoi Numbers

There are several methods for working with Grabovoi Numbers, all of which involve focusing your energy and intention on the desired outcome. Here are a few common ways people use these numbers:

1. *Writing the Numbers: One* of the simplest ways to work with Grabovoi Numbers is to write them down on paper. Some people choose to write them daily in a journal, while others write them on sticky notes and place them around their home or workspace.
2. *Visualizing the Numbers:* Another effective method is visualization. Close your eyes, take a deep breath, and visualize the sequence of numbers in your mind's eye. See the numbers glowing with energy and feel yourself aligning with their vibration.
3. *Repeating the Numbers Aloud:* Just as affirmations have power, repeating Grabovoi Numbers aloud can help imprint their energy into your subconscious. You can repeat them as a mantra during meditation or while doing daily tasks.

A List of Common Grabovoi Numbers and Their Uses

Love & Relationships	
8884121289018	Attracting a romantic partner
5254917	Harmonizing relationships
888874888	Unconditional love
285555901	Restoring love in a relationship
548491	Meeting your soulmate
Career & Success	
9148148	Success in your career
318514517618	Success in career and life
71974131981	Manifesting success

52243657569	Finding your life's purpose
498518498	Attracting opportunities

Protection

9187756981818	Protection from negativity
71974131947	Shielding from harmful influences
8947197848	Spiritual and energetic protection
11179	Universal safety and security
9187948181	Protection for loved ones

General Healing

9187948181	Healing and restoration
4812412	Physical and emotional healing
2145432	General health improvement
567432198	Accelerating recovery
8154891	Perfect health and holistic balance

Weight Loss & Fitness

4812412	Ideal body weight
1891014	Weight loss and fat reduction
5343168	Boosting metabolism

8234941	Success in body transformation
498518498	Strength and physical fitness

Gratitude & Happiness

519608719	Gratitude and appreciation
888885888	Joy and happiness
719741319	Manifesting positive emotions
214543719	Inner peace and gratitude
975318537	Universal harmony and happiness

Money & Wealth

5207418	Financial flow
71427321893	Attraction of wealth
318798	Manifesting money
4264998	Abundance and prosperity
8974989	Success in financial matters
520	Sudden money or unexpected financial gain
741	Solution to financial problems

Success in studies & Learning

212585212	Success in education
319817318	Enhanced learning abilities

71381921	Concentration and focus
914285714	Memory improvement
914318319	Academic success

Spiritual Growth and Awakening

719317218	Spiritual enlightenment
8884121289018	Aligning with higher consciousness
214317489	Awakening inner potential
5197148	Connecting with divine energy
817498198	Accelerating spiritual growth

Emotional & Mental Health

48971281948	Emotional balance
514248538	Mental clarity and focus
318514517	Overcoming anxiety
814418918	Emotional healing
519471941	Inner peace and resilience
5197148	Relief from depression
489514821	Positive thinking and optimism
8145432	Stress relief and relaxation
318612518	Emotional stability and calmness

218341211	Mental peace and serenity

Miracles & Divine Interventions

777	Manifestation of miracles
5197148	Divine intervention
8888888	Infinite blessings and miracles
7180197	Realisation of miraculous events
91481988	Connection with divine guidance
777888	aligning with higher frequencies of miracles and abundance

Manifesting Desires

741	Manifestation of goals
498714	Attracting desired outcomes
5197148	Fulfilment of wishes
318798	Manifesting success and abundance
9147198	Accelerating manifestations

Understanding the Angel Numbers

These are just a few of the many sequences attributed to Grabovoi's work, and people often adapt or find new codes based on their own needs. Some use these numbers in various ways, like writing them down, visualizing them, or repeating them as mantras.

While this practice has no scientific backing, many people claim to find personal or spiritual benefits from focusing on these numerical sequences.

In my belief, we have the power to infuse anything with our energy. If we strongly believe that, for example, the number *2145432* will promote tooth health, the more we focus our energy on that number, the more potent it becomes. Our intention, at the quantum level, carries energy in the form of frequency. This frequency has the potential to influence and charge a number positively (or negatively). The more we engage with this charged number, the more effective it becomes, ultimately manifesting the desired outcome.

1.6 My First Encounter with Vivid Angel Numbers

That particular point in my spiritual awakening journey remains vivid in my memory even now. I recall a day, etched clearly in my mind, when I kept seeing sequential number frequencies from early morning. It started at 11:11, and it continued in such an uncanny manner that I had to share it with a friend – I even have a screenshot of the message I sent, expressing my astonishment.

I remember reaching a point where I deliberately avoided my phone to escape these numbers, but the universe had

other plans. The numbers kept appearing—on my PC clock, on my husband's phone... it was relentless. I went to sleep that night with a final glance at my mobile, only to see one more Angel Number: 22:22. Then, the exact same thing happened the next morning to 11:11, followed by 12:12, and finally, it halted at 19:19. A whirlwind of emotions swept over me—excitement mingled with an undefined apprehension. I was clueless about what this prolonged occurrence of sequential numbers was trying to signal to me.

This unforgettable experience happened back in Janiary 2023. Little did I know, it was the beginning of a profound and transformative journey into the world of Angel Numbers.

1.7 When Angel Numbers Appear

Angel Numbers began to make their presence known to me during a pivotal moment in my life. This period marked a significant transition: I had just transitioned from managing a successful online business, which I had nurtured for four years and received multiple awards for, to opening my retail shop. This was a milestone I achieved independently, without financial assistance or support from my friends or family, in a new country where my husband and I were crafting a fresh start.

The appearance of Angel Numbers coincided with a time of introspection and ambition. One year after having accomplished the substantial goal of opening my shop, my mind was brimming with plans for further growth, both professionally and personally. My thoughts were steering towards business consulting, leveraging my two decades of business experience and academic background in Business Management.

But life had a different path in store for me. It was a moment of unexpected redirection, marked by a unique sequence of numbers that captured my attention. The timing of their appearance was particularly meaningful. At that time, I was becoming more open to embracing my mediumship abilities, which seemed to surface spontaneously. I would find myself connecting with souls linked to the clients shopping in the store, an unscheduled, natural ability that I was delighted to practice daily. With each encounter, my gift seemed to grow stronger. There I was, delivering spiritual messages to unsuspecting shoppers, watching their faces light up as the details I shared were confirmed. It was an ordinary afternoon in May 2023, just another regular day on my way home from the shop. The routine was familiar—same bus, same time, six days a week. And then, the numbers appeared. In Scotland, the scenery outside the bus window is too majestic to miss, so I always find myself gazing outside, especially since looking inside the bus or car makes me dizzy. But on this particular day, something unusual happened. As if guided by an unseen force, I felt an irresistible urge to turn my head and look at the bus panel. And there it was, a number sequence that I couldn't overlook—17:17 on the 17th of May. The triple appearance of 17 was striking. On the panel I was seeing: 17:17 17-5. This wasn't just a coincidence; it felt like a message intended for me. I even captured this moment in a video and shared it on my TikTok, expressing my excitement and intrigue. At that time, the full meaning of these numbers was unclear to me, but now, in retrospect, the message seems so obvious.

Trust me, when you finish this book, you will be in a place to easily decode these messages.

That day was more than just an encounter with a sequence of numbers. It marked the commencement of a deeply transformative journey—one that went beyond understanding Angel Numbers. It was the beginning of a profound path towards spiritual growth and connecting with my true self.

As you can see from my own experience described above, it's clear that Angel Numbers emerge in our lives precisely when we're in need of guidance. Their appearance is intricately linked with what is known as the Spiritual Awakening of our consciousness, a topic I will delve into more deeply later. Essentially, these numbers make their presence known to us when we are prepared and open to receiving the messages they carry.

1.8 The Change

As I had shared before, my thoughts were steering towards providing business consulting services. Having gained extensive experience in handling social media for my enterprise, Estia Soaps Ltd, the idea of venturing into video content began to take root in my mind. These videos would focus on kick-starting businesses, embracing independence, and transforming lives. Although English isn't my first language, I had to step out of my comfort zone and do it. This would be an approachable and helpful way to reach out to those eager to break free from the typical 9-5 routine and step into self-sufficiency. This venture felt like a natural progression, aligning with my skills and the knowledge I was keen to share. Even now, if you scroll down to my TikTok feed, you will see these first videos. That was before everything changed...

One particular day marked a turning point. I created a video unlike any I had made before. In it, I spoke to my modest but growing group of followers, sharing a message that was new and deeply personal: "Join me on this journey of transformation into my new self." It was that time when Angel Numbers had just begun appearing in my life. The nature of this video was uncharacteristic for me. I was in a state of mild confusion, not fully grasping why I felt compelled to make such a video. In retrospect, it seems as though it was a catalyst, a sub-conscious herald of my impending transformation, or perhaps even a premonition of the profound changes that lay ahead.

Back then, I didn't really understand what the Angel Numbers meant. I kept seeing these sequences of numbers, and they definitely caught my attention. But the idea that they were sending me a message? That never crossed my mind. It was just a bunch of numbers showing up in my life, or so I thought.

Reflecting on my journey now, I see things with newfound clarity. The Angel Numbers that once puzzled me have become a language I understand. Take, for example, the numbers I saw on the bus that day—the sequence of 1s and 7s. I now realise that these numbers were sending me a profound message about embarking on a new chapter in my life. The number 1 symbolised the beginning, a fresh start. And the number 7, deeply spiritual, signified a connection with my higher self, a beckoning towards spiritual enlightenment, not just awakening.

This sequence of 17 17 17 was a clear message of an impending new kind of enlightenment. It was an indication that my life was about to take a turn, but not in the direction I had anticipated. I had plans to expand my financial advice services, focusing on the practical, tangible aspects of my career. Yet, these Angel Numbers were gently steering me towards a different route, one that was more aligned with spiritual growth and transformation.

Back then, I was blind to this guidance. The Angel Numbers were there, consistently trying to steer me, but I lacked the knowledge to interpret their message. It's only in hindsight that their meaning becomes clear to me. They were nudging me towards embracing a spiritual path, one that would lead to a deeper understanding of myself and my purpose. And now, having traversed this path and learned the language of these numbers, I am here to help you decipher the messages hidden in the Angel Numbers that appear in your life.

2

The Spiritual Awakening Journey-Phase 1

You're likely starting to see how Angel Numbers have a special timing in our lives. They appear at moments perfectly aligned with our spiritual path. Whether it's the beginning of our spiritual awakening or a significant turning point, these numbers serve as a gentle nudge from the universe, waking up our consciousness to its true potential and purpose.

Imagine these numbers as markers on your life's journey, guiding you toward your life's purpose or even a pre-destined mission. It's a fascinating concept, and I understand if it feels a bit overwhelming at first. But there's no need to worry. I'm here to guide you through it all, step by step, in the upcoming chapters.

For now, let's delve into what 'Spiritual Awakening' really means. It's a term that gets thrown around a lot, but understanding its essence is key to grasping the whole concept of Angel Numbers. A spiritual awakening is like opening a door to a new dimension of perception and understanding, where you become more aware of the deeper truths of life and your place in the universe. It's an incredible journey, and Angel Numbers are one of the ways the universe helps us navigate this path. So, let's take this journey together and explore the fascinating world of spiritual awakening.

Spiritual awakening is a deeply individual experience, unique to each of us. Much like the journey of understanding Angel Numbers, it unfolds in various stages. This book, while primarily focused on Angel Numbers, will touch upon some aspects of this mystical journey. The insights I share are drawn from a deep, hidden well of knowledge that I've awakened, along with a profound connection to my Spirit Guides.

My understanding of spiritual awakening revolves around two key concepts: **Remembering** and **Activation**. It's about recalling your true essence—where your soul comes from and what it has learned through its journey so far. This process also involves activating the purpose or mission you are meant to fulfil in this lifetime. (I'll dive deeper into these concepts in the upcoming chapters.) It's a journey embarked upon after a pivotal event that shifts your perception of reality. For many, it begins with the loss of a loved one or a tragic event, leading to questions about life, death, and what lies beyond. For others, it's a quest for a missing sense of purpose, a dive into the rabbit hole where they start to see that the world isn't quite what we've been led to believe, and the reality we perceive might be an illusion.

The journey of spiritual awakening varies in pace for each individual. While some might rapidly traverse through its various stages, others might move more slowly, sometimes even lingering or feeling stuck in a particular phase. This variation is neither right nor wrong; it's a deeply personal journey, intricately linked to one's life purpose or mission. If your soul has chosen to thoroughly explore a stage of this journey and fully immerse in this experience in the current timeline, it's important not to rush. Your journey is unfolding as it was meant to, serving a specific purpose.

Trusting your intuition and the process is key. The signs and signals along the way are there to guide you through each phase. Be open, receptive, and if you find yourself seeking guidance or feel drawn to someone who has progressed further along their spiritual path, don't hesitate to seek mentorship. After all, learning is an unending process, and we can all benefit from the insights and experiences of others as we navigate our spiritual awakening.

So, in conclusion, I would describe this initial phase of the spiritual awakening journey as the fall of a veil, revealing a world that was always there yet hidden from our sight. This first stage is characterised by an awakening to a reality that's richer and more profound than we previously understood. It's a moment of revelation, where a sense of deeper purpose starts to unfold, nudging us toward a journey that promises to be both enlightening and transformative.

2.1 Awaken from Birth

There exists a unique group of souls, those who have been spiritually awake since their very beginning. These individuals entered the world awakened, with their psychic abilities fully active—a rarity in a world where most people's spiritual senses begin to fade around age three, and by seven, they are often entirely forgotten. Yet, these abilities are never truly lost; they lie dormant within us, awaiting reawakening. These gifts are part of our essence, capable of being reactivated and embraced. I am part of this distinct group.

Before you think, "How fascinating this must be," let me share my reality. Possessing open psychic abilities is both a blessing and a curse. Born in 1978, in a Christian Orthodox country like Greece, expressing my experiences with the spiritual realm was incredibly challenging. Discussing my encounters with spirits—not just of family members who had passed but also of friends or acquaintances—often led to ridicule. I was labelled as crazy or worse, accused of engaging in the Devil's work. This was a time before the widespread use of the internet, where information and support for such experiences were scarce. I couldn't find a mentor to guide me, leaving me feeling isolated, almost witch-like, or simply an oddity.

At 33, coinciding with my marriage, I made a conscious decision to suppress my psychic abilities. I did this by deliberately ignoring all spiritual communications and even trying to suppress my dreams, as they often became mediums for premonitions or encounters with spirits. I stopped discussing anything spiritual and vowed to myself that I would only reopen these abilities when I felt truly ready. As a physical symbol of this decision, I boxed up my Tarot decks and other spiritual tools, like a few cherished crystals and pendulums.

Prior to this, I had been navigating through a dark phase, struggling without guidance on how to positively harness and manage my clair senses. This struggle led to frightening encounters with lower-frequency entities—experiences so daunting that they felt hostile at times. At that point in my life, I certainly didn't want to expose my partner, or any future children, to such influences. Indeed, a decade later, I was blessed with two children. I became a typical person, deeply immersed in the mundane, earthly rat race, utterly 'asleep' in my 3D world. That is, until that fateful day on 28th September 2021...

I'm sharing this part of my journey with you as a cautionary tale, to highlight the importance of opening your psychic abilities at a time when you're operating at a higher frequency, have control over these gifts, and have access to a mentor for guidance and support. Now, having reopened my abilities, the experience is profoundly different. I've reconnected with seven of the nine clair senses, showcasing a more controlled and enlightened engagement with my spiritual capabilities. I now work with:

Clairvoyance, clairaudience, clairsentience, claircognizance, clairintellect, clairempathy, and clairsmelling. The two I don't (yet) have are clairgustance and clairtangency.

List of Clair Senses

1. **Clairvoyance (Clear Seeing)**

   Clairvoyance involves the ability to see visions, symbols, spirits, or auras beyond the physical realm. It's like having an internal screen where you see images or scenes play out, offering insights or messages.

2. **Clairaudience (Clear Hearing)**

This sense allows you to hear messages from the spiritual world. It could be voices, music, or sounds that others can't hear, providing guidance or important information.

3. **Clairsentience (Clear Feeling)**

With clairsentience, you feel emotions or physical sensations that aren't your own. It's like sensing the energy in a room or feeling the emotional state of another person or spirit.

4. **Claircognizance (Clear Knowing)**

This is the ability to just know something without knowing how you know it. It's like having sudden insights or understandings about a situation or a person without prior knowledge or logic.

5. **Clairintellect (Clear Thinking)**

Clairintellect involves a deep inner knowing that comes through thoughts. It's like having a stream of thoughts or ideas that provide clear guidance and understanding.

6. **Clairempathy (Clear Emotional Feeling)**

Similar to clairsentience, clairempathy is specifically about feeling the emotions of others. You might feel someone else's joy or pain as if it were your own.

7. **Clairsmelling (Clear Smelling)**

This sense allows you to smell scents that aren't physically present. It might be the perfume of a deceased loved one or a smell associated with a specific spirit or message.

8. **Clairgustance (Clear Tasting)**

Clairgustance is the ability to taste something that isn't actually there. It could be a specific flavour that brings a memory or message from the spirit world.

9. **Clairtangency (Clear Touching)**

Also known as psychometry, this involves receiving information through touch. Holding an object might give you insights into its history or the emotions of the person who owned it.

As I sit down to share this with you, there's a sense of excitement mixed with a deep feeling of responsibility. You see, the journey of spiritual awakening is a profoundly personal one, and as I've walked this path, I've come to understand a few truths that might resonate with you as well.

For starters, spiritual awakening isn't just about one's personal growth or a series of "aha" moments. It's much more profound. It's about peeling back the layers of societal conditioning to reconnect with your higher self. It's like rediscovering a treasure that was always there, hidden under the sands of social norms and expectations.

This journey, for many, begins at a point of questioning the very fabric of our existence. It's not confined to the boundaries of personal development but extends to how we contribute to the collective consciousness. Imagine realising that your existence, your choices, and your actions ripple across the universe, impacting the collective journey of humanity. That's what awakening is about – understanding your role in this grand tapestry of life.

But let me tell you, this journey transcends religion. While religion can be a beautiful path for many, spiritual awakening is about exploring a realm that's above human-made doctrines. It's about discovering universal truths that bind us in love and authenticity. It's about learning to listen to your inner voice without the filters of fear or societal biases.

I've always believed that this journey requires an open mind. It's about questioning everything, researching, and seeking your own truths. It's about being brave enough to challenge the norms and being receptive to new ideas and perspectives. And most importantly, it's about understanding that spirituality is a personal journey. Each of us has a unique path, a unique way of connecting with our higher self and the universe.

In sharing my experiences, I hope to shed some light on your path, to offer you a compass as you navigate this beautiful, sometimes bewildering journey of awakening. Remember, it's not just about discovering who you are, but also about contributing to a greater understanding and love in the world. Your journey is significant, not just for your personal evolution but for the elevation of collective consciousness. So, embrace this journey with an open heart and mind, and watch as the universe unfolds its magic in your life.

2.2 The Psychic Abilities

At this stage, I want to delve into psychic abilities, which are intricately linked to the spiritual awakening journey. Contrary to popular belief, psychic abilities are not gifts but inherent capabilities. They are the essence of our higher self, interacting with our energetic body. We are composed of various energetic layers: the physical vessel (our body), the energetic body (our aura), and our consciousness, which includes a deeper layer of our soul. While I won't go into extensive detail about these bodies, as they do hold different layers, it's crucial to grasp how interconnected they are and how they function as a unified whole, albeit not always in harmony.

From birth, our consciousness is the dominant layer, more attuned to the spirit world from which it emerged, and less so to the physical, 3D world. This affinity explains why many children experience dreams of flying, which are instances of astral projection or even remote viewing and can describe seeing their parents in another room while they are "sleeping." Their consciousness can easily separate from the body due to its strong connection with the spiritual world and other dimensions. This connection naturally activates psychic abilities, enabling children to see, hear, and communicate with spirits, experience premonitions, and, in many cases, demonstrate telepathy, telekinesis, and other psychic skills.

As we grow, particularly around the age of three, these psychic senses begin to diminish. This period marks a transition where children engage more with the physical world, start schooling, and by the age of seven, become more integrated into the 3D world, often losing or "forgetting" their psychic abilities. Several factors contribute to this loss. Family environments typically discourage these abilities, deeming them irrelevant to the physical world. Phrases like "stop that nonsense" are common, leading children to indeed stop talking or being engaged with their abilities. Social and religious norms further suppress anything beyond the physical, imposing restrictions that foster a disconnect from our true essence and, in many cases, confining the spiritual self within the limits of religion.

This shift results in a focus on the physical body at the expense of our true essence, creating an imbalance. Our energetic body becomes unregulated, our aura absorbs energies that manifest as stress, anxiety, or depression, and we resort to chemicals instead of caring for our energetic well-being. As we grow older and immerse ourselves in the rat race, we lose our connection to the spiritual realm. This disconnection manifests in various ways, such as interpreting voices or shadows as anxiety, severing our natural bond with nature, and adopting behaviours that further distance us from our higher self. The journey to reconnecting with our psychic abilities and higher self involves recognising and nurturing these inherent capabilities, moving beyond societal norms and expectations to embrace our true, spiritual essence.

Inevitably, embarking on your spiritual awakening journey, often signalled by the emergence of Angel Numbers, triggers a natural reawakening of your psychic abilities. Initially, this reactivation prominently enhances your intuition, which directly influences your physical responses—a phenomenon commonly referred to as "gut feelings." Essentially, your body becomes a conduit, translating the energies perceived by your aura into physical sensations. It's not a coincidence when you experience a knot in your stomach in the presence of certain individuals or a chill down your spine upon entering particular places. This early stage of psychic activation offers a glimpse into your reestablished connection with the spiritual realms. The Angel Numbers that start appearing serve as a bridge, facilitating your communication with these higher dimensions. They are not just random sequences but messages, guiding and affirming your intuitive insights, marking a significant step in rediscovering your inherent psychic potential.

2.3 28th September 2021 – My 2nd Awakening Point

On September 28th, an ordinary appointment for microblading led me to an extraordinary encounter. The beautician, whom I had found through a Facebook post, had her studio set up at her home. I didn't know her personally, but as soon as I stepped into her space, I was captivated by an amazing collection of crystals. They were everywhere, each emanating a unique, inviting energy. I instantly felt a buzzing surrounding me!

Seeing my excitement, she began showing me her collection, passing each crystal into my hands and explaining its abilities and benefits. It felt like being a child in a candy shop – the energy of each crystal profoundly resonated with me. We both got so carried away with the crystals that we almost forgot the reason for my visit. We started giggling with excitement as she passed her crystals into my hands, asking, "How does this feel?", "Now tell me about this", "Here, hold this one!"

She then led me to another room that housed some of her rarer pieces. There, I felt an inexplicable pull. Guided by this unseen force, I reached behind a stack of books on a side table and pulled out a hidden stone. It was an Ajoite, a crystal I had not consciously known about, but felt deeply connected to. The beautician was astonished. "How did you know?" she asked. My reply was simple yet filled with wonder, "I didn't."

Holding the Ajoite, a long-suppressed part of me awakened. I found myself channelling messages from her grandmother, providing intricate details that were later confirmed. This moment was a turning point for me. I left her place with an immense headache, a blend of dizziness and joy – a feeling of being intoxicated with energy. I was recharged and reborn. Thirteen years later, I had returned to my true self. It was as though the universe had conspired to lead me back to my path, reigniting the spiritual awakening that had started at my birth. This was more than just a return; it was a reaffirmation of my purpose and a reconnection with my authentic self.

A few days after that transformative encounter, I decided to treat myself to an Ajoite, a crystal that had quickly become one of my favourites. Its origins are as fascinating as its energy; Ajoite hails from the Musina mine in Limpopo, South Africa. This detail added an extra layer of personal connection for me, as I've always felt a strange and inexplicable connection to Africa. The thought that this beautiful piece of the earth travelled from such a distant and unique place, from a continent that always held a mysterious allure for me, to find its way into my life, felt like a profound sign. For me, it's more than just a crystal; it's a bridge to a broader, more mystical world, a reminder of my own journey and the deep, spiritual connections that transcend time and space.

3

The First Stage of Angel Numbers

Now, I think it's important to talk about how I began to recognise what I call 'stages' in understanding angel numbers. The first stage is crucial. It's all about when you first start noticing them. This is usually at the beginning of your spiritual awakening journey when you're open and receptive, ready to see and feel the changes in the environment around you. So, they usually first appear either in phase 1 or 2 of your spiritual awakening journey.

3.1 Recognising the First Stage

In this initial stage, angel numbers appear in a very intense way. This intensity is necessary because it's meant to catch your attention, to make you really see them. For example, you might start seeing 111 repeatedly and in various forms.

You could see 111 or 11:11 everywhere. It might be on the clock, like 11:11 AM or PM. Or you might notice it on a receipt where the total comes to £111.11. It could be on a car's registration plate, or even in someone's phone number. The last digits might read 1111.

This stage can last quite a while. It's like the numbers are sticking around, making sure you notice them. It's their way of saying, 'Hey, look here, something is happening.' This persistence is a key part of the journey. It's the universe's method of ensuring you're paying attention to the signs it's sending you.

3.2 Exploring the Baader-Meinhof Phenomenon

In our journey of understanding angel numbers, it's crucial to discuss the Baader-Meinhof phenomenon, also known as the frequency illusion. This is a psychological effect where something you've recently noticed, like a specific car, starts appearing everywhere. It can also happen with a name. You meet someone with a rare name, and soon after, you start seeing this name very often. It happens because your brain is now tuned into seeing this particular thing, making it seem more common than it really is. It's like your awareness has a spotlight, and it's shining on this new thing you've noticed.

This phenomenon explains why, once you become aware of something like angel numbers, you might start seeing them more often. It's similar to learning a new word and then hearing it everywhere. This doesn't make angel numbers any less significant. Instead, it shows how our awareness can increase our perception of these numbers in our lives.

Now, you might be wondering: are these really angel numbers, or is it just the Baader-Meinhof phenomenon at work? The key to recognising the difference lies in how it feels. Seeing angel numbers isn't just about noticing them; it's about when they appear, how they appear, and the feelings they evoke. There's often an urgency or a sense of importance when you see them. You might also experience other signs, which I'll talk about later. Plus, there's your intuition, your gut feeling, which is different from the simple recognition of a pattern, as explained by the Baader-Meinhof phenomenon.

3.3 The Significance of Ear Ringing

During my Spiritual Awakening journey, I became aware of the significant role of frequencies in our lives. Albert Einstein is often credited with saying that "everything has a frequency set point" and that matching the frequency of the reality you want is the only way to get that reality. Daryl Anka (Bashar), in 1988 also said: "Everything is energy and that's all there is to it."

I totally agree with this, and expanding my thoughts, I add that:

Everything is a continuous moving energy, operating in different frequencies that can be manipulated. This frequency manipulation can move the particles to create something tangible and intangible.

Have you ever thought about how everything in the universe, including our bodies, vibrates at its own unique frequency? It's like every person, object, and thought has its own musical note. When we talk about the frequencies of our body, we're diving into a world of subtle energies that many of us don't usually notice. But they are there, humming along with the rhythm of life.

On the other side, there are frequencies of higher realms. These are like special radio stations broadcasting at a frequency higher than our usual senses can pick up. Think of them as the secret, invisible channels where spiritual guides or higher beings communicate, or lower frequency entities using lower vibrational signals.

But I want to talk more about that ringing in your ears. Sometimes, it's just a health thing, what doctors call tinnitus. It's like a glitch in your ear's system, often harmless but annoying. Tinnitus often comes with other physical symptoms. These can include a feeling of fullness in your ears, hearing loss, or dizziness. If you're experiencing these along with the ringing, it might just be tinnitus. Tinnitus usually lasts for an extended period or happens consistently. If the ringing in your ears is persistent and doesn't vary much, it's likely tinnitus. On the other hand, spiritual connections through ear ringing are often more sporadic and come with variations in tone and frequency.

Have you ever felt a sudden ring in your ear that makes you feel like you're tuning into a radio frequency from another dimension? This could be a message from your spirit guides or a connection to a different energy form. It's not just random noise; it's like getting a phone call from the spiritual world.

Ear Ringing and Frequency Tones

Ear ringing has different tones corresponding to the frequency it aligns with, serving as a subtle way for energy entities to communicate with us. Recognising these tones can help you understand the nature of the messages you are receiving. If you have ever heard of the healing frequency forks used by energy healers, the sound you experience is very similar.

1. **High-pitched Ear Ringing**

   This occurs when your frequency aligns with a higher vibrational entity, such as spirit guides. The high-pitched sound, which might feel quite loud and even irritating, signals this connection. It often has a wavy quality, starting at a lower pitch, rising, and then falling again. This sound is similar to the three higher Solfeggio frequencies: 852 Hz, 963 Hz, and 741 Hz.

2. **Middle-tone Ear Ringing**

   This occurs when we align our vibrational energy state with a soul that has passed. In this case, it feels more like a buzzing sound, with a continuous flow and middle-tone quality. It's easier on the ear and feels "warm." This ear ringing is closer to the three middle Solfeggio frequencies: 528 Hz, 639 Hz, and 741 Hz.

3. **Low-tone Ear Ringing**

   This is a low sound that is deeper and has a more pronounced buzzing feeling, moving in a wavy pattern. It is more difficult to recognise. This sound occurs when our frequency aligns with lower energy frequencies, such as elemental spirits or "dark" energies. It can also signify passed human souls that, due to their choices in life, lowered their frequency. When they reside in the 4th dimension, they remain very connected to our dimension. Additionally, this can be related to energies that are not consciousness-related, such as accumulated negative energy in a place. All these give an ear ringing closer to the last two Solfeggio frequencies: 396 Hz and 417 Hz.

Ear ringing, or "spiritual tones," can manifest in an array of distinct frequencies and qualities, each carrying unique characteristics that often correspond to the source or entity sending the "call." While many of us are familiar with the common higher-pitched tones that feel like traditional ringing, these sounds can vary immensely, presenting as everything from light chirping and melodious whirlings to deeper buzzing or pulsating tones. Each frequency offers valuable insight into the nature of the energy or being reaching out.

For example, the more melodic, chirping, or whirling tones are often attributed to passed human souls or loved ones who may be trying to connect. This gentler sound can feel comforting and familiar, carrying a frequency that aligns more with earthly energies while still vibrating in a way that reaches our spirit.

Angels, archangels, and deities, on the other hand, tend to communicate through high-pitched, pure, and clearly defined frequencies. These sounds are distinct in that they often feel as if they are vibrating from above or from a space beyond our immediate physical surroundings. They can come across as strikingly "unreal," signaling an interaction with energies from higher realms. Angelic frequencies may even carry a subtle, uplifting tone that feels enlightening or serene, reassuring us that the guidance is of divine or high-vibrational origin.

Conversely, lower-vibrational or malevolent entities often give off heavier, buzzing, or pulsating sounds. These tones can feel dense or unsettling, resonating with an unsteady or vibrational quality that seems to disrupt rather than soothe. These types of tones may feel intense or uncomfortable, prompting us to acknowledge their energy while possibly serving as a reminder to shield ourselves and remain grounded.

Each ringing tone is unique and can vary based on our sensitivity, our energetic state, and the source attempting communication. By learning to distinguish these subtleties, we can enhance our discernment, understanding more about the vibrational landscape of these tones and the spiritual connections that accompany them.

Additional Occurrences with Ear Ringing

Ear ringing is often accompanied by other spiritual or energetic phenomena that can provide further insights into the nature of the communication or alignment you are experiencing. Here are some occurrences that might happen simultaneously with the different types of ear ringing:

1. **High-pitched Ear Ringing:**
   - *Physical Sensations*: You might feel a tingling sensation in your crown chakra or a gentle pressure on your head, indicating a connection with higher vibrational entities.
   - *Emotional Shifts*: A sudden sense of peace, clarity, or heightened intuition may accompany the high-pitched ringing, suggesting guidance from spirit guides.
   - *Visual Phenomena*: You may see flashes of light, colours, or symbols in your mind's eye, often associated with the presence of spiritual beings.
   - *Synchronicities*: Spirit guides might also use angel numbers or other synchronicities to communicate their messages, offering further guidance and reassurance.

2. **Middle-tone Ear Ringing:**
   - *Temperature Changes*: A noticeable warmth or a gentle breeze might surround you, indicating the presence of a passed soul.
   - *Memory Recall*: Unexpected memories or feelings associated with a loved one who has passed may arise, providing comfort and connection.
   - *Scent Recognition*: Familiar smells, such as a loved one's perfume or a particular flower, might suddenly appear, serving as a sign of their presence.

- ◦ *Electrical Disturbances*: Flickering lights or disturbances in electrical devices can occur, signifying the presence of passed souls trying to make contact.
- ◦ *Clair senses activation*: You will receive more messages through the rest activated clair senses you have.

3. **Low-tone Ear Ringing:**

- ◦ *Environmental Sensations*: You might feel a heaviness in the air or a subtle pressure in your chest, reflecting the presence of lower energy frequencies or accumulated negative energy.
- ◦ *Emotional Responses*: Feelings of unease, anxiety, or even slight agitation can accompany low-tone ear ringing, indicating the need for energetic cleansing.
- ◦ *Visual Cues*: Shadows or dark shapes in your peripheral vision may be noticed, often associated with elemental spirits or darker energies.
- ◦ *Electrical Drain*: Unlike passed souls, lower frequency energies can drain electricity rather than just causing flickering, making the environment feel energetically heavy and depleted.

By paying attention to these additional occurrences, you can gain a deeper understanding of the nature of the energies or entities communicating with you and take appropriate actions to align, cleanse, or protect your energy as needed.

During my research and personal experiences so far, I have recognised a pattern regarding ear ringing from our spirit guides and angel numbers. In the initial stages of our spiritual awakening journey, we will receive the ear ringing first to capture our attention. It is then up to us to observe our surroundings and identify any synchronicities or angel numbers that appear. This is a training stage, preparing our brains to interpret these messages better later on.

It's like calling you, and if you answer, the message is revealed.

As our journey progresses, the sequence changes. In the more advanced stages, you might see the angel numbers and simultaneously receive the ear ringing, which calls for you to connect through internal telepathic communication. Of course, since every individual is unique, and so is their relationship with their spirit guides, the pattern may vary. But have faith—they will use the best method for you to awaken and embark on this magnificent journey of connection with the spirit world.

On top of that, I recently came across new information regarding ear ringing. A comment on my TikTok revealed that someone had been experiencing ear ringing that acts like Morse code. This was fascinating to learn and adds another technique to help us identify this coded communication.

This discovery opens up new possibilities for understanding and interpreting the messages we receive through ear ringing. By paying attention to the patterns and variations, we can further decode the communications from our spirit guides. This highlights the importance of remaining open to new methods and continuously expanding our knowledge in our spiritual journey.

Ear ringing is like receiving a call, and
angel numbers are the voicemail message.

3.4 Synchronicities Accompanying Angel Numbers

Embarking on a journey with angel numbers often leads to encounters with synchronicities, where seemingly random elements align in a meaningful way. These synchronicities, appearing alongside angel numbers, are not mere coincidences but are laden with significance, acting as markers or guides on our spiritual path.

Animal Encounters

You might consistently encounter a particular animal or bird at the same moment you notice specific angel numbers. Take, for example, the recurrent sighting of a butterfly whenever the number 333 makes its appearance in your life. This occurrence isn't mere coincidence; it's a profound symbol of transformation and growth, deeply intertwined with the vibrational essence of the angel number you're seeing. The repeated presence of an animal alongside angel numbers serves as a nuanced layer to the message being conveyed to you.

Butterflies, in spiritual terms, represent not just transformation but also freedom, the cyclical nature of life, delicate sensitivity, and the acceptance of change. They embody the concept of significant life transitions, mirroring the journey from caterpillar to butterfly—a transformation that, although it leads to the end of one phase (as symbolised by the caterpillar), ushers in a new era of existence and awareness (the butterfly phase), all while maintaining the essence of the same soul.

When this symbol of metamorphosis accompanies an angel number like 333, the message is clear: you are on the cusp of significant personal evolution and holistic expansion. If the accompanying number is 777, the transformation takes on a deeply spiritual connotation, suggesting a journey toward enlightenment or the awakening of spiritual gifts. On the other hand, the presence of 999 alongside the butterfly might indicate the conclusion of a significant chapter in your life, prompting you for the emergence into a new phase of your soul's journey, much like the butterfly emerges, reborn with the same consciousness but in a new form.

When you find yourself encountering an animal at the same time as an angel number, it's an opportunity to pause and reflect on the deeper significance of these simultaneous appearances. Consider the attributes and abilities of the animal, and ponder on how these qualities might relate to your current life situation or personal journey. The animal's characteristics can provide insights into the message being conveyed through the angel number, offering guidance, reassurance, or a nudge in the right direction.

If you notice the same animal accompanying various angel numbers over time, it might not just be a recurring symbol of guidance—it could very well be your spirit animal making itself known to you. A spirit animal is a specific type of spirit guide that embodies the qualities, strengths, and instincts of the animal it represents, providing support, wisdom, and protection as you navigate through your life's path.

This intriguing intersection of angel numbers and spirit animals opens up a rich dialogue between you and the spiritual realm, highlighting the interconnectedness of all things. It serves as a reminder that our spirit guides, in their many forms, are always reaching out, trying to communicate with us in a language that transcends words.

Repeated Names or Words

Imagine frequently encountering the same name or word, either right before or after you spot an angel number. This pattern isn't random; it's likely a gentle push towards something—or someone—vital to your spiritual journey. Names, in particular, can be incredibly potent, possibly alluding to a person with whom you share a soul contract. This recurring name might be signalling that it's time to fulfil or conclude this soul contract, thereby completing a significant task or cycle. Alternatively, it might serve to stir memories from a past life where this name played a crucial role, influencing a chain of events that continue to impact your current existence.

Sometimes, the repeated appearance of a name could stem from your intuition, hinting at a forthcoming interaction with this name. It's important to remember that a name isn't confined to just individuals; it could refer to places, objects like ships, or even something as outlandish as a spaceship. When faced with such synchronicities, it's beneficial to keep an open mind and explore every angle. The universe communicates in myriad ways, and these repeated names or words are just one of its methods to guide us on our path.

Songs and Melodies

When you come across a specific song or melody at the same time as noticing an angel number, there's an added richness to the message being conveyed. Consider a song that might stir up memories or spark certain feelings, complementing the significance of the angel number you've seen. This musical encounter could be a gateway to exploring a past life, deciphering the lyrics for answers to questions you've recently posed, or finding clarity in a looming decision. It might offer assurance of support and guidance.

Reflect on your emotional response to the song. When was the first time you heard it? Could it be tied to a loved one who has passed, hence its resurfacing alongside an angel number? Analyze the specific angel numbers that appear in tandem with this music. Their combination could be guiding you toward recognising an unresolved trauma, signalling that now is the opportune moment to embark on a journey of self-healing.

Music's inherent frequency and the emotions it evokes, when intertwined with the vibrational energy of angel numbers, create a powerful medium for receiving profound insights and guidance. Whether it's a reminder of support, a nudge toward healing, or a beacon for spiritual exploration, the synchronicity of music and angel numbers holds valuable messages waiting to be deciphered.

Phrases from Books or Poems

A line from a book or a poem that stands out, especially when accompanied by an angel number, could offer profound insights. It's like the universe communicating through literature, providing guidance or affirmation. If the phrase doesn't "speak" to you, think about who the author is, what the story is, or when it was published. Every piece of information could give you one more piece of the puzzle.

I want to share with you a personal experience with a phrase that came as an answer. One of my boys wasn't feeling very well, so my husband and I were both quite worried. As I was searching for comfort, I randomly opened a book, and the phrase that stood out to me was, "This too shall pass." That phrase, combined with the angel number I had just seen, gave me the peace and reassurance I needed in that moment. It wasn't just a coincidence—it felt like a direct message from the universe, guiding me through that difficult time.

These small synchronicities—whether they come from a book, poem, or even a passing conversation—often carry profound significance. They may appear subtle, but when paired with angel numbers, they can offer a deep sense of clarity, guidance, and confirmation.

Colours

A colour that suddenly seems prominent is one more synchronicity you might encounter. For example, noticing a bright green car frequently after seeing the number 5 might symbolise growth and change, resonating with the angel number's energy. Green is also associated with the heart chakra, so seeing it repeatedly could be a message about healing, love, or emotional balance.

Always try to expand your perspective when decoding the message. It could be about more than just the colour itself—it might be tied to a specific area of your life, such as personal growth, healing, or even a relationship that needs attention.

Symbols

When a specific symbol starts appearing repeatedly in your life, especially around the same time as angel numbers, it holds a deeper meaning. This symbol could be a fragment of your light language, a sacred and soulful form of communication that transcends conventional language barriers. Light language is a universal form of expression that originates from the soul, often activated during significant spiritual awakenings or deep meditative states. It can be used for healing, as its vibrational energy directly interacts with our spiritual and energetic body, facilitating a profound form of healing that transcends the physical. It's also a powerful tool for channelling, enabling a direct line of communication with higher dimensions and our spirit guides.

Moreover, symbols that resonate with us on a deep level might be remnants of our experiences in past lives. These symbols could provide clues about the period or geographical location we once inhabited, offering insights into our soul's journey across lifetimes. They might also signal an affinity or connection that is significant in our current incarnation, possibly indicating roles or relationships that will profoundly impact our life's path.

Understanding the appearance of these symbols, especially when they emerge alongside angel numbers, invites us to delve into the intricacies of our spiritual heritage. Whether it's deciphering the messages encoded in light language or unravelling the mysteries of our past lives through symbolic language, these experiences enrich our spiritual journey. They serve as reminders of our interconnectedness with the universe, the timeless nature of our souls, and the intricate tapestry of life that we are part of. Engaging with these symbols opens a gateway to a deeper understanding of our existence and the universal forces that guide us.

For example, a symbol alongside the angel number 888 offers a fascinating insight into the universe's messaging system. Such a symbol, when encountered, might not just be a random coincidence but a powerful sign pointing towards abundance and prosperity. The repetition of 888, known for its strong association with financial and spiritual abundance, could be emphasising the importance of this symbol in your journey toward manifesting wealth and success.

Imagine this symbol as a spiritual tool, one that you might have utilised in a past life to attract abundance or facilitate spiritual practices. Its reappearance in your life, especially in conjunction with 888, suggests a divine reminder of your innate ability to channel prosperity and positive energy. This could be an invitation to reacquaint yourself with this symbol's energy through meditation, using it as a focal point to affirm your intentions and desires.

Incorporating this symbol into your meditation practice could serve as a powerful catalyst for change. Visualising the symbol while meditating and aligning it with the energy of 888 enhances your connection to the vibrational frequency of abundance. It's as if the universe is handing you a key, one that unlocks the doors to wealth and well-being, reminding you of the tools and knowledge you carry within your soul from lifetimes past.

This unique combination of angel number and symbol serves as a guide, encouraging you to explore and utilise the spiritual practices that resonate with your soul's history. It's a testament to the layered and interconnected nature of our spiritual journey, where numbers, symbols, and past life experiences converge to guide us toward our highest path.

Plant Synchronicities

When you repeatedly come across a certain type of plant or flower, especially in conjunction with an angel number, it's not merely a coincidence; it's a nuanced form of synchronicity. Each plant and flower brings its unique symbolism and energetic signature, offering specific messages or guidance when paired with angel numbers. This interaction between the botanical world and numerical sequences opens a rich channel for spiritual communication.

Plants and flowers, with their myriad colours and fragrances, serve as multifaceted symbols. The colour of a flower may resonate with the vibrational frequency of one of your chakras, offering insights or healing. For instance, seeing a lot of red roses alongside the angel number 111 might be a nudge to focus on your Root Chakra, signalling a time for grounding or asserting your power.

The fragrance of a flower or plant can also evoke deep memories or emotions, serving as a bridge to past experiences or connections. If a particular scent reminds you of a beloved family member who has passed away, this could signify their presence or guidance, especially if this sensory experience coincides with seeing an angel number. It's as if the universe is using this olfactory memory to convey comfort, love, or perhaps a message from the loved one.

Moreover, your personal connection to a plant or flower can reveal layers of meaning. If you find yourself repeatedly drawn to a specific flower, consider its symbolism or personal significance. Was it a favourite of someone close to you who has passed, or does it carry meanings in folklore or mythology that resonate with your current life situation? For example, encountering lavender, known for its calming properties, alongside the angel number 222 might suggest a need for peace and balance in your life.

When encountering specific herbs alongside angel numbers, it's a signal worth exploring deeper, as it might carry messages related to healing. Herbs have been utilised for centuries for their medicinal properties, offering natural remedies for various conditions. The appearance of a particular herb in conjunction with an angel number could be a nudge toward focusing on aspects of your physical or emotional well-being.

Adding to the layers of meaning provided by the colour and fragrance of plants, the therapeutic properties of herbs introduce a new dimension to the messages conveyed by angel numbers. For example, if you keep seeing the angel number 444—a sign of protection and encouragement—alongside sightings of rosemary, a herb known for its purifying and protective qualities, it might be an encouragement to cleanse your environment or to protect yourself energetically to help you find balance in life.

Moreover, this synchronicity can serve as a precautionary signal. Reflect on the healing attributes of the herb that's making its presence known to you. What conditions does it treat? Is its appearance a gentle warning from the universe about paying attention to certain aspects of your health or lifestyle? For instance, if echinacea, known for boosting the immune system, repeatedly appears in your life alongside the angel number 333, a number signifying support from the universe, it could be a hint to strengthen your immunity or to be mindful of your health.

Unique Encounters with Angel Numbers

Mentioning the 333 reminded me of my unique encounters with 333. Even though I provide a list of decoded angel numbers at the end of the book, I am a strong believer that the message from the same angel number can vary a lot according to specific life events and occurrences. For example, when I first started seeing the 333, I was trying to decode the message as a way to go out of my comfort zone—to be the unit above the duo, to lead the group, to be more creative.

But after a day during which the 333 was very prominently visible, I had an oesophagal spasm—a horrible chest pain that led to me being admitted to the hospital. It could be a coincidence if six months later the exact same pattern hadn't occurred. I saw the 333 repeatedly, and one day later, I was back at the hospital for the same problem. As you can see, the same angel number was now giving me another message, highly connected to my health. Now if I were to see it again, I would be more prepared.

Keeping a journal of these synchronistic experiences is highly beneficial. Record the details—the angel number, the accompanying element, and the context. This practice helps in piecing together the puzzle, allowing you to decode the universe's language tailored for your journey. Later in this book, I'll delve into interpreting these signals, helping you to understand and utilise them as guiding posts on your spiritual path.

4

The Shift – A New Era in Spiritual Awakening

4.1 The 5D Earth

On July 18th, 2023, something remarkable happened in the realm of spiritual experiences. Many people, including myself, noticed that angel numbers became more intense. This wasn't just a coincidence. It happened at the same time as a significant spike in the Earth's frequency, as measured by the Schumann Resonance. Usually, this frequency is around 7.86 Hz, but in July 2023, it jumped to an astonishing 168 Hz, to then go down to 40Hz and ever since it spikes high unexpectedly.

This huge change in Earth's frequency had a profound impact, especially on people who were going through their spiritual awakening. We are more sensitive to these shifts in frequency. When the Earth tried to raise its vibration, it created a kind of split. Some people tuned into this higher frequency, which helped them on their spiritual journey. Others stayed more connected to the material world—the 3D world—and didn't feel this shift as much.

During this time, more and more people started seeing angel numbers. It wasn't just a few people here and there; it was people from all different backgrounds. This wasn't random. It was directly linked to the Earth's vibrational change. It's like this global event opened up new ways for us to communicate spiritually, making angel numbers more clear and important for guiding us.

Regarding energetic shifts, and as it has been almost a year since I began writing this book, I want to share the symptoms you might experience as your physical and energetic bodies try to align. Over the course of these shifts, many changes have occurred in distinct phases:

1. **First Shift (Initial Spikes in Earth's Frequency)**
   During the first significant spikes in Earth's frequency, there was a collective exhaustion. Many people wanted to sleep more, felt energetically drained, and lacked motivation in their daily lives.

2. **Second Shift (Energising and Revitalising Phase)**
   In the second stage, this tiredness transformed into a revitalising energy. People felt more awake, more open to connecting, discovering, and exploring. During this phase, the veil between the two worlds thinned significantly, and more people began to activate their psychic abilities, allowing them to "see" and sense energies more clearly.

3. **Third Shift (Separation from the 3D World)**
   After approximately three months, we experienced a deeper shift, creating a larger separation from the 3D world. Many people found themselves leaving behind relationships that no longer resonated with their higher purpose. Some disconnected from family members or friends, while others made drastic life changes, such as moving to new locations, changing jobs, or altering their lifestyles. This phase initially felt heavy, but it eventually brought a sense of relief and alignment.

4. **Fourth Shift (Collective Cleansing and Purging – August 2024)**
   The most recent energetic shift, beginning in August 2024, led to a massive collective cleansing and purging. Those whose bodies needed to release harmful substances or habits went

through a detox, expelling foods, substances, and even addictions. Personally, during this shift, I began fasting naturally and quit drinking coffee, which had been my only remaining indulgence. After more than 25 years of daily coffee consumption, my body no longer tolerated it, or large amounts of food, except for one meal consisting mainly of fresh fruits, vegetables, and home-cooked food. Embracing this change, I realised this final phase was purging everything unnecessary, moving us closer to the 5D Earth.

As you read this, you might wonder: are you being left behind? What about future generations? Trust me, the universe and our Creator count each one of us. There will be many more shifts to help everyone who is ready, at their own time, to move forward. If you haven't felt the effects yet, know that it will happen when the time is right for you.

Understanding this link between cosmic changes and our spiritual experiences is incredibly important. It shows that as the Earth changes, we change too. The signs we see, like angel numbers, are part of this. They help us understand what's happening in our own lives and in the world around us.

We're living in a time where more and more people are experiencing spiritual awakenings. People are remembering what they're here to do, their life's purpose. Angel numbers are a big part of this awakening. They help us wake up to who we really are and bring us messages from the divine.

It's also important to think about how different this is from the past. In the 16th and 17th centuries, during the witch hunts, anything spiritual or out of the ordinary was seen as dangerous. People who talked about their spiritual experiences were often accused of witchcraft, which could lead to terrible punishments. Today, we're much more open to these ideas. We're more willing to think critically, research, and share our experiences.

The fact that we're seeing more angel numbers now is tied to this greater openness and the collective spiritual awakening happening around us. If we were living in a different time, like the Dark Ages, we wouldn't be able to talk about these experiences or get help understanding them. But now, in this era of heightened spiritual awareness, everything feels more intense, and we're able to connect more deeply with the spiritual realm.

4.2 The Journey So Far

By now, you've gathered a wealth of information on this journey of understanding angel numbers. You've explored their significance, the timing of their appearance, and the personal transformations they often herald. You've delved into the psychological aspects, like the Baader-Meinhof phenomenon, and recognised the difference between mere coincidence and genuine spiritual communication.

Reflecting on my own experiences, you've seen how angel numbers appeared at crucial moments in my life, signalling changes and guiding my decisions. From the shift in focus from business consulting to a deeper, more spiritual path, to the intense awakening marked by Earth's frequency change on July 18th, 2023, these numbers have been constant companions.

You've also learned about the role of synchronicities in this journey. The appearance of angel numbers alongside specific names, colours, or other phenomena is not random. These are intricate messages, tailored to guide and enlighten us. Recording and interpreting these occurrences in a journal can help decode their deeper meanings.

As you move forward, it's important to remain open and receptive. The journey with angel numbers is ongoing. Each new sighting, each synchronicity, and each moment of heightened awareness brings with it a message, an opportunity for growth, and a step closer to understanding your spiritual path.

In the next part of this exploration, you'll dive deeper into specific angel numbers and their meanings, learn more about synchronicities, and discover how to apply these insights in your daily life for personal and spiritual development.

5

The Messengers-Understanding Our Spirit Guides

We've already established that angel numbers serve as a unique system of communication, a mystical language bridging the human and the divine. These sequences of numbers catch our attention, nudging us towards deeper insights and understanding. However, a fundamental question arises: Who is behind these angel numbers? From where do these guiding sequences originate?

5.1 Identifying the Messengers: Spirit Guides

The answer lies in the realm of spirit guides. My journey and insights have led me to recognise these entities as the ones sending us angel numbers. These spirit guides operate at a higher frequency, existing in the 5th dimension and beyond—a realm parallel to our own, yet typically beyond our regular sensory perception. Spirit guides are distinct from our loved ones who have crossed over, whose consciousness remains in the 4th dimension before deciding their journey beyond.

Spirit guides are not bound by the physical laws that govern our world. They have never walked on Earth (except in rare emergencies when they can make use of a body to fulfil a purpose). They exist in a higher vibrational state, which allows them to communicate through subtle, energetic means such as numbers and synchronicities.

These guides are assigned to each of us from our first birth and come from various backgrounds. Some may be ancestral spirits, others could be enlightened masters, and others might be celestial beings with specific roles in guiding humanity. Each spirit guide is uniquely aligned with our journey, attuned to our life's purpose, challenges, and the lessons we need to learn.

As we delve deeper into spiritual communication, it becomes evident that our spirit guides employ a diverse array of tools to convey their messages and guidance. Each one of us is accompanied by a group of spirit guides, and depending on their nature and purpose, they prefer different mediums to establish their connection with us.

- Animal spirit guides, entities that embody the essence and attributes of the animal kingdom, often communicate through synchronicities involving animals.
- Healer guides lean towards the natural world for their communication, making use of plants and herbs.
- Ancestral guides, connected to our lineage and heritage, might choose names, phrases, or songs to reach out to us, often carrying deep personal or familial significance.
- Teacher and guardian guides, dedicated to our intellectual and protective needs, favour colours and symbols as their mediums of choice, particularly when they stand out or appear repeatedly.
- Ascended masters, beings of high spiritual wisdom and enlightenment, use a blend of these mediums. Their guidance is often multidimensional, combining animal encounters, plant and herb synchronicities, names, songs, colours, and symbols.

In addition to these unique mediums, all groups of spirit guides also incorporate a combination of synchronicities, including angel numbers and the phenomenon of ear ringing, to communicate with us.

Now, you might wonder: since it's our Spirit Guides sending us the angel numbers, why do we call them "Angel" numbers? Are our Spirit Guides angels? At this point, it's important to explain the hierarchy of the spiritual world.

While our Spirit Guides reside in the 5th and 6th dimensions, above them are the angels, and even higher are the Archangels. Angels are higher entities working in groups and are assigned to assist humanity collectively. Archangels hold an even higher position in the hierarchy, supervising both angels and Spirit Guides. Archangels can interfere with humanity in extremely rare situations, as they are considered the most powerful entities, often associated with protection and, if necessary, war.

The key difference between Spirit Guides and angels lies in their roles and relationships with us. Spirit Guides are uniquely connected to each individual—they are our personal, supportive team, guiding us on our spiritual journey. Angels, on the other hand, work collectively for the benefit of humanity as a whole.

So, why do we call them "Angel" numbers? The term "Angel" is used because these numbers come from the divine realm, which is often referred to as the Angelic realm. While our Spirit Guides are the ones delivering these messages, the numbers themselves originate from a higher, divine source, which is why we associate them with angels.

5.2 Why Spirit Guides Use Numbers

After discovering the origin of angel numbers, you might wonder, "Why numbers?" There's a profound simplicity and clarity in using numbers for communication across dimensions. Their universality breaks down barriers of language and culture, making them a universally accessible medium. Numbers effortlessly capture our attention. You can't help but notice the repeat appearance of 1111, can you?

The choice of numbers by spirit guides is intentional and significant. Each number sequence vibrates with distinct energy and conveys specific guidance, perfectly tailored to our unique life paths and experiences. It's fascinating how this universal language of numbers can address each of us individually, carrying a personalised message.

These number sequences are far more than just coincidental patterns; they're directional beacons, celestial signposts. They guide us through the maze of life, illuminating paths, offering support, and providing reassurance when we most need it. They're constant companions on our journey of spiritual awakening, subtle reminders of a higher presence always looking out for us.

To truly grasp the messages conveyed through these numbers, you need to cultivate a heightened sense of awareness and maintain an open heart. Trusting your intuition is crucial in unravelling the deeper meanings embedded in each numerical sequence. The context in which these numbers appear often holds the key to their interpretation. Reflecting on your current life situations, the challenges you face, and your deepest aspirations can provide valuable insights into understanding the guidance being offered.

In essence, comprehending the origin and purpose of angel numbers enriches our relationship with our spirit guides. Realising that these numbers are not random but intentional messages from entities in higher frequencies transforms every encounter into a moment of potential enlightenment. As you become more attuned to these numbers, your journey through life becomes an interactive experience with the universe, a dance of cosmic communication filled with wisdom and wonder.

I'd like to share a personal belief that's pivotal to understanding the essence of our journey with angel numbers. My open-mindedness is a core part of who I am. I've always been someone who eschews labels and resists constraints. Bearing this in mind, I encourage you to broaden your own perspectives and delve deeper into these concepts.

While I refer to these entities as spirit guides, your intuition might resonate with different terminologies. You might perceive them as aliens, energetic beings, angels, the architects of the Matrix, or even manifestations of God. The key takeaway here isn't the specific label we assign to these entities, but the recognition that we are guided and supported throughout our journey.

This understanding transcends the limitations of names and definitions. It's about embracing the underlying truth that we are not isolated in our experiences. There's a guiding force, regardless of the name we give it, that's constantly with us, helping us navigate the complexities of our lives. It's this realisation that's crucial, and I urge you to look beyond the superficial labels and truly embrace the messages and guidance that come your way. In doing so, you open yourself to a world of profound insights and cosmic connections, all aimed at enhancing your journey through life and your spiritual awakening. For those eager to deepen their connection with their spirit guides, I have developed a comprehensive course available on my website. This course is specifically designed for individuals seeking a more profound understanding and a stronger connection with their spirit guides.

You can access the course on my website at www.olgaawaken.com Look for the course titled 'Connect with Your Spirit Guides' or scan the QR code:

6

Deepening Your Connection with Angel Numbers

In this chapter, we delve into practical ways to deepen your engagement with angel numbers. These techniques are unique and immensely valuable for anyone looking to enhance their spiritual journey. Let's explore these.

Key Practices for Engaging with Angel Numbers

Acknowledgement

The first step is always to acknowledge the angel numbers when you see them. This act is like opening a portal to your spirit guides, signalling to them that you're aware and attentive. By acknowledging these numbers, you're essentially telling your spirit guides, "Yes, I see your message, and I'm ready for more guidance." This strengthens your connection and keeps the lines of communication open. So, whenever you encounter angel numbers, confirm it by saying, "Thank you, I have seen it," whether out loud or in your mind.

Affirmation

Once you acknowledge the angel numbers and feel the portal is open, it's a powerful time to make a wish or set an intention. This practice harnesses the energy of the moment. While different numbers have different meanings, making a wish applies to all angel numbers. It's about using the opportunity presented by their appearance to focus on your desires and aspirations.

In the fascinating journey of manifestation and affirmations, there's a subtle yet powerful shift in approach that can significantly enhance our ability to manifest. Let me share a secret that has profoundly influenced my practice. Traditionally, many have used expressions like "I wish for" or "I ask for," which places us in a state of wanting—emphasising a gap between us and our desires.

In recent years, there's been a shift towards more assertive forms of manifestation, such as "I demand the Universe to..." or "It is mine, I claim this...". This approach embraces a commanding stance, acknowledging our deservingness and right to abundance, love, or success based on our efforts and existence.

However, my preferred method of manifestation takes a different route—one that aligns closely with the concept of creating our reality through free will. Instead of asking or demanding, I advocate affirming our desires as already fulfilled. This method uses affirmations framed in gratitude and present possession, such as, "I am grateful for having abundance," or "I feel full of love." This approach is not about wanting or demanding; it's an acknowledgment, a confirmation that what we seek is already a part of our reality.

Manifesting through confirmation harnesses the power of belief and the law of attraction in a highly effective way. By affirming our desires as already present in our lives, we align our energy with the frequency of having, not lacking. This alignment attracts what we affirm into our physical reality and nurtures an internal state of gratitude and fulfilment, regardless of external circumstances.

This technique transcends traditional dynamics of asking or demanding from the universe. Instead, it creates a partnership with the universe, where we co-create our reality through balanced giving and receiving. By affirming our desires as already manifested, we open ourselves to receive, recognising that the universe is abundant and ready to fulfil our affirmed reality.

Embracing this method fosters a deeper connection with the universe and strengthens our power as creators. It invites us to live in a state of gratitude and abundance, acknowledging that everything we desire is already within our grasp, awaiting our recognition and acceptance.

Reflection

Reflect on the last question you silently asked yourself. It could be a recent thought or a significant event that left you wondering what to do next. The timing of the angel number often correlates with the issue you are facing. Later in this book, we will explore how timing is a crucial element in decoding angel numbers.

Identification

Pay attention to any changes in your life after seeing angel numbers. Notice if there are shifts in your decisions, thoughts, or choices. Your spirit guides use these numbers not only to show their presence and support but also to guide you through specific life situations. By identifying what happens after you encounter these numbers, you will begin to decode the personal messages meant for you.

While this book will provide guidance to help you decode the messages, your own intuition and connection with your spirit guides are equally important. We will delve deeper into this later in the book.

Gratitude

Always express gratitude for the guidance and support you receive. A simple "Thank you" can go a long way in acknowledging the presence and assistance of your spirit guides. Gratitude keeps the communication channel open and vibrant, encouraging your guides to continue providing insights and messages.

By showing gratitude and staying open, you create a positive flow of energy, signalling that you're ready to continue this spiritual dialogue. This practice ensures that you remain receptive to future messages and guidance.

In conclusion, engaging with angel numbers is a journey of partnership with your spirit guides. By acknowledging the numbers, making wishes or setting intentions, observing personal messages, and expressing gratitude, you cultivate a deeper connection with the spiritual realm. This practice opens up a world of guidance, insight, and transformation, enriching your spiritual journey and personal growth.

7

Understanding the Persistence of Angel Numbers

Many times, people experience a phase where the same angel numbers keep appearing, like seeing 111 repeatedly over a long period, sometimes even years. This can be quite puzzling. If you're in this stage, you might be wondering about the meaning behind this repetition and why these numbers seem to follow you so persistently.

When you keep seeing the same numbers without variation, it may indicate that there is stagnation in your spiritual communication. It's as though the message hasn't been fully received or understood, leading to a repetitive cycle. This repetition is your spirit guides' way of saying, "There's something important here that you haven't fully grasped yet."

Moving Beyond the Repetition

To break this cycle, start by focusing on the timing of when these numbers appear. Acknowledge them, and don't hesitate to do this out loud. Simply saying, "Yes, I see that," reinforces your awareness and acceptance of the message.

Follow this acknowledgement with gratitude. Say, "Thank you. I received it, and thank you for showing me." This expression of thanks demonstrates that you're open and ready for further guidance. By doing this, you signal to your spirit guides that you're paying attention and are prepared to move forward.

Transitioning to the Next Phase

Once you actively engage with the angel numbers by acknowledging and expressing gratitude, you'll likely find that the repetitive cycle begins to break. New number sequences will start to appear, and they may be longer, such as 22222, or mirrored and paired numbers like 1221 or 1212.

A Test of Awareness

This shift acts like a test, encouraging you to notice the differences in each new sequence and how they correlate with changes in your life. Each new number sequence carries its own unique message and guidance, pushing you to become more attuned to the signs around you.

As you begin to see these new sequences, you are effectively transitioning into the second phase of your journey with angel numbers. This phase involves a deeper understanding of the messages and how they relate to the specific changes, challenges, and decisions in your life.

In summary, when you find yourself seeing the same angel numbers repeatedly, it's a signal to enhance your communication with your spirit guides. By acknowledging these numbers and expressing gratitude, you open yourself up to a wider range of messages and begin a new chapter in your spiritual journey. This progression into different number sequences marks an evolution in your understanding and interaction with the spiritual realm.

8

____

The Spiritual Awakening Journey-Phase 2

8. 1 The Rabbit Hole

At this stage of our spiritual awakening, we embark on an exhilarating journey of exploration. This is when we dive deep into new concepts and ideologies, eagerly soaking in every bit of knowledge we can find. It's a period marked by a hunger for learning, as we broaden our understanding of both our reality and the spiritual realm.

This exploration phase often leads us down fascinating paths. Many of us find ourselves captivated by the world of conspiracy theories. We delve into topics like the mud flood theory, the flat earth hypothesis, the nuances and controversies surrounding COVID-19, the mysterious red shoe club, the enigmatic Illuminati, the moon landing's authenticity, the intricacies of the 9/11 incident, the secrecy of Area 51, and the influence of families like the Rothschilds. It's like venturing down a rabbit hole, with each twist and turn revealing more questions than answers, expanding our horizons and challenging our perceptions.

Concurrently, others might be drawn more towards the mystical aspects of this journey. This involves exploring the realms of witchcraft, psychic abilities, Tarot cards, the healing powers of crystals, the significance of different frequencies, and spirit communication. It's a dive into a world that bridges the tangible with the intangible, blending the physical with the metaphysical.

This exploration isn't just about gathering information; it's a transformative process that opens our minds to a multitude of possibilities. Whether we're unravelling conspiracy theories or delving into the mystical, this stage is about questioning, learning, and expanding our understanding of the world around us.

8.2 Spirituality and Psychic Abilities

As we embark on this second phase of our spiritual awakening journey, a profound question often surfaces: What is the essence of spirituality, and how does it intertwine with our psychic abilities? This inquiry is deeply personal, inviting us to delve into the mysteries of existence and our inherent connection to something greater than ourselves.

Understanding spirituality and its intricate relationship with psychic exploration is pivotal at this juncture. It sets the stage for a transformative process that extends far beyond conventional perceptions of reality. Spirituality, in its broadest sense, is the acceptance of a higher force—a divine energy that permeates every aspect of the universe, binding us in a web of cosmic interconnectedness. It's about recognizing our place within this vast expanse and nurturing a connection that transcends the physical, reaching into the depths of our souls.

Conversely, psychic abilities represent a more introspective aspect of this journey, focusing on the personal exploration of our innate capacities. These abilities, ranging from intuition to clairvoyance, offer a unique lens through which we can perceive the subtleties of the spiritual realm, fostering a deeper understanding of our connection to the universal energy.

At this stage, grappling with the concepts of spirituality and psychic abilities invites us to explore the profound layers of our existence. It challenges us to expand our consciousness, opening our hearts and minds to the possibility that we are more than physical beings navigating life's trials. We are spiritual entities endowed with psychic potential, capable of experiencing and influencing the world in ways that defy conventional understanding.

This exploration is not a solitary journey. It's a collective voyage that connects us with others on similar paths, seeking to uncover the truths that lie hidden beneath the surface of our everyday reality. As we delve into the realms of spirituality and psychic exploration, we begin to unravel the fabric of our existence, discovering that the answers we seek are woven into the very essence of our being.

Spirituality encourages us to look beyond the physical realm, guiding us toward self-discovery, purpose, and interconnectedness. It's about finding harmony with the universe, recognizing the sacredness in all things, and understanding our place within the cosmic order. Through spirituality, we cultivate values like compassion, empathy, and gratitude, seeing ourselves in others and recognizing the universal spirit that dwells within all beings.

As you continue on your spiritual awakening journey, one of the most intriguing and transformative aspects is the discovery of your psychic abilities. These abilities aren't exclusive to a select few; they are inherent within all of us, waiting to be awakened and nurtured. The more in tune you become with your spiritual self, the more these abilities begin to surface, offering a deeper connection to the spiritual realm and enhancing your perception of the world around you.

Psychic abilities are essentially extensions of our natural senses, but they operate on a higher, more subtle frequency. They allow us to perceive beyond the physical, tapping into energies and information that aren't immediately visible or tangible. Understanding and developing these abilities can enrich your spiritual practice, helping you navigate your path with greater clarity and insight.

In previous chapters, we discussed the *clairs*—the primary psychic abilities linked to clear seeing, hearing, feeling, and knowing. Now, let's dive even deeper into a broader range of psychic abilities that you may encounter and develop as your spiritual journey progresses:

Psychic Abilities

1. **Clairvoyance (Clear Seeing)**
   As previously discussed, clairvoyance is the ability to perceive images, visions, or spiritual entities beyond the physical realm. This ability allows you to "see" into the spiritual realm and gain visual insights from your guides.

2. **Telepathy**
   Telepathy is the psychic ability to communicate mentally with others, exchanging thoughts, emotions, or messages without spoken words. This deeper mental connection allows for a direct exchange of information between two minds, often bypassing language barriers.

3. **Pyrokinesis**
   Pyrokinesis is the ability to influence and manipulate fire or heat using focused energy. Although rare, this ability is often explored by those deeply involved in energy work and metaphysical practices.

4. **Energy Healing**
   The ability to channel universal life force energy to heal others, whether physically, emotionally, or spiritually. Practitioners of Reiki, pranic healing, and other modalities often develop this ability, tuning into the subtle energies of others to balance and restore well-being.

5. **Telekinesis (Psychokinesis)**
   Telekinesis, or psychokinesis, is the ability to influence or move objects with the mind. This ability is a powerful example of mind-over-matter and is explored in advanced metaphysical and spiritual practices.

6. **Mediumship**
   Mediumship involves communicating with spirits, guides, or

entities from other dimensions, especially those who have passed away. A medium acts as a bridge between the spiritual and physical worlds, delivering messages or insights from the other side.

7. **Precognition**

Precognition is the ability to foresee future events. This can manifest as visions, dreams, or sudden flashes of insight, allowing individuals to glimpse events that have not yet occurred in the physical world.

8. **Retrocognition**

The ability to perceive or experience past events through psychic impressions or visions. Retrocognition allows one to tap into the energy or residual memories of people, places, or situations from the past.

9. **Aura Reading**

Aura reading is the ability to perceive the energy fields, or auras, surrounding living beings. Through this ability, one can "see" the colours and vibrations of a person's aura, which reveal insights into their emotional, physical, and spiritual well-being.

10. **Psychometry**

Psychometry is the ability to receive information from objects by touching them. By holding an item, a psychic may perceive impressions of its history, the people who used it, or the emotions connected to it.

11. **Astral Projection**

Astral projection, or out-of-body experiences (OBEs), is the ability to consciously leave one's physical body and travel through other dimensions or planes of existence. This ability is often experienced during meditation or sleep, allowing the spirit to explore beyond the physical world.

12. **Telempathy**

Telempathy refers to the ability to sense or communicate emotional states with others, whether they are near or far. This ability is especially useful for empathic individuals who can tap into the emotional energy of others on a psychic level.

13. **Light Language**

Light language is a form of spiritual communication that transcends traditional languages. It is a channelled, multidimensional form of communication that connects directly with the soul and higher realms. Light language often manifests through sounds, symbols, gestures, or written codes and carries healing energy and information from higher dimensions. Those who speak or write in light language use it to heal, activate DNA, and communicate with star beings or guides.

14. **Channelling**

Channeling is the ability to connect with higher beings, spirit guides, or even extraterrestrial entities, allowing them to speak or communicate through you. In channelling, the psychic becomes a vessel for messages, wisdom, or healing energy from non-physical beings. This ability requires a deep level of trust and surrender to the spiritual realm, as the psychic allows these higher energies to flow through them.

15. **Remote Viewing (Remote Reading)**

Remote viewing is the ability to psychically "see" or perceive information about a distant location, person, or object without being physically present. This ability is often used to gain insights into events, people, or places that are far away, and it has been explored by scientific communities for military and intelligence purposes as well.

16. **Psychic Surgery**

Psychic surgery is an advanced healing technique that involves the psychic manipulation of the body's energy fields to remove negative energies, blockages, or imbalances. It is often performed energetically, without any physical contact, and aims to heal at a deep spiritual level by correcting the flow of energy.

17. **Shapeshifting (Energetic)**

    Shapeshifting is the ability to energetically alter one's appearance or presence, either in the physical or astral realm. While not literal physical transformation, energetic shapeshifting involves shifting one's energetic signature to mimic or embody another being or form, often used in meditative or shamanic practices.

18. **Elemental Communication**

    This is the ability to communicate with and influence natural elements like water, earth, fire, and air. Those who have developed this ability can psychically connect with the spirit of these elements and use this connection for healing, insight, or working with nature.

19. **Automatic Writing**

    Automatic writing is a psychic ability that involves writing down messages received from spirit guides or other entities without conscious thought. The psychic allows their hand to be guided by spiritual forces, producing words, symbols, or messages from beyond.

20. **Psychic Dreaming (Lucid Dreaming)**

    Lucid dreaming and psychic dreaming are the abilities to remain conscious during dreams and receive messages or insights from the spiritual realm. During lucid dreams, the dreamer can control their actions and experiences, while psychic dreaming involves receiving premonitions or spiritual guidance through dreams.

Each of these psychic abilities offers a unique way to perceive and interact with the world beyond the physical. They don't separate us from reality but rather deepen our understanding of the spiritual energies that permeate everything around us. These abilities, when nurtured and developed, can help us navigate our spiritual paths with greater clarity, insight, and connection.

As your spiritual awakening progresses, you may notice some of these abilities becoming stronger. Embrace them as part of your journey, and remember that developing these abilities takes time, practice, and patience. Approach them with an open heart and mind, and they will enrich your life with deeper meaning and connection to the universe.

Psychic Exploration: The Inner Journey

While spirituality provides the framework for our connection with the universal, psychic exploration delves into the personal dimensions of these connections. It involves a deep, introspective journey into our own abilities, understanding how to harness and enhance our inherent psychic potential. Psychic abilities, such as intuition, clairvoyance, and telepathy, are viewed as extensions of our spiritual selves, offering pathways to understand the universe's mysteries.

Both spirituality and psychic exploration are intertwined, each influencing and enhancing the other. Spirituality offers the philosophical and ethical foundation, grounding our psychic explorations in a context of purpose and meaning. In contrast, psychic exploration provides practical pathways and experiences that deepen our spiritual understanding.

Ethical Considerations

Both realms emphasize the importance of ethics. Spiritual principles guide us in using our psychic abilities for the greater good, ensuring that our explorations are aligned with compassion and the intention to benefit others.

8.3 Maintaining Balance in Spiritual Awakening

As we embark on our spiritual awakening journey, integrating spirituality with psychic exploration, maintaining balance becomes essential. Here's how we can navigate this journey effectively:

- **Grounding Practices**: Engage in practices like meditation, mindfulness, and spending time in nature to stay grounded and connected to the physical world. This ensures that our explorations enhance our lives without losing touch with reality.
- **Continuous Learning**: Embrace a mindset of continuous learning, seeking wisdom from various traditions and experiences.
- **Ethical Living**: Let your spiritual and psychic practices inform how you live your life, making choices that reflect your values and contribute to the well-being of the world.
- **Community Connection**: Seek out a community of like-minded individuals for support, shared experiences, and growth.

The journey through spirituality and psychic exploration offers endless opportunities for growth, discovery, and connection. By embracing both realms, we open ourselves to a richer understanding of the universe and our place within it. The key is to navigate this journey with balance and an open heart, allowing the insights and experiences to transform us and the world around us.

8.4 The Test

During this second phase of spiritual awakening, the journey becomes a blend of curiosity and discovery. We find ourselves in a state of constant learning, where every piece of information adds another layer to our evolving understanding of life and spirituality. It's a crucial step in our journey, laying the groundwork for deeper insights, personal development, and a richer understanding of the universe.

At this point, our spirit guides may begin testing us with more complex angel numbers. This marks a transition into the next stage of understanding and interacting with angel numbers. In this phase, you might start noticing a shift from simpler sequences like 111 or 222 to more elaborate patterns such as 1234 or 1212. These intricate combinations are meaningful messages from our guides, designed to engage us in a deeper understanding of our spiritual path.

The complexity of these numbers reflects the depth of the messages they convey. They resonate more profoundly with our personal experiences and challenges, indicating that we are ready for more advanced insights. It's a sign of spiritual progress, moving beyond surface-level awareness into a space where we can appreciate and decode the subtleties of divine communication.

As you continue reading this book and learning about angel numbers, remain open to receiving these messages. Avoid forcing interpretations or rushing the process. Trust in the natural flow of your spiritual awakening, allowing the understanding of these numbers to unfold organically. They will guide you accurately and beneficially on your path.

9

The Second Stage of Angel Numbers

In this evolved stage, the angel numbers you encounter are imbued with more nuanced and specific messages. This shift calls for a more personal and introspective approach to decoding these numbers. Unlike the earlier phase, where the meanings might have been more general and universally applicable, the sequences you now encounter demand interpretation within the unique context of your own life and personal experiences. Decoding these messages becomes an intensely personal endeavour, where your intuition and understanding play pivotal roles.

To assist you in navigating this complex stage, I plan to provide a general chart at the end of this book. This chart will offer basic interpretations of sequences such as 111, 222, 333, and so on, serving as a foundational guide. Additionally, I will discuss the concept of mirrored numbers and their general significance. However, it's crucial to approach these resources as starting points, basic frameworks upon which to build your personal interpretations.

Consider it like decoding a vivid dream where specific symbols appear, such as a turtle, which may hold different meanings for different people. Personally, whenever I see turtles in my dreams, I tend to have challenging days afterward. Conversely, my husband associates this symbol with good fortune. In the same way, your interpretation of angel numbers should reflect your personal life story, beliefs, and current circumstances. After all, your spirit guides will send you the messages you can decode best.

9.1 Two-Way Communication

This stage is pivotal because it unlocks the potential for you to use angel numbers proactively, rather than just receiving them passively. It's a significant development in your spiritual communication, one that empowers you to take a more active role.

In the initial stages, your experience with angel numbers might have felt like receiving signs or hints from the universe or your spirit guides. You were in a position of interpreting and understanding these numbers as they appeared randomly in your life. However, as you progress and become more attuned to these numbers, a remarkable transformation happens. You move from being a passive recipient to an active participant.

This active participation means that you can now use angel numbers as a tool for direct communication with your spirit guides. It's akin to opening a two-way street where you're not just listening but also speaking. Imagine having a direct line to higher wisdom, where you can ask questions about your life, decisions, or feelings, and receive guidance in the form of these powerful numbers.

Just as someone might use tarot cards to gain insights into a situation, or a pendulum to seek answers to yes-or-no questions, you can now pose questions to your spirit guides and receive answers through angel numbers. This could be as simple as asking a question in your mind and being alert to the numbers that appear soon after. The specific sequence or pattern of these numbers can be interpreted as responses to your queries.

This ability to "speak" using angel numbers is a testament to your growing spiritual awareness and connection. It's a more nuanced and sophisticated level of interaction where you're not just at the receiving end of spiritual wisdom but are actively engaging with it. This interaction marks a deeper involvement in your spiritual path, where you're learning not just to understand the messages but also to use them as a guide in your decision-making and personal growth.

Here's a method to experiment with this interactive aspect of angel numbers: whenever you're seeking guidance, pose your question internally, using your inner voice. Remain vigilant for the angel numbers that appear following your inquiry. Don't worry if you don't receive your answer right away. Trust me, you'll be surprised by how angel numbers will appear to give you the answer. Approach this practice with patience and openness. You can even try asking questions before bedtime—often, during the dream state, messages and answers, including numerical ones, come through. Your spirit guides might wake you up at a specific time, compelling you to notice the clock showing an angel number like 05:55, as a direct answer to your questions.

Now you know who's waking you up at those specific times!

In summary, the second stage of your journey with angel numbers is about harnessing their power for active spiritual dialogue. This stage offers you a profound opportunity to not only receive but also to seek specific guidance, thereby enhancing your connection with the spiritual realm and enriching your personal spiritual journey.

9.2 Three-Six-Nine Unlocking the Universal Code

In the journey of understanding angel numbers, you may notice the sequence 369 or any combination of the numbers 3, 6, and 9 appearing to you repeatedly. Whether it's a reminder on your phone that flashes at 3:06, a receipt total of £36.90, or even glimpses of 369 in dreams or daily life, these numbers are more than mere coincidences. Often called the "key to the universe," the sequence 369 holds a special place in numerology, spirituality, and even science, thanks to the pioneering work of the famous inventor Nikola Tesla.

Nikola Tesla, the brilliant scientist and inventor, was famously captivated by the numbers 3, 6, and 9, referring to them as keys to unlocking the mysteries of the universe. He believed that these numbers held the blueprint of reality, seeing them as essential to understanding the nature of frequency and vibration *(Tesla, 1900).* Tesla often suggested that if one could grasp the significance of 3, 6, and 9, it would unlock universal secrets, a testament to his conviction that energy, frequency, and vibration are the foundation of all existence. But why did Tesla view these numbers as so crucial? This question opens a doorway into Tesla's visionary world, where mathematical patterns reveal deeper truths about reality itself. According to Tesla, the universe operates on energy, frequency, and vibration. In Tesla's theory, 3, 6, and 9 are the fundamental numbers representing the underlying framework of the universe:

- **The number 3** represents the energy of creation and expansion. It symbolizes growth, connection, and manifestation in both the spiritual and physical realms.
- **The number 6** represents balance and harmony, often seen as the frequency that connects the material world with the spiritual. It is associated with nurturing, healing, and unity.
- **The number 9** is the frequency of completion and divine wisdom, holding the vibration of enlightenment and higher spiritual understanding.

Tesla believed that the interplay of these numbers—3, 6, and 9—created a vibrational blueprint for the universe. He observed that these numbers hold unique mathematical properties that can be seen in the patterns of nature, energy cycles, and even in the frequencies that govern human consciousness.

Interpreting 369 as an Angel Number

When the sequence 369 appears in your life, it may be the universe prompting you to explore its layers of meaning. Here's what each number signifies individually and as a collective message:

- **3** urges you to tap into creativity, joy, and self-expression, reminding you of your power to manifest your desires.
- **6** encourages you to create balance and harmony in all areas of life, especially between the physical and spiritual.
- **9** prompts you to seek wisdom and release anything that no longer serves you, fostering a higher state of awareness.

Together, seeing the angel number 369 may be a call to align your intentions, embrace balance, and complete cycles that contribute to your personal evolution. The message is that your life's journey is in harmony with the vibrational energy of the universe, and you're supported in creating, balancing, and completing stages of your soul's path.

Tesla was fascinated by this mathematical dance and believed that 3, 6, and 9 govern the frequencies of the universe. For those on a spiritual path, the appearance of these numbers may be a reminder that we're part of a vast, interconnected design that speaks to us through numbers.

How can you apply the significance of 3, 6, and 9 when they show up as angel numbers?

1. **Tune into Creativity (3):** Use this energy to think outside the box, cultivate new ideas, and connect with your creative side.
2. **Seek Harmony (6):** Practise balance, whether through mindfulness, meditation, or nurturing relationships with others.
3. **Embrace Higher Wisdom (9):** Recognise what you've learned, let go of what no longer serves you, and step into a state of greater understanding.

Tesla's legacy reminds us that by tuning into these frequencies, we are aligning ourselves with the universe's flow. The numbers 3, 6, and 9 invite us to connect deeper with the vibrational blueprint of existence, guiding us on a journey of creation, harmony, and enlightenment.

A powerful way to manifest your desires is by harnessing the energy of 3, 6, and 9. Begin by creating an affirmation that aligns with your intention. Then, either write it down or repeat it aloud, following the sequence: say it three times in the morning, six times in the evening, and nine times at night.

Personally, I love using these numbers to charge my water with intention. I hold a glass of water, focus on my affirmation, and speak it directly to the water, infusing it with my desire. Since water holds memory, drinking it allows that intention to align with my energy, drawing the manifestation closer to me. I repeat this ritual three times in the morning, six in the evening, and nine at night. I've found that whenever I do this, I see results within the first three days! Remember, the key is to believe and truly feel the intention—that's where the magic lies!

9.3 A Dive into Complexity

Remember when I talked about the time I saw those 171717 sequences? It was right when I was getting ready to launch my business consulting services. I had this whole plan laid out—I was going to make videos on TikTok about startups, business strategies, and financial advice. But something happened after I saw those numbers.

After a while, I found myself changing course. Instead of focusing on business and finance videos, I started creating content about spiritual awakening, the different stages people experience, and especially about angel numbers. Looking back, I realize that seeing the 171717 sequence was a message for me. Back then, I was convinced that my path was all about business consulting. But those numbers were trying to tell me something else.

At first, I didn't fully understand why these numbers kept showing up. But now, it's clear to me that the angel numbers were guiding me away from my original plan. They were pointing me towards a path more in line with my true purpose. It wasn't about business advice—it was about helping others understand their spiritual journeys and the role of angel numbers in their lives.

This experience was eye-opening. It taught me that sometimes, we have a plan in mind, but the universe has a different, often better, plan for us. And sometimes, the universe communicates that plan through signs like angel numbers. It's fascinating to think how these numbers were a way for the universe, or my spirit guides, to communicate with me, to redirect me towards a path that was more fulfilling and aligned with my deeper calling.

That period of my life, with the 171717 sequence popping up, really changed my direction. It shifted my focus from what I thought I should be doing to what I was meant to do. It was more than just a coincidence—it was a guiding force that led me to where I am now. And it's incredible how something as simple as repeating numbers can have such a profound impact on our lives and decisions.

9.4 Advanced Number Sequences and Mirrored Numbers

As you move into this second stage of working with angel numbers, you'll likely notice the appearance of more advanced number sequences. These are no longer just the basic repeating numbers like 111 or 222; instead, they might be longer, more intricate combinations like 1234 or 7474, or even mirrored numbers such as 1221 or 2112.

Mirrored numbers, in particular, hold a special significance. They represent balance, reflection, and harmony, often signalling that something in your life needs to be reflected upon or aligned. They can indicate that you're entering a phase where introspection is necessary, calling for you to look at the "mirror" of your actions, thoughts, and emotions. This symmetry in the numbers is a reminder to focus on balance, not just externally but within yourself as well.

For instance, if you repeatedly see mirrored numbers like 1212 or 1221, it could be your spirit guides urging you to evaluate your decisions and choices. What is being reflected back at you? Are you aligned with your higher self and life's purpose, or are there areas where adjustments are needed? Mirrored numbers are a call to self-awareness and to ensure that your outer actions are in harmony with your inner desires and spiritual journey.

The more advanced sequences, such as 1234 or 2345, often symbolize progression and growth. They may appear when you are on the verge of leveling up spiritually or in your personal development. These numbers could be a sign that you are moving in the right direction, steadily advancing toward your goals. They may also remind you that growth is a process, one step leading naturally to the next, and you are encouraged to trust this unfolding.

Other number sequences that combine repeating digits and progression, like 7474 or 8181, emphasize cycles, breakthroughs, and transformation. They indicate that you may be approaching a pivotal moment of change in your life, and your spirit guides are encouraging you to embrace it. These sequences often bring messages of encouragement, reminding you that cycles—whether challenging or rewarding—are temporary and part of a larger spiritual journey.

9.5 Trusting Your Inner Voice

At this stage, the complexity of angel numbers means that you must trust your inner voice more than ever. The personal significance behind each sequence will resonate deeply with your intuition. Your spirit guides are now delivering messages tailored specifically to your current situation, and the answers will become clearer as you tune in and trust your inner knowing.

It's important to remember that while these numbers carry universal meanings, the way they interact with your life and your energy is unique. You might find that 444 signals stability and foundation in your life, while for someone else, it's a call for grounding and self-care. This is why decoding angel numbers is a deeply personal and intuitive process.

To strengthen your intuitive connection, spend more time in stillness and meditation. Quieting the mind and tuning into the subtle messages within will help you decipher the angel numbers with more clarity. Journaling is another effective tool in this phase—writing down the numbers you see and the context around them can offer invaluable insights into their meanings and patterns.

Remember that your spirit guides are working closely with you, tailoring their messages to your spiritual progress. If you feel uncertain about the meaning of a particular number, ask for clarity, and trust that the answer will come in time. It might appear as another number, a dream, or even through a conversation you overhear that suddenly resonates with you.

9.6 The Journey Continues

As you progress through this stage of working with angel numbers, you'll notice that these sequences become more dynamic. They are no longer just signs to catch your attention—they are active guides, helping you make decisions, offering reassurance, and even pushing you towards necessary changes. This stage is not just about receiving guidance but about integrating that guidance into your everyday life, learning how to walk in step with your spiritual path and the messages you receive.

Angel numbers in this second stage are often an invitation to take more responsibility for your spiritual growth. It's no longer just about noticing and acknowledging the numbers but about consciously acting on the guidance you receive. As you grow spiritually, your guides may challenge you to step out of your comfort zone, confront fears, or take bold steps toward your true purpose. They may even guide you through difficult decisions, ensuring that you are following a path that aligns with your highest good.

The beauty of this stage is that the communication becomes a dialogue—a back-and-forth conversation with the universe. You are not just the receiver of messages; you are an active participant, engaging with the guidance you receive and using it to shape your path.

In the upcoming chapters, we'll explore how to integrate these more advanced messages into your daily life, how to strengthen your connection with your spirit guides, and how to use these angel numbers as powerful tools for spiritual and personal transformation. The journey continues, and with each new number sequence, you're being guided toward a deeper understanding of your true self and the divine purpose you're here to fulfill.

10

The Four Categories of Angel Number Messages

As I delved deeper into this captivating world of numerical communication, I made an enlightening discovery: angel numbers can be categorized based on the underlying intentions or messages they convey. This realization opened up a new dimension in my understanding of these mystical sequences.

Each category reflects a distinct purpose or message, shedding light on the diverse ways our spirit guides communicate with us through numbers. It's like uncovering layers of a complex language, with each layer revealing a new aspect of communication.

This categorization isn't just an academic exercise; it's a practical tool. By understanding the intention behind each sequence, we can more accurately interpret the messages being sent to us. It's akin to learning the nuances of a foreign language, where understanding the context and tone can drastically change the meaning of a phrase.

In this chapter, I will introduce you to the four primary categories of angel number messages: supportive, confirming, advisory, and guiding. This understanding will deepen your connection with your spirit guides and enhance your ability to receive and comprehend their guidance.

The Supportive Angel Numbers: 111–444

The first category is the *supportive* angel numbers. These numbers often show up during times of hardship or uncertainty. They act as a form of encouragement, reminding you that you are not alone and that the universe has your back.

For instance, sequences like 111 or 444 often appear when you feel overwhelmed, facing challenges that seem insurmountable. When you see these numbers, it's as though the universe is gently whispering, "I'm with you." These numbers serve as a reminder that your spirit guides are offering you support, even if everything seems to be falling apart.

When you encounter 111, it often signifies that you are entering a period of new beginnings, and your spirit guides are reassuring you that you're not starting this journey alone. Meanwhile, 444 is a message of stability, grounding, and protection, urging you to stay strong and trust that the foundations you've built will hold, no matter the external turbulence.

The Confirming Angel Numbers: 222–333

The *confirming* numbers are another key category. These sequences appear when you are on the right track, offering affirmations that you're moving in the right direction. When you see numbers like 222 or 333, it's a message from the universe saying, "Keep going, you're doing great." These numbers reinforce that your actions and decisions are aligned with your higher purpose.

For example, the number 222 is often associated with duality, harmony, and relationships. It confirms that balance is being restored in your connections with others, and positive outcomes are likely in your relationships. Meanwhile, 333 signals empowerment, often urging you to step into a leadership role or embrace your personal power. It confirms that you have the ability to take control of a situation and lead with confidence.

The Advisory Angel Numbers: 555–666–999

Some numbers serve as *advisory* messages, signaling preparation for change or the need for course correction. Numbers like 555, 666, and 999 fall into this category.

Contrary to popular misconceptions, 666 isn't a negative number. It often serves as a prompt to reevaluate your path, suggesting that something in your life may be out of balance or alignment. It's a gentle nudge to take stock of your actions and recalibrate where necessary.

Similarly, 555 is associated with major transformations. When this number appears, it's a sign that change is on the horizon, and you need to embrace it rather than resist it. It's a reminder that while change may feel uncomfortable, it often leads to growth and new opportunities.

Finally, 999 signals the completion of a cycle. It might indicate the end of a chapter in your life, urging you to let go of what no longer serves you and make space for the new. This number brings a message of closure and invites you to step forward into the next phase of your journey with an open heart.

The Guiding Angel Numbers: 777–888

The *guiding* numbers direct you toward deeper spiritual insight and purpose. Sequences like 777 and 888 often appear when you are being called to explore your spiritual path more fully.

The number 777 is a powerful signal of spiritual enlightenment. It encourages you to delve into your spiritual practices, engage with your higher self, and seek a deeper connection with the divine. When you see this number, it's a call to expand your consciousness and embrace your spiritual gifts.

The number 888, on the other hand, is closely associated with abundance—both material and spiritual. It's a sign that prosperity is flowing your way and that you are on the right path to manifesting your desires. This number often appears when you are entering a phase of fulfillment, reminding you to remain open to receiving the blessings the universe has in store for you.

When 777 and 888 appear in combination or in sequences like 171717 (a combination of 1 and 7), the numbers can signal both new beginnings and spiritual awakening. This was exactly the message for me during my personal journey when I kept seeing 171717. It was a profound sign that I was stepping into a new phase of my spiritual journey, one filled with growth, abundance, and deeper understanding.

Applying These Categories to Your Life

As you move forward with your journey, it's essential to recognize these categories and understand that each sequence carries its unique vibration and message. As you become more attuned to these numbers, you will start to see the intricate ways they guide, support, and communicate with you.

Understanding the complexity of angel numbers, especially when they come in intricate sequences, can seem overwhelming at first. If you're feeling unsure about how to decode these messages, don't worry—that's completely normal. This journey is not always straightforward, and it's okay to take your time to grasp the nuances of this spiritual communication.

But don't worry, I've got you covered. At the end of this book, you'll find a comprehensive guide. This guide is designed to take you step-by-step through the process of decoding angel numbers, no matter how complex their sequences may appear. It's laid out in a way that's easy to understand and follow, ensuring that by the time you reach the end of this book, you will have gained a thorough mastery of communicating with angel numbers.

Through this guide, you'll learn the meanings behind different numbers and sequences, and how they apply to various aspects of your life. The goal is to equip you with all the tools and understanding you need to confidently navigate this form of spiritual communication.

As you continue on this journey, remember that all the insights and knowledge you need to become proficient in understanding angel numbers are waiting for you. By the end, you'll not only be familiar with these heavenly messages but will have learned to embrace them as a natural and enlightening part of your daily life.

11

The Spiritual Awakening Journey – Phase 3

11.1 The Dark Night of the Soul

You've reached a pivotal point in your spiritual journey, one where your entire worldview has been turned upside down. The exploration stage has been a whirlwind of new ideas and perspectives, challenging everything you've been taught. Questions about your existence, your true identity, and the very nature of life itself begin to surface, creating a profound sense of introspection. It's as if a veil has been lifted, revealing a world of possibilities and mysteries that were previously hidden.

At this stage, your focus shifts inward. The external fascinations—the energy of crystals, the intriguing theories about our reality—while still captivating, no longer quench your deep thirst for understanding. They have served their purpose in opening your mind, but now you find yourself yearning for something more, something deeply personal and introspective.

You are now stepping into what many refer to as the *dark night of the soul*—the challenging phase of your spiritual awakening. This phase is characterized by deep self-reflection and often, a sense of isolation. It's a time when the external distractions fall away, and you are left to confront your deepest truths, fears, and questions.

This "dark phase" is a crucial part of the journey. It's where you confront your inner shadows, question your deepest beliefs, and start to uncover your true self. It can be a challenging time, filled with uncertainty and introspection, but it is also a period of immense growth and transformation. This phase serves as the gateway to discovering your authentic self and embracing the vast potential within you.

11.2 The Dive into Deeper Realizations

In this profound phase of the dark night of the soul, a significant shift in perspective occurs. You begin to see life beyond the routine of a 9-5 job, recognizing that there's much more to existence than the daily grind and the relentless pursuit of traditional success. You come to realize how precious time truly is.

The traditional path of spending hours commuting, working tirelessly, and waiting for the weekend or retirement to truly "live" starts to lose its appeal. You start to see the importance of every moment, understanding that life on Earth should encompass more than routine and obligations. It's about appreciating the present and making the most of your time here.

This awakening brings forth questions: *Why couldn't I see this before? Why has my life been so challenging, consumed by the rat race? Why have relationships felt fleeting and ephemeral? What is the true meaning behind all these struggles?*

Your soul begins a journey of introspection, seeking to understand and heal. This isn't about dwelling in the past, but rather about gaining insight into the lessons life has offered and how they have shaped you. It's about reevaluating priorities, reassessing life goals, and redefining what truly matters.

The dark night of the soul pushes you towards deeper meanings. It's a time to question everything, reflect, and grow. Ultimately, this phase is about transitioning from viewing life as a series of tasks and duties to embracing it as a rich tapestry of experiences, connections, and spiritual evolution.

11.3 The Cocoon Phase

During this transformative stage, a natural inclination towards solitude often emerges. You may find yourself pulling away from certain relationships, especially those that no longer resonate with your evolving self. This isn't about rejection but about realignment. Just like a caterpillar retreats into its cocoon, you may feel the need to create a personal space of reflection and introspection. This time of solitude is vital for nurturing your inner self, preparing for significant transformation.

The sense of loneliness that often accompanies this phase is natural. However, remember that you are not truly alone. The recurring numbers you see, such as 666 or 999, are gentle yet powerful reminders that you are being supported.

The number 666 often carries misconceptions, but in the realm of angel numbers, it signals necessary change and realignment. It encourages introspection, urging you to shed old patterns and find balance. Meanwhile, 999 symbolizes the completion of a cycle, inviting you to embrace a new chapter in your spiritual journey.

This phase calls for you to trust your intuition, to stay attuned to your true self, and to allow the process of transformation to unfold.

11.4 Navigating Through the Darkness

Here are some valuable tools to help you navigate this challenging stage:

Meditation and Mindfulness

Meditation offers a refuge of peace during this tumultuous period. Start with brief moments of focused breathing, gradually extending the time as you become more comfortable. Guided meditations are also helpful, and you can explore various options until you find the one that resonates with you.

Journaling

Journaling is a powerful tool for self-reflection. Keeping a daily journal allows you to process your thoughts and emotions. Free writing can help tap into your subconscious mind, revealing hidden insights. Pay attention to any angel numbers that might appear as you write—these may offer further guidance.

Grounding

Connecting with nature is essential during this phase. Whether through a walk in the park or simply sitting under a tree, nature has the power to heal and ground you. Remember, grounding isn't just about connecting with nature but also about cleansing your energy and realigning with the Earth's frequency.

Creativity and Physical Expression

Engage in creative activities like art or music to express emotions that words cannot capture. Physical outlets like yoga are also beneficial, releasing emotional blockages and aligning your body and spirit.

Healing Frequencies

Healing frequency music, especially at 432Hz, can profoundly impact your journey. Start with this frequency and explore others, such as the Solfeggio frequencies, which are known for their healing properties. Each frequency carries its own vibrational energy, guiding you toward balance and harmony.

11.5 The Light at the End of the Tunnel

The *dark night of the soul* is a profound period of deep introspection and transformation. For many, it feels like a long winter hibernation, lasting months or even years. This phase strips you back to your very essence, forcing you to confront your shadows, but it also provides the opportunity for immense growth.

During this time, you'll gain clarity about your true self and purpose. Like the caterpillar in its cocoon, you are in a state of becoming, preparing to emerge as a more spiritually evolved being. The dark night of the soul, while challenging, is an essential part of your spiritual awakening, leading you toward a more enlightened and fulfilled existence.

Through meditation, reflection, grounding, and creativity, you will navigate this phase and emerge with a deeper understanding of yourself and your place in the universe. There is indeed light at the end of the tunnel, and as you progress, you will see that this journey was necessary for your transformation.

12

The Spiritual Awakening Journey - Phase 4

12.1 The Rebuilding

In the aftermath of navigating through the shadowy depths of the Dark Night of the Soul, there comes a pivotal moment of rebirth. It's a time when you start piecing together the fragments of your being, but this time, with a profound awareness and a fresh perspective. This stage, aptly called *The Rebuilding*, is not just about recovery; it's about transformation and the deliberate creation of a life that resonates with the deepest truths discovered during your journey inward.

During this phase, the spiritual insights and lessons learned are no longer abstract concepts but become integral to your daily existence. You start to see the world through a new lens—one that is more aligned with your true essence and higher purpose. This doesn't mean that life becomes free of challenges, but rather that you are now equipped with a deeper understanding and the tools to navigate them more effectively.

The *Rebuilding* phase is marked by a conscious effort to apply your spiritual insights to shaping a life that reflects your true self. This could mean making significant changes in your career, relationships, and hobbies, or it could manifest as subtle shifts in your values and priorities. The essence of this phase is *alignment*—ensuring that every aspect of your life is in harmony with your spiritual path.

This is also a time for action. Armed with a clearer understanding of your purpose and what brings you joy, you start to make choices that reflect this newfound clarity. Whether it's pursuing a long-held dream, adopting a healthier lifestyle, or dedicating yourself to service, the actions taken during *The Rebuilding* are steps toward a more authentic and fulfilling life.

An essential aspect of this phase is the transformation in your relationships. You may find that individuals who no longer serve your life's purpose have naturally drifted away. Remarkably, the departure of even those close to you often brings a sense of relief rather than sadness. Your frequency has shifted, and so has your environment. This clarity paves the way to forming new, more aligned relationships effortlessly and magically. Unlike before, connections now seem to gravitate toward you, creating a community that, though smaller, feels infinitely more significant. A single smile or glance can fill you with an unparalleled sense of joy.

Additionally, you'll notice changes in your physical habits. Old vices like alcohol or tobacco no longer appeal; your body rejects what no longer serves it, initiating a holistic purge that encompasses body, mind, and spirit. This natural detoxification process underscores your readiness for further growth.

As you embrace this new version of yourself, even if it means letting go of parts of your old self, you find yourself magnetically drawing in like-minded souls. This burgeoning community around you, though numerically smaller, enriches your life in ways large gatherings never did.

And it is at this juncture, having shed your cocoon and basking in the light of transformation, that your spirit guides acknowledge your progress by sending new angel numbers. You are now on the threshold of the third stage, the most crucial yet, for you have never been more prepared to embrace what lies ahead.

In conclusion, *The Rebuilding* is a testament to the resilience of the human spirit and its capacity for renewal. It's a phase where the spiritual and the tangible merge, guided by newfound clarity and the relationships that now define our journey. As we ready ourselves for the next chapter, we do so with a heart full of gratitude for the journey thus far and an eagerness to welcome the new connections, experiences, and lessons that await.

12.2 The Lightworkers

The *Rebuilding* phase also marks the activation of your psychic abilities in relation to your Life's Purpose. Recall how our structured world initially forced these abilities into dormancy. Now, you possess the power to shape your authentic world, strengthening your bond with your higher self. During this phase, you'll naturally gravitate toward not only exploring your abilities, as you did in the second phase of your journey, but also integrating them into your everyday life. This is when Lightworkers are truly activated, ready to embrace and wield their innate gifts.

Lightworkers come from various backgrounds, lifestyles, and professions. They may be found in the arts, science, education, healing professions, and more. Regardless of their outer roles, their core mission remains the same: to bring about positive change and enlightenment by spreading compassion, kindness, and understanding. They possess an innate ability to uplift others, often feeling a profound sense of responsibility toward the well-being of the planet and its inhabitants.

Lightworkers, a term that encompasses a diverse group of souls known for their healing and transformative energies, includes not only those who have awakened to their Earthly mission but also starseeds, indigos, and higher consciousness Eartheans. These beings are united by a common purpose:

to elevate the vibrational frequency of the planet and assist in the collective journey toward enlightenment and spiritual awakening.

Starseeds

The concept of multidimensional consciousness suggests that starseeds are deeply connected to higher realms, embodying wisdom and guidance from advanced beings. Many believe starseeds bring ancient knowledge and healing from beyond Earth to support humanity's evolution *(Marciniak, 1992).* This understanding of extraterrestrial origins highlights the spiritual missions of starseeds, reflecting their role as bridges between cosmic realms and earthly life. Starseeds are souls that originate from other planets, star systems, or galaxies but have chosen to incarnate on Earth to aid in its evolutionary leap. They bring with them knowledge and a higher frequency that can help shift the collective consciousness of humanity toward a more harmonious state.

Indigos

Indigo children, known for their deep blue auras, are characterized by their strong wills, intuitive natures, and resistance to conventional systems and authority. Their role is often to challenge and dismantle outdated societal structures to make way for new paradigms of living that are in harmony with Earth's ascension.

Higher Consciousness Eartheans

These are consciousnesses who have been Earth-born but have awakened to their higher consciousness through spiritual practice, self-inquiry, and a dedicated commitment to personal and planetary healing. They work from within the framework of their human experience to bring about change, healing, and transformation.

12.3 The Seven Categories of Lightworkers

1. **Empaths**: The Emotional Alchemists

   Empaths stand as the emotional alchemists of the Lightworkers, gifted with the profound ability to sense and transmute the energies surrounding them. This natural attunement allows them to perceive not just the emotions of humans but also the subtle vibrations of animals and places. Their energetic field operates as a sieve, absorbing energies, discerning their essence, and then releasing them back into the universe, purified and healed.

However, this remarkable ability comes with its vulnerabilities. Empaths must vigilantly shield their energy fields to avoid becoming conduits for overwhelming negative forces, which can manifest in physical symptoms such as anxiety or depression—a direct consequence of processing unfiltered energies. Practices like salt baths and grounding become essential tools for empaths, aiding in the maintenance of their energetic hygiene and well-being.

2. **Channellers**: The Spiritual Intermediaries

Channellers serve as the bridge between the spiritual and physical realms, facilitating communication with spirits to convey messages that offer solace and closure. This role is vital for the continuity of souls' journeys and for providing the living with comfort amid grief.

However, channellers may encounter challenges in managing their chakra portals, which, if left unregulated, can become gateways for lower-frequency entities. These encounters can affect them emotionally and physically, underscoring the importance of grounding meditations and periods of isolation. Creative outlets like free writing or drawing offer channellers a form of expression that aids in managing their connections with the spirit world.

3. **The Guides**: The Enlightened Mentors

The Guides are the visionary leaders among Lightworkers, gathering like-minded souls to further the collective good. With an innate capacity to impart knowledge and wisdom, they act as mentors, directing others on their spiritual journeys. Despite their broad understanding of psychic abilities, Guides often find their true calling in teaching and guiding rather than direct service.

Challenges arise when their teachings are not received as anticipated, leading to feelings of overwhelm and retreat. In such times, Guides may turn to writing as a means to continue their mission. Their profound wisdom often comes with a sense of loss, as their focus on others' paths can sometimes detract from their own journey. Surrounding themselves with empaths and engaging with natural elements like water and fire helps Guides to rejuvenate and stay connected.

4. **The Peacemakers**: The Harmonizers of Humanity

Peacemakers wield their psychic abilities to instill balance and tranquility within the human sphere. Masters of telepathy and telekinesis, they can subtly manipulate energies and elements to foster peace and beauty. Their presence alone can transform environments, activating their powers in times of turmoil to avert further discord.

Yet, mastering these tele-abilities often eludes Peacemakers, leading to a lifetime quest for understanding and control. Mentorship from Guides can be instrumental in unlocking their potential, building self-confidence, and refining their skills. Recharging through air and aether elements and close collaboration with spirit guides enables Peacemakers to fully embrace and utilize their gifts.

5. **Healers:** The Custodians of Vitality

Healers embody the capacity to channel and transform energy, using their own beings as conduits for facilitating healing. This selfless exchange can, paradoxically, lead to their own energy depletion, as their healing efforts inadvertently prioritize others over themselves.

To counterbalance this, Healers benefit from forming supportive communities with fellow practitioners, where shared energies can replenish and nurture all members. Retreats and the exploration of diverse healing modalities allow Healers to deepen their practice and expand their repertoire, ensuring that their well of vitality remains abundant for both themselves and those they serve.

6. **The Visionaries**: Architects of New Realities.

The Visionaries stand out as the dreamers and creators among Lightworkers, blessed with the ability to see beyond the present into the realms of new possibilities and futures. They are the catalysts for change, using their powerful imaginations and unwavering faith to manifest new realities that align with the highest good of humanity and the Earth.

Visionaries often face the challenge of being misunderstood or seen as outcasts due to their unconventional ideas and perspectives. Their path requires courage to stand firm in their convictions, even when facing skepticism or resistance. To thrive, Visionaries benefit from practices that nurture their creativity and confidence, such as visualization, meditation, and engaging with inspirational art or nature. Their greatest strength lies in their ability to envision and manifest transformation, making them indispensable in the evolution of consciousness.

1. **The Protectors:** Guardians of Energy and Nature
   The Protectors emerge as stalwart guardians, imbued with a deep commitment to preserve the vibrational sanctity of individuals, locales, and the Earth itself. With a keen sensitivity to the presence of malevolent energies and entities, they act as the spiritual defense mechanism, repelling forces that disrupt the natural equilibrium and unity. Their protective embrace extends beyond humans, encompassing a heartfelt dedication to the welfare of animals and plants, viewing the conservation of nature and the prevention of extinction as their sacred charge. The relentless confrontation with negative energies presents a significant hurdle for Protectors, potentially ushering in weari-

ness, disenchantment, or a sense of seclusion if left unchecked. There exists a paradox in their journey, as they might find solace in withdrawing from human contact to forge deeper bonds with the natural world—a calling that replenishes their spirit yet may sever human ties, risking solitude. To uphold their vigor and purpose, Protectors are encouraged to engage in rituals that purify their energetic essence and connect with sanctified retreats that restore their vitality. Employing methods like earthing, utilizing guardian crystals, and invoking spiritual protectors are essential practices that sustain their health and capability. The Protectors' mission is pivotal in upholding the collective's energetic wholeness, ensuring a fortified and nurturing environment for all Lightworkers to thrive.

In conclusion, Lightworkers, in all their diversity, share a common purpose: to guide, heal, and elevate the collective consciousness. Each category, with its unique abilities and challenges, plays an integral role in the cosmic dance of energy and transformation. Through understanding and supporting each other, they continue to weave the fabric of spiritual evolution, embodying the very essence of light and love.

12.4 Chakra Association with Lightworkers

Integrating the profound connection between Lightworkers and the chakra system offers a fascinating perspective on how these spiritual beings align with the energy centers within the body. Each category of Lightworker resonates predominantly with a specific chakra, which not only influences their abilities but also highlights the path for their spiritual development and challenges.

Empaths: The Heart Chakra (Anahata)

Empaths, with their innate ability to feel and transform the energies around them, are deeply connected to the Heart Chakra. This chakra, located at the center of the chest, represents love, compassion, and empathy. Empaths embody these qualities, using their heart-centered energy to heal and harmonize the emotions of others and the environment. To maintain their well-being, Empaths must focus on practices that keep their Heart Chakra open and balanced, ensuring they can give and receive love in a healthy, protected manner.

Channellers: The Crown Chakra (Sahasrara)

Channellers' profound connection to the spiritual realm aligns with the Crown Chakra, the gateway to higher states of consciousness. Located at the top of the head, this chakra is the point of divine connection, understanding, and enlightenment. Channellers, through their communication with spiritual entities, demonstrate an open and vibrant Crown Chakra, facilitating messages that serve the greater good. Balancing and nurturing their Crown Chakra allows Channellers to access higher wisdom while remaining grounded in their physical existence.

The Guides: The Throat Chakra (Vishuddha)

The Guides, known for their leadership and ability to impart wisdom, resonate with the Throat Chakra. This energy center, located in the throat, governs communication, expression, and truth. The Guides excel in articulating spiritual truths and mentoring others, showcasing a balanced Throat Chakra that enables clear and inspiring communication. For The Guides, maintaining the health of this chakra is essential for their teaching and leadership roles, ensuring their messages are received with clarity and integrity.

The Peacemakers: The Solar Plexus Chakra (Manipura)

The Peacemakers, who bring balance and harmony, are aligned with the Solar Plexus Chakra. This chakra, situated above the navel, is the core of our identity, personal power, and confidence. Peacemakers utilize their inner strength and determination from a balanced Solar Plexus Chakra to mediate conflicts and restore peace. Strengthening this chakra helps Peacemakers to assert their will in challenging situations, empowering them to create harmony in the external world.

Healers: The Sacral Chakra (Svadhisthana)

Healers, with their profound ability to transmute energy for healing, resonate with the Sacral Chakra. Located in the lower abdomen, this chakra governs creativity, healing, and our relationships with others. Healers, through their nurturing and transformative energy, demonstrate a vibrant Sacral Chakra, facilitating physical, emotional, and spiritual healing. Keeping this chakra in balance is crucial for Healers to continue their work without depleting their own energy reserves.

The Visionaries: The Third Eye Chakra (Ajna)

Visionaries, the creators of new realities, align with the Third Eye Chakra. This energy center, located between the eyebrows, is the seat of intuition, insight, and vision. Visionaries, with their ability to envision and manifest new possibilities, showcase an open and clear Third Eye Chakra, enabling them to see beyond the physical realm and into the realm of potential. Cultivating this chakra allows Visionaries to refine their foresight and bring their visionary ideas into reality.

The Protectors: The Root Chakra (Muladhara)

Protectors, guardians of the energetic realm, are deeply connected to the Root Chakra. Situated at the base of the spine, this chakra represents grounding, stability, and our connection to the Earth. Protectors, with their role in safeguarding against negative energies, embody a strong and healthy Root Chakra, providing them with the stability and strength needed to perform their duties. Focusing on grounding practices helps Protectors maintain their resilience and effectiveness in their protective roles.

In conclusion, the synergy between Lightworkers and the chakra system reveals the intricate balance between the cosmic and the corporeal. By understanding and nurturing their leading chakra, each category of Lightworker can enhance their abilities, overcome their challenges, and fulfill their unique role in the collective mission of enlightenment and healing.

12.5 Witches as Lightworkers

Witches, as Lightworkers, embody a unique and powerful aspect of the Earth's consciousness, deeply connected with the natural elements that make up our world. These individuals, through their innate connection to nature, harness the energies of water, fire, metal, wood, earth, aether, and air to effect change, healing, and balance both within their personal sphere and in the broader environment.

The Essence of Witches as Lightworkers

The core essence of a witch working as a Lightworker is to collaborate with the elements in a harmonious and respectful manner. This practice involves:

- Water: Utilizing its cleansing and emotional healing properties to bring about emotional clarity and purification.
- Fire: Harnessing its transformative power to facilitate change, passion, and the manifestation of will.
- Metal: Working with metal to invite strength, resilience, and protection into one's life and the lives of others.
- Wood: Employing its growth and expansion qualities to foster new beginnings and nurture development.
- Earth: Drawing on its grounding and nurturing attributes to promote stability, fertility, and physical healing.
- Aether: Connecting with the spiritual and mystical aspects of existence, facilitating communication with higher realms.
- Air: Using its qualities of intellect, communication, and movement to inspire new ideas and spread positivity.

The Positive Work of Witches as Lightworkers

Witches who align themselves with the Lightworker path use their connections to these elements to bring about positive outcomes:

- Healing: Creating rituals and spells that draw upon the elements to heal the body, mind, and spirit.

- Protection: Crafting protective charms and wards that safeguard individuals and spaces from negative influences.
- Guidance: Offering wisdom and insight gleaned from their deep understanding of the natural world and its cycles.
- Transformation: Assisting in personal and collective transformations by working with elemental energies to clear blockages and open pathways to higher consciousness.

While it's acknowledged that some individuals may choose to work with lower frequency entities for less benevolent purposes, the focus here remains on those witches who embody the Lightworker's mission. These practitioners strive to enhance the energy of their surroundings positively, contributing to the healing and betterment of the Earth and its inhabitants.

For those who resonate with the path of the witch as a Lightworker, embracing this aspect of your being means committing to a life of deep connection with nature and its elemental forces. It involves learning to listen to the whispers of the earth, the flow of water, the crackle of fire, the breath of air, and the silent strength of metal and wood. By understanding and working with these energies, you can become a conduit for healing, transformation, and the awakening of higher consciousness.

Witches and Chakras

Witches, as Lightworkers connected with nature's elements, primarily utilize the Heart Chakra (Anahata). This chakra, located at the center of the chest, symbolizes the bridge between the physical and spiritual worlds, embodying love, compassion, and a deep connection to nature. Through the Heart Chakra, witches harmonize their practices with the rhythms of the Earth, channeling elemental energies for healing, transformation, and balance. This focus allows them to work effectively with natural elements like water, fire, earth, air, and aether, aligning their magic with the essence of life and the nurturing force of the planet.

Witches can also significantly utilize the Root Chakra (Muladhara) due to their profound connection with Mother Earth. The Root Chakra, situated at the base of the spine, represents our foundation, stability, and grounding to the Earth. Through this chakra, witches draw upon the grounding and nurturing energies of the Earth, enhancing their natural abilities to work with herbs, stones, and the elemental forces. This deep-rooted connection not only amplifies their magical practices but also fortifies their bond with nature, allowing them to harness Earth's elemental energies for protection, healing, and manifestation. Their intrinsic understanding and use of earth elements and herbs for magical and healing purposes are a testament to the powerful alignment between their practice and the stabilizing energy of the Root Chakra.

While I've outlined specific categories of Lightworkers, this classification isn't meant to limit your journey as a Lightworker. In fact, many Lightworkers blend attributes from several categories, drawing upon their vast array of experiences from past Earthly incarnations. Despite this variety, there's often one trait that stands out as your dominant characteristic, guiding your path and influence as a Lightworker.

12.6 The Role of Lightworkers in Collective Ascension

As we step into this new age of collective ascension, the role of Lightworkers becomes even more significant. The world is undergoing a tremendous vibrational shift, and Lightworkers are at the forefront of this transformation, holding space for healing, growth, and enlightenment. Each of us, through our unique gifts and abilities, contributes to the collective awakening that's happening on a global scale.

Whether you resonate with the energy of an Empath, the visionary guidance of a Guide, or the protective strength of a Protector, your work as a Lightworker is an essential part of this planetary evolution. The lessons and insights gained during your spiritual journey, especially through the challenging phases like *The Dark Night of the*

Soul and *The Rebuilding*, are the tools you now use to assist others in their journeys.

Lightworkers are here to elevate consciousness, whether by healing emotional wounds, guiding others through their spiritual paths, or simply being a beacon of light in a world that often feels dark. The energy you hold, the light you spread, and the love you embody are transformative forces in the world. This collective effort from Lightworkers is what helps to raise the vibration of humanity, ushering in a new era of higher consciousness, unity, and compassion.

In this *Rebuilding* phase, as you align your own life with your spiritual insights and truths, you also inspire others to do the same. Your personal transformation becomes a ripple that affects everyone you come into contact with. Whether consciously or unconsciously, people are drawn to your energy, your authenticity, and your light. In this way, the work of Lightworkers goes far beyond the individual—it becomes a collective mission to uplift and transform the world.

Embracing Your Role as a Lightworker

The journey of a Lightworker is not always easy, but it is deeply rewarding. As you move through the phases of spiritual awakening—*The Dark Night of the Soul, The Rebuilding,* and beyond—you become more aligned with your true purpose and your role in the greater cosmic plan.

Now, in this phase of *Rebuilding*, you are called to step fully into your power as a Lightworker. Embrace your gifts, trust your intuition, and know that the work you do—whether it's healing, guiding, protecting, or creating—matters. The world needs the light that you bring, and by staying true to your path, you contribute to the collective ascension of humanity.

Remember, you are never alone on this journey. Your spirit guides, your higher self, and the vast network of Lightworkers across the globe are all connected in this mission to elevate the planet. Together, we are building a new Earth, one that reflects love, harmony, and higher consciousness.

As you continue to align with your purpose and embrace your role, know that the Universe is always supporting you. The signs, synchronicities, and angel numbers you encounter along the way are reminders of this divine guidance, affirming that you are on the right path.

The *Rebuilding* phase is both a personal and collective transformation. Through your light, you inspire others to embark on their own journeys of awakening. And together, as Lightworkers, we move toward a future filled with hope, love, and infinite possibility.

13

The Third Stage of Angel Numbers-Unv

13.1 The Discovery

Throughout my exploration of angel numbers, I encountered a profound shift in their nature. These numbers, which I had always perceived as spiritual symbols, began to morph into something far more substantial and palpable. I remember vividly a day when, within the span of just half an hour, I was bombarded with three distinct sets of angel numbers. The sequence of events was so rapid and precise that it defied the notion of mere chance. This extraordinary experience inspired me to share my insights on my Tik-Tok account @olga.awaken. Little did I know, this decision would resonate with countless others on their spiritual paths. The video rapidly gained traction, reaching over 1.3 million views.

In my video, I shared an intriguing experience about a sequence of numbers: 4343 from a shopping receipt, 888 from a car's license plate, and 19,191 from our car's mileage. Oddly enough, these numbers all popped up within a few minutes of each other. It was strange because they weren't the typical angel numbers I usually notice. They seemed random and disconnected at first, but they kept echoing in my head, compelling me to think think deeper. It was a moment unlike any other; I've noticed angel numbers close together before, but never in such an unusual sequence. That's when a lightbulb went off: could these numbers be coordinates? Remembering that coordinates often consist of around 7 to 14 digits, and here I was, staring at a 12-digit number sequence. So, I tried my luck on Google Maps, and to my amazement...The coordinates pointed me straight to a historic chateau in France, dating all the way back to the 12th century, Château Saint-Félix-Lauragais. Now, this really piqued my curiosity. Why was I being led to this place? I've never been to France, I don't know anyone from there, and my knowledge about it is pretty much nonexistent. But then it clicked. It perfectly matched a past life regression session I had, revealing I once lived in France around 1463. The castle shown by the coordinates was built in the 12th century, predating my past life there. This couldn't just be a coincidence. Yet, with this discovery, even more questions started bubbling up inside me. I made a drawing right after returning from my past life regression in September 2023.

These are the images I found online after receiving my angel numbers coordinates, in November 2023.

I found them 2 months after my drawing! This discovery about angel numbers functioning as coordinates was a turning point for me. It represented a fusion of spiritual guidance with the tangible, physical world, revealing that these numbers could indeed guide us to real locations that hold deep personal significance. This revelation has

propelled me to delve even deeper into the mysteries of angel numbers. It leaves me in awe, contemplating the myriad other secrets and insights these divine sequences might hold, waiting to be uncovered. As I continue my journey with these numbers, I am constantly reminded of the profound connection between our spiritual journey and the physical world we navigate.

After this incident, I remembered a reiki session I had months ago. During the session, the reiki practitioner told me she was connected with me, and she "saw" me walking on a white shoreline, giving her the sense that I was in France. At the same time, I was seeing the same thing!

What is even more fascinating, though, is the reason everything happened! Because now I had a big question mark in my head. Why was I guided there? What is the reason for this information? Should I go there?

13.2 The Past Life Regression: From France 1463 to Scotland 2023

So, after this discovery, it kept playing in my head that I should do one more past-life regression to see what new information I would get. And so I did. This time, I managed to see even more details because I made the past life regression intending to see the specific time from 1463 that I had seen in my previous lifetime, and indeed, I managed to see a lot of details.

I vividly remember standing on a hill, surrounded by cypress trees, with the castle visible in the distance. I wasn't alone; I was accompanied by people who served as my aides. Wearing white gloves was the first detail that struck me, emphasizing the elegance of my attire.

Another detail that remains etched in my memory to this day was the smell emanating from the castle. It was as if someone was cooking a stew, but it was a scent of food I have never encountered since. It's a very specific aroma that lingers in my mind even as I write this book.

The smell was a blend of a wood stove burning mixed with the stew, intertwined with the fresh air from the cypress trees and the forest, creating an intensely vivid sensation.

I then proceeded to walk and enter the castle, where every detail was etched in my memory. I visited the kitchen, where the maids were busy cooking. Two of them had dark skin, and one was notably young, appearing to be around eleven. I felt a deep sense of affection for her and was saddened by her presence there, working for me. It was clear to me that she was still a child, and the idea of her labouring in such a manner was discomforting.

I made my way to my bedroom, which, while not overly large, it was adorned with beautifully carved wooden furniture. Standing before the mirror, I removed a hat that was holding my hair back. It was a pointy cone shape with linen underneath covering my hair. Once the maid removed my hat, I saw my hair. I had long brown hair. I removed my gloves, and my hands were so thin, skinny, and white. It seemed like I'd never really done any housework or much of anything else. The maids were busy getting me ready for a visit. The name Antoine kept echoing in my mind. Antoine was on his way, and I needed to be prepared for his arrival.

Flashbacks from this past life kept surfacing. I found myself waiting for my husband, gazing out my bedroom window. Below, outside the cold stone walls, the village sprawled out, smoke curling up from the houses. The distant sound of music and laughter floated up, yet I was engulfed in a profound loneliness. Despite my royal status, which provided me with everything, a deep void lingered inside. I was sad, feeling utterly purposeless. My role was to always be presentable for royal visits and to accompany my husband to royal gatherings. He was a significant figure, often away, leaving his duties and care in the hands of others. Life was luxurious, yet it left me feeling empty.

13.3 The Realization of Choices

Reflecting on my past life regression, I suddenly understood everything. It became crystal clear, and I found myself overwhelmed with emotion. I realized the stark contrast between my past and current lives. In this life, I chose to be born into a family that struggled financially, a family that wouldn't offer the support I needed emotionally and financially. It felt like a life filled with obstacles—lacking financial aid, unable to pursue education freely, and struggling to find my footing. Yet, I understood that experiencing this hardship was the only way to grant me the freedom I deeply yearned for.

Freedom became a central theme in my life. Growing up with no support, I learned to rely on myself, to work tirelessly towards my goals. The realization that no one would provide for me, forced me to break my Life Patterns. It also forced me to innovate and find solutions for every obstacle. I instinctively knew that a marriage based on wealth wouldn't align with my purpose. Despite attracting successful men, I sought something more meaningful—a relationship built on partnership and shared time.

Breaking away from societal norms, especially in Greece where early marriage and family are expected, I focused on carving my own path. I started my entrepreneurial journey with a coffee shop at 26, self-funding it through relentless hard work. This independence was a stark contrast to my past life of luxury and inactivity. Now at 46, the struggles of my youth make sense. I see the strength in my choices, and the wisdom in my journey.

Moving to Scotland with my husband, when I was 9 months pregnant and with our first boy being just 15 months old was a decision born out of necessity, a bid for a better life amidst financial struggles. This shift wasn't just about survival; it was about choosing a life that echoed my desire for creativity and self-development. Our marriage, unconventional by my past standards in partners, taught me resilience, creativity, and the power of self-reliance. My desire for creativity and innovation led to the creation of a business that defied expectations, starting with just £500 and growing into a multi-award-winning brand.

After my second Awakening, which I can also call the *Re-activation* point, I reconnected with my true self. This reconnection with my psychic abilities started the fulfilment of my Life's journey in this timeline. This journey, which later was punctuated by angel numbers, guided me to a deeper understanding of my life's purpose. It showed me the beauty of embracing my path, the strength in a partnership, and the peace that comes with acceptance. Now, as I turn more towards to my spiritual self, I see how every choice, and every struggle, has been a step towards this moment of peace and balance. It's a realization that's nothing short of magical.

Sharing these insights, I hope to illuminate the underlying reasons behind your life choices. As a holistic coach, my guiding principle for clients is to "focus on the reason, the 'Why things happen for you,' rather than the events themselves." Everything that unfolds in our lives does so for a reason, influenced not solely by our current experiences but also by the accumulated memories of our soul across all its reincarnations.

If you ever feel out of place in your life, as if the reality you're living doesn't quite match up with what you envisioned, you may have chosen to be born into circumstances vastly different from those you've experienced in past lives. I aim to clarify this concept further, to assure you that there's a deeper significance to every aspect of your journey.

13.4 We Choose Our Parents

In exploring the journey of our consciousness, it's crucial to delve into the profound decisions it makes, including the selection of our parents, the country of our birth, and the environment we are born into. This process, which might seem bewildering at first, is deeply intentional and intricately planned in the realm beyond our physical existence.

When our consciousness transitions beyond the physical body, finding itself in higher dimensions, it enters a phase of reflection and planning with the guidance of our spirit guides. This reflective process is not just a review of our past life experiences—lessons learned, progress made, and repeated mistakes—but a strategic planning session for our soul's evolution in its next earthly journey.

The decision to choose our parents, the socio-economic conditions of our birth, and even the challenges we might face are made with a clear purpose: to foster our soul's growth, to experience life through a specific lens, and to navigate through chosen obstacles for our development. This choice is based on the understanding that certain conditions can propel us towards fulfilling our life's purpose and mission. After all remember you are playing a game! Your time on Earth is about learning, developing and having fun!

You might question the rationale behind choosing a challenging family dynamic, a single parent, or being born in a country marred by conflict or poverty. These choices are rooted in the desire for specific earthly experiences that offer lessons essential for our spiritual and emotional growth. For instance, being born into a non-supportive family environment poses a unique set of challenges and choices. It's an opportunity for the soul to learn resilience, empathy, and independence, to break cycles of negativity, or to champion support and love in the face of adversity.

These decisions underscore the power of free will—a central theme in our spiritual journey.

It's not about the actions done to us but
how we choose to respond to them.

Do we succumb to despair, or do we find strength and purpose in our struggles? Do we replicate harmful patterns, or do we forge new paths of kindness and understanding?

Moreover, if you originate from a nurturing and compassionate environment, your consciousness may select this as a fundamental starting point for your journey, providing you with sturdy foundations for an easier life. This can enable you to dedicate more attention to self-care and extend love to those around you. Often, souls who appear to be withdrawn from the world, both socially and spiritually, do so as a period of rest, allowing for ample time for introspection and a clear mind to make informed decisions. It's essential to remember that everything boils down to choices. Regardless of your initial circumstances in this life, you always retain the power to choose.

This stage of our spiritual journey emphasizes that our responses and the choices we make shape our experiences and our evolution. It's a reminder that, despite the circumstances of our birth or the challenges we face, we possess the innate power to craft our destiny through our reactions and decisions. This understanding of free will and choice is fundamental to navigating the earthly experience, guiding us toward a life of fulfillment and growth.

13.5 Life's Purpose

Reflecting on the concept of life purpose, it's fascinating to consider how our consciousness chooses diverse earthly experiences to fulfill its Life purpose. These choices might vary from one life to another or repeat until mastery and complete fulfillment are achieved.

The Travellers

In some incarnations, the soul opts for contrasting experiences to gain comprehensive understanding and wisdom, which it later applies in serving the collective more effectively.

Throughout these journeys, our consciousness may embody different genders, live in various countries, and experience wide-ranging socioeconomic backgrounds. Such diversity can sometimes result in complex dynamics in one's current life, especially for old souls who have amassed holistic experiences. These individuals often exhibit certain characteristics:

1. **Innate Wisdom:** From an early age, they possess knowledge on subjects they have never formally learned, suggesting a deep, intuitive understanding carried over from past lives.

2. **Fluidity and Growth:** They frequently change environments or relationships, not due to instability but because their accelerated growth often outpaces that of their peers. This rapid development can create gaps in understanding with close associates, fostering a sense of independence as they continually evolve and forge new paths without being weighed down by the past.

3. Service to the Collective: Regardless of their career paths, they seek ways to contribute to the greater good, whether through volunteer work, supporting those around them, or offering guidance. Their actions are not just for personal gain but for uplifting others, embodying the roles of teachers, guides, or counsellors.

4. **Justice and Protection:** Having experienced various aspects of life across many incarnations, including witnessing injustices, they possess a strong sense of right and wrong. This drives them to protect others and strive for balance, challenging injustices and advocating for ethical solutions to societal issues.

Old souls carry the weight of their extensive experiences, facing numerous challenges in each lifetime. Yet, it's through these struggles that they demonstrate resilience and the capacity to inspire change, showing that there's always a path to transformation and collective betterment through ethical actions.

Throughout their earthly journeys, these old souls may exhibit traits and characteristics that blur traditional gender norms, both physically and in their personalities. It's not uncommon for them to feel a sense of misalignment with their physical form, driving them to explore their sexuality and identity more freely. This exploration isn't necessarily about homosexuality but could manifest as displaying characteristics typically associated with the opposite gender. This phenomenon stems from the dominant gender identity carried over from their past lives influencing their current existence, leading to a man expressing his feminine side more openly or a woman showcasing traditionally masculine traits.

Moreover, these souls often possess a unique skill or ability that persists across their lifetimes, enhancing with each reincarnation. This could be a consistent ability to perceive beyond the veil as a clairvoyant, to heal others, or to guide and counsel those around them. This singular talent becomes a thread weaving through their many lives, each experience honing and mastering this gift to serve both their evolution and the collective good. It's as though a specific aspect of their spiritual capabilities is destined to be developed and perfected across their earthly sojourns, contributing to their overarching mission of upliftment and enlightenment.

The Harmonizers

These consciousnesses have a journey of deepening into self-development, choosing to reincarnate with specific themes or energies, and harmonizing their soul's knowledge and experience around a core aspect of existence. These souls seek to achieve mastery and harmony within a specific domain of life, whether it be love, service, creativity, or wisdom, by immersing themselves repeatedly in similar conditions or roles.

"The Harmonizers" embark on a path of concentrated learning, choosing environments and life circumstances that resonate closely with their soul's chosen area of focus. Each reincarnation is an opportunity to refine their understanding, improve their approach, and achieve a more profound level of integration with their chosen theme. This deliberate choice of similar lives allows these souls to become beacons of expertise, wisdom, and compassion in their area of focus, ultimately serving as guides and teachers for others on similar paths, but in a different way than the Travellers. They do not teach, but they can "show."

These souls, deeply intertwined with the journey of self-healing, are on a mission to transcend a trauma—be it a result of their own decisions leading to impactful events on themselves and their surroundings, or due to the actions of others that left a mark too profound to easily overcome. Their choice of similar life scenarios across reincarnations is a deliberate path towards healing and completing their soul's mission. Here are some defining characteristics of these resilient souls:

1. **Natural Magnetism and Loyalty:** They are the epitome of loyalty and truth, possessing an innate ability to attract and nurture close-knit relationships. Their lives are deeply rooted in family ties and long-lasting friendships, embodying the essence of true companionship.

2. **Interconnected Existence:** Unlike the Travellers who are driven by a thirst for independence, they thrive in creating and maintaining a stable and harmonious environment for themselves and their loved ones. Their existence feels inextricably linked to the well-being of those around them.

3. **Periods of Reflection:** Although they may seek solitude, it's always within a supportive setting. Their journey is marked by fluctuating moods, especially when echoes of a greater purpose begin to surface, clouded by a lack of clarity yet underscored by a profound sense of destiny.

4. **Mastery of a Healing Skill:** Each of these souls is gifted in a particular skill that not only defines their journey but also serves as a tool for self-healing. Whether it's through the enchanting power of beauty or artistic expressions like drawing, singing, or dancing, their chosen skill is a means of personal therapy and transformation.

These are the souls that effortlessly radiate light, often leading lives that appear smooth and enviable on the surface, yet are fraught with internal battles. Their ultimate quest is to recognize and mend the wounds of their trauma, thereby liberating themselves from the grips of emptiness that could otherwise spiral into depression or a lack of drive. In healing their deepest scars, they fulfill their life's purpose, illuminating the path not just for themselves but for others who may find solace in their journey.

I'm sharing all this to help you figure out what you're here for. Your Spirit Guides have a timing for everything, and they send you angel numbers to nudge you towards remembering your life's purpose. So, when you get these numbers and they point you to a specific place, it's all part of the plan. These places have something to do with your life's big picture. They're clues or signposts, guiding you to where you need to be or what you need to understand about yourself. It's like getting hints on a treasure map, where each clue leads you closer to discovering what you're truly meant to do.

13.6 Life's Mission

If you're grappling with the concept of our consciousness selecting its entry point into this world, including the environment and parents, it's crucial to recognize the nuanced dynamics of free will. While our consciousness indeed chooses its starting conditions, the unpredictable nature of free will means we can't predict every interaction or outcome with the individuals in our lives. This uncertainty adds complexity to our earthly journey but also enriches it with opportunities for growth and learning.

Some souls embark on this earthly journey with a specific mission, distinct from a life purpose focused solely on personal development. These souls are here to navigate and surmount challenges, to disrupt and transform enduring patterns, not just for their own evolution but to inspire and guide a collective shift toward a higher consciousness. Their presence serves as a catalyst, propelling not just individual but collective progress.

Such souls have typically experienced numerous lifetimes, accumulating a wealth of experiences and lessons that prepare them for their mission. They possess a profound understanding and empathy, enabling them to connect with and influence a broad spectrum of souls. Their mission is to usher in change, to illuminate new paths of thinking and being that transcend personal fulfillment and contribute to the greater collective good.

Understanding that some of us are here with a broader mission helps frame our struggles and challenges in a new light. It shifts the narrative from a purely personal journey of self-discovery to a vital part of a larger, communal evolution. This perspective encourages us to look beyond our immediate circumstances and consider our role in the tapestry of collective consciousness. It's a reminder that, while our path may be fraught with challenges, each step forward contributes to a grander vision of collective awakening and transformation.

Understanding the journey of our consciousness and its transition between dimensions reveals a fascinating aspect of our existence that transcends time and space. In the earthly realm, we experience life from a linear perspective, with a clear progression of past, present, and future. This linear perception is confined to the third dimension, where our physical lives unfold. However, once our consciousness ascends to the fourth dimension and beyond, the conventional constraints of time and space dissolve.

In these higher dimensions, our consciousness is liberated from linear timelines, enabling it to traverse freely across what we perceive as past and future. This non-linear existence allows for a unique perspective on life and the universe. It's from this vantage point that some highly vibrational souls bring back to Earth groundbreaking ideas and innovations that seem far ahead of their time. These insights can rapidly advance human understanding and technology, propelling collective progress in leaps and bounds.

This phenomenon is not merely about individual enlightenment or progress. It speaks to the existence of highly evolved souls among us, whose missions extend beyond Earth experiences. These are the souls who have journeyed through numerous lifetimes, planets, and dimensions, gathering a wealth of experience and wisdom. They return to the earthly plane with a specific purpose: to awaken, guide, and catalyze positive change within the collective consciousness.

Such souls often carry with them knowledge and ideas that may appear to originate from the future but are, in fact, drawn from the limitless expanse of the higher dimensions. Their ability to access and bring forth this knowledge is a testament to their advanced spiritual development and their commitment to the collective evolution of humanity.

Understanding this aspect of our spiritual journey offers a profound perspective on the role of consciousness in shaping not only our individual destinies but also the collective fate of humanity. It highlights the interconnectedness of all things and the boundless potential of the human spirit to transcend the apparent limitations of our physical existence.

13.7 The Reason

And now, you might be curious about how all of this ties into the concept of angel numbers, particularly as we explore the advanced stage of using them as coordinates. This aspect of angel numbers as a communication system unfolds when we reach a critical point in our awakening journey. It's during this stage that the use of angel numbers as coordinates becomes particularly significant, serving as a tool to deepen our understanding of our life's purpose or mission.

The reception of angel numbers as coordinates is not random; it occurs at pivotal moments, specifically designed to guide us toward greater self-awareness and enlightenment. This method of communication is intricately linked to our spiritual evolution, acting as a beacon that lights the way to our true path. When we begin to receive these numerical sequences as coordinates, it signifies that we're ready to unlock deeper layers of our existence, to explore connections and revelations that have been waiting for us.

This concept underscores the profound relationship between us, our spirit guides, and the universe. It emphasizes that our journey is not solitary; we are constantly supported and guided through signs and symbols that resonate with our soul's frequency. The use of angel numbers as coordinates is a clear indication of this support, offering us a unique and direct way to interact with the higher dimensions and receive guidance that is tailored specifically to our spiritual journey.

So, when you start noticing angel numbers that seem to suggest coordinates, pay close attention. This is a direct message from your spirit guides, inviting you to explore, remember, and understand the deeper aspects of your life's purpose or mission. It's a call to embark on a journey of discovery, one that leads you to the answers you've been seeking and aligns you more closely with your true self and your role in the universe. It's time for Activation!

13.8 Which Angel Numbers Can Be Used as Coordinates?

By now, I can imagine that you must be feeling excited, reading all this, and you can't wait to figure out how to use your angel numbers as coordinates. And I will tell you about this right now. So first of all, not all the angel numbers that you see are coordinates. There have to be three specific conditions: *Timing, Length, and Reason.*

Timing is everything. The numbers that serve as coordinates don't just pop up occasionally; they appear all at once, almost bombarding you with their presence. It's like the universe is tapping you on the shoulder, insisting you pay attention. These aren't the familiar sequences you're used to; they're new, fresh, and impossible to overlook. It's a sign that you're ready for this deeper, more profound level of communication. Your mind has been trained to recognize these patterns, and now it's time to see what they truly mean. Remember I saw mine in less than 30 minutes.

Length is the second crucial aspect. For angel numbers to transform into coordinates, they need to be long enough. We're talking about sequences that can fill at least two sets of seven digits, which is essential for pinning down a location on Google Maps. In my personal experience, the numbers 4343, 888, and 19191 combined to form a 12-digit sequence. Ideally, you'd want 13 digits for precision, but even 11 can work. This length is important because it gives you a specific point on the map, a destination with potential significance to your personal journey.

There is also a third parameter, which is *Reason*. The period my angel number coordinates appeared was significant as I felt everything was collapsing. I was ready to quit, and for the first time in my life, I felt I had no way out. My spirit guides sent me these specific angel number coordinates to lead me to my past life, which would give me the solution for the present. There was an urgency to the matter, and that's why the Universe gave me this sign. It was an awakening to my Life's purpose and Mission.

It's fascinating to think about what these numbers could reveal. Maybe they point to a place connected to a past life or somewhere that holds the key to your next big step in life. The possibilities are endless and deeply personal. It's like the universe is giving you a treasure map, and the numbers are the X marking the spot.

13.9 How to Use Angel Numbers as Coordinates on Google Maps

Alright! Let's say you saw your angel numbers with all the above parameters. You know you can use them as coordinates. But you don't know how.

Let's explore how to enter the angel number sets as coordinates on Google Maps. We'll use different formats to see how they might translate into potential coordinates. Remember, the format for coordinates on Google Maps is generally in degrees (latitude and longitude), and can be input in various ways.

Example: Angel Numbers Set - 1221 333 1515 (11 digits)

First Format (2 digits .5 digits, dash 2 digits .5 digits):

Using Numbers: 12.21333 - 15.1515

On Google Maps: This format will lead to a specific latitude and longitude on the map. The first part (12.21333) is the latitude, and the second part (15.1515) is the longitude.

Second Format (1 digit .5 digits, dash 1 digit .5 digits):

Using Numbers: 1.22133 - 3.31515

On Google Maps: This is another valid format, potentially pointing to a different location due to the changed value of the coordinates.

Example 2: Angel Numbers Set - 1221 3333 1515 (12 digits)

First Format (2 digits .5 digits, dash 2 digits .5 digits):

Using Numbers: 12.21333 - 15.1515

On Google Maps: Similar to the first example, this would pinpoint a location based on these latitude and longitude values.

Second Format (1 digit .5 digits, dash 1 digit .5 digits):

Using Numbers: 1.22133 - 3.33151

On Google Maps: This altered format will again provide a different location on the map.

Example 3: Angel Numbers Set - 1221 3333 15151 (13 digits)

First Format (2 digits .5 digits, dash 2 digits .5 digits):

Using Numbers: 12.21333 - 15.15151

On Google Maps: This will pinpoint a unique location, different from the previous examples due to the slight change in the longitude value.

Second Format (1 digit .5 digits, dash 1 digit .5 digits):

Using Numbers: 1.22133 - 3.33151

On Google Maps: Similar to the second example, this format might lead to a different location.

It's fascinating to see how these angel number sequences can be interpreted into coordinates, leading to various places around the globe. Each set of numbers, when input differently, can guide you to a unique location, offering a blend of mysticism and geography.

The places revealed by these coordinates could hold a profound connection to your past life, a significant moment in your soul's journey, or even offer guidance for the next steps in your current life. When you receive these angel numbers, it's as though your spirit guides are laying out a map for you, showing you where to go next on your path of spiritual awakening.

In Chapter 13, we've explored the deep connection between angel numbers and coordinates, delving into how these numbers act as guides on your journey. Whether pointing to significant places from past lives or directing you toward the next pivotal stage in your spiritual path, the understanding and use of angel numbers as coordinates represent an advanced level of spiritual communication. This chapter illustrates that angel numbers are far more than just messages; they are the universe's way of guiding us toward places and experiences that are integral to our soul's evolution.

As you continue your spiritual journey, always be open to the possibility that the numbers you're seeing hold deeper meanings, guiding you not just metaphorically but literally, to places where your soul is being called. You may find yourself uncovering ancient memories, reconnecting with lost parts of your spiritual history, or finding the answers you've been seeking—all through the powerful and mysterious world of angel number coordinates.

By recognizing these coordinates and understanding their significance, you unlock a deeper layer of spiritual insight. It's not just about receiving a message; it's about being guided to a place where you can learn, heal, and grow. This is the third stage of angel numbers, and it reveals an even greater potential for spiritual expansion and transformation.

Keep your eyes open, and trust that the universe is always guiding you. Whether through numbers, dreams, or other signs, the path is always unfolding before you, leading you to the places where your soul can thrive and evolve.

14

Decoding the Reason

Now, imagine you've transformed those intriguing angel numbers into coordinates, leading you to a distinct location on Google Maps or perhaps even in the vast expanse of the sky. What comes next? How do you forge a deeper connection with this new-found place? Let's explore how to further unravel the mysteries of this discovery.

14.1 Past Life Regression

Now that you have identified a place, it's time to uncover the reasons behind it. Why have your spirit guides shown you this location? What insights could it offer about your current life choices or even your life purpose? Why now?

To gain more clarity, consider undergoing a past-life regression. You can either consult a hypnotherapist you trust or try a guided meditation. I also offer a hypnosis meditation on my website, in the courses collection, designed to help you explore your past lives: www.olgaawaken.com

Remember, the experiences you uncover are meant to provide you with a new perspective on life. Exploring past lives is not only intriguing but also enlightening, as it could reveal your life purpose or explain certain inclinations and choices in your current journey.

Reflecting on whether there's a connection to the place revealed by the angel numbers, I realized it offered me profound clarity on my life's choices. It illuminated why I've always felt a strong sense of equality and a protective urge towards those unfairly treated. The revelation of a specific location I once inhabited shed light on past endeavors to address injustices—efforts that were unfulfilled then but have permeated this life with a drive for fairness and a rebellious spirit against the oppression of the vulnerable.

This insight also provided an understanding of why my second son, born with Down syndrome, chose me as his mother. His consciousness recognized in me the ability to ensure he experiences a life marked by justice and equality. It's a realization that deepens my bond with him and underscores the responsibility I feel to provide an environment where he can thrive without prejudice.

Moreover, this journey has clarified my inexplicable connection to Africa and, particularly, to its black population—a continent I've never visited but feel deeply drawn to.

The mysterious origins of the phrase "Akuna Matata," which I inexplicably used as a child growing up in Greece, have finally been unraveled, thanks to the journey through my past lives and the exploration of angel numbers. This phrase, which predates its popularization by a Disney song in 1994, was a puzzle piece from my childhood that seemed out of place until now. The connection it has with my past life experience in 1463, where I witnessed African women, likely slaves, working in my household, has shed light on its significance in my life.

"Akuna Matata," a Swahili term meaning "no problem," mirrors the "ce la vie" attitude I might have adopted back then. The revelation that this phrase could have been used in the kitchen of my past life by a young girl working for me opens up a floodgate of realizations. It suggests a direct link to South Africa, potentially indicating the origin of the young girl and possibly implicating involvement in the slave trade. This connection not only highlights a personal historical tie to a time and practice of profound injustice but also deepens my understanding of the karmic threads that weave through my lifetimes.

Understanding this connection brings to light the reasons behind my innate sense of justice, equality, and my deep-seated need to correct the wrongs of the past.

This profound insight gained from a simple childhood phrase I used unwittingly reveals the complexity of our souls' journeys. It underscores how experiences from our past lives continue to shape our present, pushing us towards fulfillment, understanding, and perhaps redemption. The realization that part of my soul's mission involves addressing and healing the injustices of my past lives adds a layer of purpose to my current endeavors aimed at supporting equality and justice. It's a poignant reminder of how interconnected our past, present, and future are, guided by the unseen hand of our spirit guides through signs like angel numbers, leading us towards a greater understanding of our place in the universe and our contributions to the collective consciousness.

This exploration through angel numbers, revealing coordinates of past significance, is not just a journey through time but a profound dive into the essence of who I am and what I stand for. It's a reminder of the interconnectedness of our lives across timelines and how past experiences shape our current realities and aspirations. My goal to assist and advocate for those who've experienced inequality feels not just like a personal choice but a mission encoded within my soul, a continuation of a journey that spans lifetimes.

14.2 Soul Contracts

Exploring the deeper implications of using angel numbers as coordinates to uncover specific Earth locations can lead to revelations about **soul contracts**. Before delving into what soul contracts entail, consider if the place revealed to you has a particular individual living there or if you've always felt a pull towards visiting. This reflection might hint at a deeper connection or purpose for you to meet with specific people.

Soul contracts are agreements made before our consciousness decides to embark on the Earthly journey. These contracts come in two main types: short-term and long-term.

Short-term Soul Contracts

Short-term soul contracts are arrangements we make with other consciousnesses to engage briefly during critical moments in our lives. These interactions are designed to catalyze significant events or developments, serving as a trigger for essential changes or growth. The individuals involved in these contracts often enter our lives unexpectedly, play a crucial role for a brief period, and then depart, leaving a lasting impact despite the fleeting connection. Their mission is precise and concentrated, meant to influence our journey profoundly but briefly.

Long-term Soul Contracts

Long-term soul contracts represent agreements made by our consciousness with others before incarnating on Earth, aimed at sharing extensive periods of our earthly journey together. These contracts could involve relationships with parents, siblings, close friends, other family members, or significant individuals who enter our lives and remain for an extended duration. Together, we engage deeply, completing each other in ways that facilitate mutual growth and fulfillment of tasks, often subconsciously, to aid the evolution of both parties involved.

Long-term soul contracts are about significant, enduring relationships that, despite challenges or perceived adversities, we are compelled to maintain until a specific purpose or task is accomplished. Such relationships can sometimes appear as if they are testing our limits, possibly even resembling abusive dynamics. However, the true essence of these contracts is not to cause harm but to prompt necessary growth and evolution. It's when either party recognizes the need to break harmful patterns and develop further that these soul contracts fulfill their purpose, facilitating a journey of mutual enlightenment and support, enriching the soul's experience on Earth.

14.3 Twin Flames and Soul Mates

Twin flames fall into the category of long soul contracts, a bond that extends beyond one lifetime, spanning multiple incarnations. This concept of twin flames suggests that, at a soul level, our consciousness was once split, creating two opposite halves. The idea is that each of us is in a perpetual search for this other half, and finding them brings a sense of wholeness. Often, one twin embodies qualities the other lacks—one may be dark while the other is light, one patient while the other is impulsive. This energetic contrast creates a dynamic, intense connection, often challenging, where the relationship can feel deeply magnetic yet difficult to sustain, sometimes leaving one or both individuals hurt. There's a common belief that leaving a twin flame equates to losing part of oneself, the "other half," which can lead to the feeling that the connection is irreplaceable.

However, I see this theory differently. In my understanding, our consciousness has always been a unified, powerful force, a whole entity directly sourced from the divine. Rather than being split, we are complete within ourselves. The twin flame relationship, as a form of soul contract, offers a profound opportunity for growth, self-discovery, and healing. Instead of viewing twin flames as our "missing half," I believe they serve as mirrors, reflecting the deeper aspects of ourselves—those qualities or challenges we may not see on our own. This relationship allows us to experience the duality within, revealing contrasting elements of our consciousness. Through this powerful bond, we are given the chance to learn, develop, and integrate these reflections, coming into alignment with our true self.

Soulmates are another form of long soul contract, one that brings multiple encounters across many lifetimes. Unlike twin flames, however, soulmate connections are often gentler and more harmonious, centred around balance, peace, and mutual growth. A soulmate relationship doesn't necessarily mean a lifelong partnership in any single lifetime—some soulmates may appear for a brief period, but their impact is lasting. The connection feels familiar, even from the first meeting, as though you've known each other forever. They might come into your life unexpectedly, yet their presence feels instantly comforting and right.

Soulmate relationships have a natural flow to them, bringing out the best in us with ease and warmth. They encourage us, motivate us, and remind us of our own strengths and values, and we do the same for them. Together, soulmates create a supportive, uplifting bond that guides each toward higher levels of understanding and self-realization. In their presence, we find encouragement and clarity, and through this mutual support, both souls are lifted on the path of ascension.

In conclusion, your angel numbers as coordinates can serve as divine guidance, pointing you toward these soul contracts. Whether leading you to a twin flame connection or drawing you to a soulmate, these numbers act as gentle beacons, helping you navigate to the relationships that are integral to your soul's journey. Maybe your soulmate lives there, or is a meeting point for you. Isn't it fascinating?

14.4 The Place

When decoding the message behind angel numbers presented as coordinates, a critical aspect to consider is the specific location they pinpoint. This location may hold significant relevance for your spiritual and life journey, suggesting a potential move or visit that could catalyze personal growth and align more closely with your life's purpose. For instance, being directed towards a new country might not just be about geographical change but about the transformative experiences and opportunities such a move could provide.

Imagine, for a moment, that the coordinates lead you to a country vastly different from your current residence. Reflect on the implications of such a move. How would immersing yourself in a new culture, with its unique customs and societal norms, challenge you? What aspects of your personality could this experience help develop?

Consider the potential hurdles and opportunities for growth this relocation could introduce.

This guidance towards a specific location is your spirit guides' way of nudging you towards experiences that will enrich your life in unexpected ways. It might break you free from the constraints of your current environment, offering a fresh perspective and new challenges that align more closely with your soul's growth. Such a move could be a pivotal step in fulfilling your life's purpose, opening doors to experiences and connections that were previously out of reach.

In some cases, the place pointed out by your angel numbers might highlight a historical event. Seeing a monument or graveyard could suggest your past involvement in significant historical moments. Often, these sites are tied to the trauma of wars or pivotal events in human history, indicating that a part of your energy may still linger there. To heal and reclaim this energy, visiting the site can be powerful. While there, try to connect, ask for your energy back, and express gratitude for the lessons learned. Even if you can't be there physically, meditation offers a way to visit these places in your mind's eye. Through meditative visualization, you can engage with the site, perform the same healing rituals, and make peace with the past.

15

Angel Numbers as Coordinates on Astrological M

Just like coordinates guide us geographically, angel numbers can guide us through the astrological aspects of our lives. When it comes to integrating your angel numbers as coordinates into your astrological chart, the process can be a fascinating and deeply personal journey. Start by identifying the primary and secondary numbers within your sequence—these will offer you key insights into the energies at play. Simplify the numbers by breaking them down into single or double digits that can easily fit within the 30-degree zodiac wheel. This is often the easiest and most intuitive way to begin mapping your angel numbers onto the chart.

For those who wish to dive deeper, you can explore more intricate methods, such as the deductive process described later. While this approach requires more focus, it can reveal hidden connections and alignments that add richness to your understanding.

Always trust your instinct throughout this process. Your intuition is your strongest guide when working with these mystical sequences, and with time, you may even discover new ways to interpret and map your numbers, unlocking more personal messages from the universe.

Lastly, while self-exploration is powerful, it's always beneficial to consult with an experienced astrologer. They can help you refine your approach and offer insights into how these numbers interact with your astrological chart, adding even more clarity and depth to your readings. Together, you'll be able to decode the guidance and wisdom that your angel numbers are offering, bringing you closer to understanding your path and purpose.

15.1 Timing and Transits

Angel numbers can also correspond to astrological timing, often aligning with key transits or progressions. For instance, repeatedly seeing a number like 1111 could indicate a significant transit at 11 degrees in your chart. Transits occur when celestial bodies pass through key points in your natal chart, bringing shifts, lessons, or opportunities into focus.

If you're seeing 1111, it may coincide with a planet like Jupiter or Venus transiting 11 degrees, influencing that specific area of your life.

15.2 Angel numbers and Planetary Energies

Each number holds a specific vibrational energy that not only carries spiritual significance but also connects to planetary influences in astrology. By understanding the planetary energies, *(Parker & Parker, 2001)*, behind angel numbers, we gain deeper insights into the messages being sent by our Spirit Guides. These celestial connections add a layer of meaning that allows us to align more fully with the divine purpose behind each number.

For instance:

- *Angel Number 1* often appears to signal new beginnings, leadership, and action. Its planetary connection is with the *Sun* and *Mars*, symbolising vitality, strength, and ambition. When you see Angel Number 1 or sequences like 111, it may be a nudge from the universe to take initiative, embrace independence, and harness the fiery energy of these planets to move forward with confidence.

- *Angel Number 2* represents balance, harmony, and partnership, aligning with the energies of *Venus* or the *Moon*. These planets amplify the qualities of emotional intelligence, peace, and cooperation. When Angel Number 2 or 222 comes into your awareness, it's often a message to seek balance in your relationships and emotional life, to trust the process of partnership, and to create peace where there may be discord.

- *Angel Number 3* resonates with creativity, communication, and growth, reflecting the expansive energy of *Jupiter*. This planet's influence encourages learning, joy, and personal development. Seeing Angel Number 3 or 333 can be a sign that it's time to embrace your creative potential, express yourself openly, and allow optimism to guide you forward.

- *Angel Number 4* symbolises stability, structure, and building solid foundations, connected to the disciplined energies of *Saturn*. When Angel Number 4 or 444 shows up, it often signifies a period where hard work, order, and perseverance are needed. Saturn's influence reinforces the need to ground your efforts in reality, ensuring that what you build is both practical and lasting.

- *Angel Number 5* is associated with change, freedom, and adaptability, aligning with the dynamic energy of *Mercury*. If you encounter Angel Number 5 or 555, it signals that shifts are occurring in your life, and you are being encouraged to embrace the changes with flexibility and open-mindedness. Mercury's influence reminds you to stay mentally agile and ready for new experiences.

- *Angel Number 6* holds the energy of nurturing, love, and responsibility, resonating with *Venus*. When Angel Number 6 or 666 appears, it is often a call to focus on your home, family, and relationships, fostering love and care. It's a reminder that balance between caring for others and caring for yourself is essential, and Venus supports you in creating beauty and harmony in your personal life.

- *Angel Number 7* represents spiritual awakening, inner wisdom, and introspection, tied to the mystical vibrations of *Neptune* and *Uranus*. If Angel Number 7 or 777 appears in your life, it signals a deepening spiritual journey, encouraging you to seek answers within and trust the guidance of your higher self. These planetary energies amplify your connection to the unseen and inspire you to explore your inner world.

- *Angel Number 8* embodies power, material success, and abundance, connected to the transformative energy of *Pluto* and the structured strength of *Saturn*. When Angel Number 8 or 888 comes into your awareness, it's often a sign that financial success and personal empowerment are on the horizon. These numbers ask you to embrace your authority and use your resources wisely, ensuring that your material gains align with your spiritual purpose.

- *Angel Number 9* symbolises completion, compassion, and humanitarianism, resonating with the expansive energies of *Mars* and *Jupiter* in their higher, philosophical forms. If Angel Number 9 or 999 appears to you, it is a message to focus on the bigger picture, to embrace your role in serving others, and to recognise that you are nearing the completion of an important life chapter. Mars and Jupiter together remind you of your strength and vision, calling you to use both for the greater good.

By understanding the planetary energies that flow through angel numbers, we deepen our relationship with these divine messages. These numbers become not only signs from the universe but also powerful tools to help us align with the cosmic rhythms that shape our lives. Angel numbers, paired with their planetary influences, guide us through every step of our spiritual awakening and personal evolution.

15.3 How to Map Angel Numbers to Your Astrological Chart

When using angel numbers in your astrological chart, the primary number in a sequence (the dominant number) will correspond to the house in the chart, and the secondary number (or repeating numbers) will relate to the degree within that house. The houses represent different areas of life, while the degrees refine the focus within those areas. This way, you can assign meaning to where your angel numbers point you.

Step-by-Step Process:

1. Identify the Angel Number Sequence: Take the angel number you've been seeing, such as 8558.
2. Use the Primary Number for the House: In this case, the primary number is 5, meaning the number points you to the 5th House. The 5th House in astrology is related to creativity, self-expression, children, and pleasure. This sets the overall theme for the message.
3. Use the Secondary Number for the Degree: The secondary number in 8558 is 8, which represents 8 degrees within the 5th House. Degrees in astrology help focus the energy on a specific point in that area of your life.
4. Interpret the Message: With your angel number 8558 mapped to the 5th House and 8 degrees, consider how this applies to your current life situation. Perhaps this number is guiding you to focus on expressing yourself creatively, embracing joy, or even thinking about how children or playful activities influence your life.

This method allows you to create a powerful link between the messages from your spirit guides through angel numbers and the insights provided by astrology. By knowing the area of life (house) and the specific degree, you can better understand what aspect of your life needs attention and how you can harness the cosmic energy.

A Simple Rule of Thumb

- Primary number = House (what area of life the message is focusing on).
- Secondary number = Degree (a specific point within that area for deeper insight).

If you come across more complex sequences, such as longer strings of numbers like 434388819191, you can break them down in pairs to map them across several houses and degrees, creating a broader picture.

So, for example, if I have the number 434388819191, I would break it down into segments: 4343, 888, and 19191. Next, I would identify the primary numbers from each segment: 4 from 4343, 8 from 888, and 1 from 19191. Then, I would look at the relevant houses in an astrological chart:

- 4th House (from 4343), with a focus on 3 degrees in the 4th House.
- 8th House (from 888), which can either focus on the 8th House as a whole or hone in on the 19th degree.
- 1st House (from 19191), with attention on 9 degrees in the 1st House.

This way, the number sequence leads you to specific houses and degrees in your astrological chart, providing insights into the areas of life connected to each house and degree.

Trust Your Intuition

As always, trust your intuition when interpreting these numbers. Your spirit guides know how to present the right message at the right time. If a certain number seems to point to a specific area of your chart, follow that guidance and reflect on what it might be telling you. It's also a great idea to work with an experienced astrologer who can help you refine and interpret these cosmic signals.

16

Angel Numbers as Coordinates in the Sky

Things got interesting when someone commented on my viral video, saying, "What if we could use angel numbers as coordinates for the sky?" The idea was to see if these numbers could point us to specific places in the universe. This was something new and exciting, and I was eager to try it out.

So there I was with my angel number sequence: 4343 888 19191—the same numbers that had mysteriously led me to a specific location in France. This time, I decided to use the Worldwide Telescope, a tool that allows you to travel through space digitally. I entered the numbers as I had done on Google Maps, half-expecting nothing to happen.

To my astonishment, these numbers guided me to a star in the constellation Aquila. That blew my mind! It was fascinating to think that the numbers I received from everyday life could connect me to a constellation light-years away. And the next constellation over? Aquarius, my zodiac sign. Talk about a cosmic coincidence!

When entering celestial coordinates, you typically use the Right Ascension (RA) and Declination (Dec) system, similar to longitude and latitude on Earth.

16.1 Celestial Coordinates

Right Ascension (RA):

- Analogous to longitude on Earth but for the celestial sphere.
- Measured in hours, minutes, and seconds.
- RA lines run from the celestial north pole to the celestial south pole.
- 0 hours is set at the celestial equator, increasing eastward up to 24 hours.
- One hour in RA equals 15 degrees.

Declination (Dec):

- Similar to latitude on Earth.
- Measured in degrees, minutes, and seconds north or south of the celestial equator.
- Ranges from +90° at the celestial north pole to -90° at the celestial south pole.

These coordinates are essential for accurately pinpointing celestial objects like stars, planets, and galaxies. They allow astronomers to track specific locations in the sky, making it possible to find connections between angel numbers and celestial phenomena.

16.2 Interpreting Angel Numbers as Celestial Coordinates

If you're feeling adventurous, you can experiment with your angel number coordinates in the sky using astronomical software or websites like Stellarium Web, Sky-map.org, NASA's SkyView, or Worldwide Telescope. You can put the Angel Numbers with the same way you did on Google maps. If the format is not right for the specific website you use then consider changing the format. For example, you can input the numbers using the Right Ascension and Declination format.

Example: Converting 4343, 888, and 19191 into Celestial Coordinates

Using celestial coordinates is a bit like solving a puzzle. You might need to interpret the numbers creatively to fit the RA/Dec format. For instance, **4343 888 19191** could be split into smaller segments.

Format:

- Right Ascension (RA): **4h 34m 30s**
- Declination (Dec): **+88° 19' 19"**

When entered into astronomical software, this would show a specific location in the sky. If the coordinates lead to a notable celestial body, star, or constellation, you can explore the astrological and spiritual significance of that area. Who knows—maybe the stars are aligning to reveal something meaningful about your life's journey.

16.3 The Spiritual Connection

The discovery that angel numbers can be used to find celestial coordinates got me thinking about my past life regression sessions, where I learned that my soul originated from **Sirius B**. This sparked an idea: what if angel numbers could also guide me to stars related to my cosmic origins?

f you're guided to celestial coordinates linked to a star system, this could be your spirit guides showing you your true home. It's a reminder that your journey is not confined to Earth but spans across the universe, where you have played different roles in different lifetimes.

Could angel numbers help pinpoint where our souls came from in the cosmos? For me, this idea opened up a new chapter in my journey with angel numbers, revealing that they might connect us not just to places on Earth but also to our spiritual roots among the stars.

16.4 Consciousness Experience in the Sky – The Starseeds

For some, angel numbers and celestial coordinates might reveal something even more profound: a connection to **starseeds**. Starseeds are souls who originated from other planets or star systems before incarnating on Earth. These beings have chosen to be here to assist in Earth's evolution, bringing wisdom and knowledge from their cosmic origins.

I know from my own spiritual journey that my soul first travelled to **Sirius B** after leaving the Source. Perhaps you too are a starseed, and your angel numbers are pointing you to constellations or stars that connect to your origins. If your celestial coordinates align with star systems like Sirius, Pleiades, or Orion, this could provide insight into your life mission on Earth.

Starseeds come to Earth with a **Life Mission** that often involves assisting humanity's collective awakening. These missions are tied to the wisdom and energy they bring from their star systems. If your angel numbers point you to a star system, consider what this might reveal about your purpose on Earth.

Common traits of starseeds include:

- A deep sense of purpose.
- Strong intuition.
- A natural connection to energy and the cosmos.
- Psychic abilities that remain active throughout life.
- Empathy and a desire to help others.

Exploring these traits might provide clarity about your life path and how your cosmic origins influence your current journey.

16.5 The Source

I want to share with you the incredible journey of discovering my soul's origin. It all began during one of my meditations when I asked my spirit guides to reveal where my consciousness first travelled after leaving the Source.

As the meditation deepened, I found myself in a vast, endless, black universe. Gradually, amidst this cosmic void, small flickers of light began to emerge. These tiny sparks grew and expanded into what appeared as planets. However, they weren't solid, spherical planets like we know; they were pulsating balls of energy, ethereal and holographic, constantly shifting in motion and colour. These planets seemed to merge and move through the chaos of the universe.

Amidst this celestial dance, an immense radiant light took centre stage. The warmth it radiated was more than just heat; it was an emotional warmth, a nurturing and comforting presence that enveloped my entire being. I watched energetic beings, like luminous specks, move between this grand light and the planets, creating a spectacle of harmony in the cosmic ballet. The love from this light was indescribable, transcending any love I had ever known on Earth. It made even the deep love I have for my family, my husband, and my children seem like a faint comparison.

As I bathed in this light, I felt an unbreakable bond, a unity so profound that it moved me to tears. Emotions overwhelmed me, and as I woke from the meditation, I was filled with fear for the first time—fear that I might choose to stay in the Light and never return. The final message I received before waking up was gentle yet firm: *"You have to go back. You have to speak."*

That love, so powerful and unconditional, lingered with me for days. It felt as if I had touched the divine, the Creator, an energy so pure and magical that it transformed my entire understanding of love.

I began to understand the significance of all consciousness coming from the same Source. We are all connected, leaving and returning to the Light to experience different lives on planets—or perhaps these planets were dimensions on the same planet? Were all these entities, often referred to as aliens, actually the same as us, just existing in different dimensions and using different vessels? This cosmic revelation showed me that we are all one, free to explore diverse paths, only to return to the Source and embark on our soul's endless journey.

16.6 A Guide from Sirius B

Sirians B communicating
Image by Olga Gerogianni

Inspired by my first encounter with the Source, I set a focused intention to witness where my consciousness first travelled after leaving the Light. A few weeks later, during a deep meditation, I found myself in a magical, serene scene that's difficult to describe. I was in the middle of a vast hall, which felt like being underwater, though the density was thinner than water but heavier than air. Light blue beings floated around with energy tails like mermaids. They all appeared ethereal.Looking at my own hands, I realized I was like them—translucent, light silverish blue, and floating in this strange atmosphere. At the far end of the hall, a taller being, seated on a throne and surrounded by guards, awaited me. Other beings stood along the hall, as if waiting for my approach.

One being came forward from a small group near the throne and touched their forehead to mine. We both had crystals on our foreheads that lit up upon contact, and I immediately received a flood of information. I was being presented to the council. I telepathically asked for my name. "Welcome home, Ahmira," the being responded. "Don't be afraid. You can approach."

As I moved forward, I noticed more details: floating octopuses like birds, large whale-like creatures drifting through the sky, all in perfect silence. Symbols adorned the columns, and groups of beings communicated with soft, silent gestures.

communicated with soft, silent gestures.

"We are still on Sirius B," they said. "We will depart soon. You are coming with us to Earth." In that instant, I remembered that I was part of the council as a guide to a team assigned to document our journey to Earth. When I awoke from the meditation, everything clicked. I remembered my role, and it all made sense. Ever since this activation of memory, my whole life changed!

16.7 The Starseeds

Starseeds are unique because they come to Earth with a *Life Mission*, which is different from a *Life Purpose* focused on personal development. A Life Mission often aligns with Lightworkers from different dimensions and planets, bringing cosmic knowledge to Earth to help with collective awakening and growth.

Starseeds tend to exhibit certain traits that hint at their extraterrestrial origins, including:

- **Innate, Unexplained Knowledge**: They have a deep understanding of various subjects without formal learning.

- **Sense of Higher Purpose**: They often feel they are part of something greater, with a mission that benefits humanity.
- **Natural Connection with Energy**: They intuitively understand and feel the energy in people, animals, objects, and places.
- **Psychic Abilities**: Many starseeds retain their psychic abilities throughout life, using them for the greater good.
- **Deep Connection with the Cosmos**: They feel a profound link to the stars and the universe, sensing that their true home is elsewhere.
- **Empathy and Sensitivity**: Starseeds often have heightened empathy and sensitivity, making them excellent healers.
- **Feeling of Alienation**: They may feel out of place on Earth, disconnected from societal norms.
- **Drawn to Metaphysics and Spirituality**: They seek wisdom and are naturally inclined towards metaphysical subjects and spirituality.
- **Strong Intuition and Visionary Ideas**: Guided by strong inner voices, they often have ideas ahead of their time.
- **Sense of Urgency or Mission**: They feel driven to contribute to the world in meaningful ways.
- **Challenges in Early Life**: Many face significant struggles in early life, which shape their empathy and resilience.

While these characteristics are general, they can vary by the starseed's race and origins. Understanding your starseed origin through past-life exploration can open up new insights into your mission on Earth.

16.8 It's Not All Light

Angel numbers, when interpreted as celestial coordinates, can reveal a connection to lower vibrational starseed races, highlighting the darker aspects of our soul from previous incarnations. This realization urges us to confront and heal these shadows, transforming them into light.

For example, if your angel number coordinates lead to a starseed race such as the Reptilians or Draconians, it may signal the need for deep introspection. These races are often associated with traits like dominance and manipulation, reflecting the Draconian archetype's narcissistic and controlling tendencies.

I found this example in my husband, whose consciousness originated from the Draconians. He struggled with narcissistic traits, feeling isolated and unable to form genuine connections. Yet, through inner healing, self-reflection, and his initiation into Reiki, he began to transform.

His journey shows that the light and dark within us aren't opposing forces but aspects that, when balanced, lead to our highest potential. His once-dominant controlling nature became self-mastery, and manipulative tendencies were redirected toward harmonious energy work. This shift embodies the light side of the Draconian legacy, proving that integration of our darker aspects can unlock profound personal growth.

This chapter offers a guide for those who may see their own struggles reflected in this story. It emphasizes embracing both light and shadow to navigate the spiritual path with wisdom and compassion. In doing so, we break through the darkness to find the light, contributing to the greater good with our unique energies and insights.

17

The starseed Races

17.1 Starseed list

In the following section, you'll find an overview of some of the most well-known starseed races. This list is intended as a starting point for your own journey, rather than a deep dive into the finer details of each origin. As you explore angel numbers as coordinates, they may just lead you toward one of these constellations, sparking a sense of recognition or curiosity.

In my quantum healing sessions, I've come to see that energy, frequency, and resonance are not only central to healing but are foundational to how we experience reality. Insights from quantum physics, as discussed in *The Quantum Self* (Zohar, 1990), illuminate these dynamics, providing a scientific framework that aligns with spiritual principles. Zohar's work suggests that at a quantum level, our consciousness and energetic frequencies are intricately connected, supporting the idea of a universe where everything is linked by vibrational resonance. This understanding underpins my healing approach, where we explore how shifts in consciousness can profoundly impact both the mind and body.

During my quantum healing sessions, my clients frequently experience energetic transformations that resonate with the quantum view of reality as fluid, interconnected, and responsive to our intentions. By embracing and harnessing this resonance, quantum healing opens doors to deep self-discovery and enhanced well-being.

Through my work, I've encountered a diverse array of starseed races—and even discovered new ones about which little is known. Each session brings fresh insights into the expansive tapestry of star origins, continually revealing new layers and mysteries.

The exploration of human galactic heritage through various starseed races is thoroughly discussed in *The Prism of Lyra (Royal & Priest, 1992)*. This foundational work provides insights into the diversity and missions of starseed lineages, offering a broad understanding of their cosmic origins and roles in humanity's evolution. Each race carries unique energy, wisdom, and purpose, encouraging both personal and collective growth.

The list below, is an invitation to follow your instincts and explore the cosmic diversity waiting beyond these pages. Let this be your springboard into the cosmos, where your intuition and research can lead you toward deeper connections and understanding. Use it to spark your path, discovering the broader universe of starseed origins and perhaps even sensing a resonance that feels like home.

Amphibians Starseeds

Amphibian starseeds are thought to originate from the planets within the *Pisces constellation*, specifically linked to the mystical energies associated with water and emotion. Some spiritual sources suggest that their origins may trace back to *Kepler-62f*, an exoplanet located in the Pisces constellation, known for its potential to support water-based life. These starseeds resonate deeply with water, not only as a physical element but as a spiritual force that embodies fluidity, emotional depth, and transformation. Their aura is frequently described as a soft, translucent blue or green, mirroring the calming, mysterious depths of the sea and creating a serene presence.

Mission and Purpose: Amphibian Starseeds come to Earth with a mission of emotional healing and guidance. They are natural mediators, offering clarity and support in complex emotional situations. Their purpose often involves guiding others to explore their own depths, find healing through reflection, and learn the power of emotional resilience. Their sensitivity to subtle energies enables them to work effectively as counselors, healers, and peacemakers.

Skills and Abilities:

- **Emotional Intelligence:** Amphibian Starseeds possess profound emotional insight, understanding and empathizing with the feelings of others on a deep, intuitive level. This makes them skilled in emotional healing and empathy-driven guidance.
- **Connection to Water:** Their affinity for water goes beyond preference; they draw strength and inspiration from it. Amphibian Starseeds are likely to be found near water bodies, where they feel rejuvenated and connected to their origin. They may also use water in spiritual practices, from cleansing rituals to meditation near bodies of water.
- **Adaptability:** Reflecting the qualities of water, these starseeds adapt with ease to different situations and people, making them flexible in both mind and spirit. Their capacity to flow with life's changes allows them to be stabilizing forces during times of transition.

Spiritual Practices: Water-based ceremonies, such as purification and emotional release rituals, play a central role in the spiritual practices of Amphibian Starseeds. They view water as a transformative element that cleanses not only the body but the soul, helping others release negative emotions and find inner peace.

Andromedans

Andromedan Starseeds, originating from the Andromeda galaxy, often referred to as M31, which is the closest spiral galaxy to the Milky

Way. They are deeply aligned with the principles of freedom and independence, valuing the liberation of the spirit and mind above all. These starseeds carry an aura that is often light, soft, and ethereal in shades of violet or indigo, representing their connection to higher realms and expansive thinking. Andromedans come to Earth with a mission of awakening others, encouraging them to break free from limiting beliefs and embrace their true, unbounded potential.

Mission and Purpose: Andromedan Starseeds are here to inspire personal and collective liberation. They aim to uplift human consciousness by helping others remember their soul's purpose and empowering them to live authentically. Their purpose often involves guiding people toward spiritual awakening, revealing new paths for growth and self-discovery. Andromedans are driven to help humanity release fears and societal constraints, paving the way for a freer, more evolved way of being.

Skills and Abilities:

- **Advocates for Freedom:** Andromedans naturally inspire others to explore personal freedom, advocating for self-liberation and helping people recognize their potential beyond imposed limitations.
- **Innovative Thinkers:** Known for their visionary ideas, Andromedans are often years ahead of their time, bringing creative and transformative insights into fields like technology, art, and spiritual practices.

- **Empathy and Compassion:** Their heightened sense of empathy allows them to connect deeply with others, understanding emotions intuitively and offering support that resonates on a soul level.
- **Spiritual Awakening Facilitators:** Andromedans are gifted at helping others awaken to their spiritual purpose. Their presence can spark significant spiritual realizations and encourage people to explore deeper truths about themselves and the universe.

Spiritual Practices: Andromedan Starseeds often engage in practices that expand consciousness, such as meditation, visualization, and breathwork, to help others break free from mental barriers. Their connection to higher realms enables them to guide others through spiritual awakenings, using techniques that encourage freedom of thought, self-expression, and alignment with the soul's purpose.

Annunaki

Annunaki
Image by Olga Gerogianni

Annunaki starseeds are often linked to the ancient planet Nibiru, a celestial body referenced in Sumerian and Akkadian mythology, marking their influence on human history and civilization. Their legacy, steeped in advanced scientific and metaphysical knowledge, fuels a deep connection to ancient cultures, especially Mesopotamia, and inspires a profound sense of responsibility to share their wisdom in today's world.

The ancient alien theory suggests that extraterrestrial beings have influenced humanity's development and spiritual traditions since early history *(von Däniken, 1968)*. This connection between Earth and otherworldly beings forms a bridge between ancient mythologies and starseed lineages, highlighting how beings like the Annunaki might have interacted with

and guided early human cultures. Such lineages suggest that many of humanity's spiritual practices, architectural marvels, and even societal structures could have roots in teachings from these advanced civilizations, intertwining our evolution with celestial influences.

Physical Characteristics and Aura: Annunaki starseeds possess a commanding presence, typically characterized by a tall, regal stature and distinguished features such as sharp cheekbones, deep-set eyes, and strong jawlines. Their intense and authoritative aura is unmistakable, often drawing attention the moment they enter a space. They are often described as having a deep, golden aura that reflects their sense of authority, wisdom, and connection to ancient knowledge. This golden hue embodies their regal and powerful presence, while also symbolising enlightenment and advanced intellect. The golden aura often has undertones of earthy brown or bronze, highlighting their grounded connection to ancient civilizations and their role as both builders and visionaries. Many Annunaki starseeds have penetrating gazes that reflect ancient wisdom and a sense of awareness, as if seeing beyond the surface into deeper truths. Often, they exude a powerful, confident energy that commands respect, and some even bear unique birthmarks or physical traits that they feel connect them to their ancient lineage.

Mission and Purpose: Annunaki starseeds carry a purpose deeply rooted in leadership and innovation. They bridge the ancient past with the evolving future, using their wisdom and influence to inspire advancements that push the boundaries of possibility. As natural leaders, they are drawn to roles where they can wield authority and advocate for progress, often in ways that blend science and spirituality. Many feel a profound connection to ancient structures, traditions, and earthy environments, which resonate with their sense of identity and heritage.

Skills and Abilities:

- **Advanced Knowledge Bearers:** Annunaki starseeds often carry innate knowledge of advanced scientific concepts and metaphysical insights, which they feel compelled to share to elevate humanity.
- **Innovative and Visionary Thinkers:** Driven to explore and expand what is possible, they push technological and spiritual boundaries, advocating for progress that aligns with ethical principles.
- **Architectural and Engineering Interest:** They feel a pull towards grand designs and structures, much like the monumental architecture associated with the Annunaki in ancient lore, and are often drawn to create or work within impressive spaces.
- **Natural Leaders:** With inherent leadership qualities, Annunaki starseeds naturally gravitate toward influential roles where they can guide and inspire others.
- **Complex Morality and Philosophical Depth:** Annunaki starseeds ponder profound questions about civilization and humanity's path, their moral complexity giving them a unique perspective on society's evolution.

Spiritual Practices: Annunaki starseeds are deeply attuned to both technological and spiritual innovation. Their practices often involve ancient wisdom and modern advancements, finding ways to harmonize these realms. They may engage in meditative or reflective practices that connect them to their heritage, especially in spaces with earthy, traditional tones. By blending ancient knowledge with modern approaches, Annunaki starseeds bring forward a unique perspective, helping humanity bridge the wisdom of the past with the innovations of the future.

Arcturians

Arcturian starseeds come from the advanced star system of Arcturus, located in the constellation *Boötes.* and are known for their deep spiritual and technological expertise. As one of the most evolved starseed groups, they act as guides, helping humanity elevate consciousness and heal.

Aura Color:
Their aura often radiates a deep blue or indigo, ranging from dark indigo to vibrant electric blue. This color represents their connection to higher realms of consciousness and their role as spiritual guides.

Characteristics:

- **Intellectual and Innovative:** Arcturians are highly intelligent and excel in visionary thinking, often providing insights that seem ahead of their time, especially in science, spirituality, and technology.
- **Spiritual Healers:** Skilled in vibrational and energy healing, they focus on elevating consciousness and balancing energies.
- **Dimensional Awareness:** They have an intrinsic understanding of multiple realms and cosmic realities, helping others connect with higher frequencies.

- **Guardians of Wisdom:** Known as keepers of sacred knowledge, they feel a profound responsibility to share their insights and serve as mentors and spiritual teachers.
- **Ethical and Philosophical:** Strongly driven by ethics, they uphold high moral values and approach life with a philosophical depth.

Physical Traits:

Arcturian starseeds often have a slender, refined appearance with angular features and sharp jawlines. Their large, intense eyes radiate wisdom and calm, drawing people in with a sense of deep understanding.

Arcturian
Image by Olga Gerogianni

Energetic Presence:

They possess a calming, high-frequency aura that resonates with those around them, creating feelings of peace and clarity. People often feel grounded and uplifted in the presence of Arcturians.

Mission on Earth:

Arcturians are here to bridge the gap between earthly experiences and higher consciousness, guiding humanity with intellect, spirituality, and a commitment to truth. Their energy serves as a beacon, encouraging others to explore deeper levels of awareness.

Atlans

Atlans, often associated with the legendary civilization of Atlantis, are thought to originate from the Pleiades star cluster, specifically from the star *Maia* within the constellation Taurus. Their history is intertwined with ancient myths of lost civilizations, and they carry memories of advanced cultures that once existed.

Atlas starseeds are often seen with an aqua or sea-green aura, reflecting their connection to water, wisdom, and the energy of Atlantis. This unique hue symbolises their harmonious nature and their deep connection to the elements.

Characteristics:

- **Ancient Knowledge:** Atlas starseeds are believed to hold ancient wisdom and knowledge from lost civilizations, particularly Atlantis. They often feel a strong pull to study or preserve ancient teachings, philosophy, and forgotten wisdom.
- **Healing Abilities:** Naturally inclined toward healing, they have a deep understanding of energy work and often feel drawn to modalities such as crystal healing, sound therapy, and energy balancing.
- **Balance Seekers:** These starseeds are deeply committed to harmony in all areas of life. They strive to bring balance between body, mind, and spirit, and often act as mediators or peacemakers.
- **Environmental Awareness:** Their connection to Atlantis gives them a strong affinity for water and nature. They may be passionate about environmental causes, especially those focused on preserving oceans and natural resources.
- **Artistic and Creative:** Atlas starseeds are known for their creativity and may feel drawn to artistic pursuits. They often use art, music, or storytelling to express their inner wisdom and to inspire others.

Physical Traits:

Atlas starseeds may have a serene, peaceful appearance, with soft facial features and expressive eyes that seem to hold ancient wisdom. Their presence often feels calming, much like being near the ocean. Some may have a unique birthmark or other physical trait they feel connects them to their Atlantean heritage.

Energetic Presence:

They emit a gentle yet powerful energy that fosters a sense of peace and balance. Being around an Atlas starseed often feels soothing and grounding, especially for those seeking emotional or spiritual equilibrium.

Mission on Earth:

Atlas starseeds are here to bring harmony, healing, and wisdom back to Earth. They aim to rekindle humanity's connection to ancient knowledge and balance, helping others rediscover inner peace and a sustainable way of life. Their role as guardians of ancient wisdom inspires them to guide humanity towards a balanced and harmonious future, much like the ideals of the mythic Atlantis.

Avians

Avian starseeds are thought to originate from the Altair star system in the Aquila constellation, a place associated with high-frequency energies and profound spiritual wisdom. Often linked to celestial themes, Avian starseeds are known for their deep alignment with higher consciousness, acting as spiritual messengers and guides.

Physical Characteristics and Aura:
Avian starseeds possess an ethereal presence, often described as graceful and light, with delicate or defined facial features that give them a striking, otherworldly appearance. Their eyes are particularly captivating, usually exuding a serene, calming

gaze that makes others feel understood and uplifted. They are frequently described as having a silver or light blue aura, symbolising clarity, peace, and spiritual purity. This aura radiates a sense of openness and high-frequency energy, drawing others to their calming presence.

Mission and Purpose:
The mission of Avian starseeds is to elevate humanity's consciousness by encouraging inner peace, unity, and spiritual awakening. Acting as guides, they inspire others to seek truth, transcend material concerns, and connect with their higher selves. Avian starseeds often feel compelled to promote harmony and interconnectedness, striving to help people understand their role in the greater cosmic picture. They are drawn to paths that allow them to share their spiritual insights, often serving as teachers, healers, or mentors in ways that foster unity and enlightenment.

Skills and Abilities:

- ***Celestial Messengers:*** *Avian starseeds are adept at channeling wisdom from higher realms. They often experience intuitive flashes or downloads of information that provide guidance not only for themselves but also for others on their spiritual journeys.*

- ***Ethereal and Spiritual:*** *Their spiritual energy is deeply rooted in purity and transcendence, allowing them to serve as beacons of peace and unity, helping others align with their higher selves.*

- ***Intuitive and Insightful****: With strong intuitive abilities, Avian starseeds are naturally insightful and possess a profound understanding of the human psyche and spiritual dimensions, often sensing emotions and intentions without words.*
- ***Connection to Air and Sky****: They feel a special connection to open, airy spaces and are particularly drawn to the sky and elements of the air. This affinity for air energizes their meditative practices, such as breathwork and visualization, which they use to stay attuned to higher frequencies.*
- ***Seekers of Truth and Unity****: Driven by a desire to foster inner peace and unity, Avian starseeds work tirelessly to encourage harmony and connection between individuals and the universe.*

Spiritual Practices:

Avian starseeds are inclined toward spiritual practices that foster higher awareness and inner peace. Meditation, especially in open spaces, breathwork, and silence are key practices for them, allowing them to maintain their connection with the celestial realms. They may also use visualization techniques that draw upon their connection with air, helping them reach states of higher consciousness. These practices reinforce their role as messengers, allowing them to channel wisdom and guidance from elevated planes to aid others on their spiritual path.

By embodying wisdom and unity, Avian starseeds inspire those around them to elevate their consciousness and embrace a deeper understanding of their soul's journey, guiding humanity towards a collective state of peace, compassion, and interconnectedness.

Cetians

Cetian starseeds, often referred to as the "whale people," are thought to originate from planets rich in vast oceans, possibly within the Delphinus or Cetus constellations. Their connection to cetacean species, such as whales and dolphins, aligns with their profound affinity for harmony, playfulness, and depth in communication. They embody a joyous presence and often act as bridge-builders, harmonizing their environment and promoting peace.

Physical Characteristics and Aura: Cetian starseeds are known for their gentle yet vibrant presence. Many describe them as having an almost ethereal quality, with graceful and fluid movements that mirror the elegance of marine creatures. Their aura is typically a soothing aqua or seafoam green, symbolizing tranquility, emotional depth, and healing. This calming color resonates with their peaceful nature, often bringing a sense of relaxation and openness to those around them. They exude a comforting energy that reminds others of the serenity found in natural, water-filled spaces, and their gaze often holds a depth that reflects their intuitive understanding of the world around them.

Mission and Purpose: Cetian starseeds are here to foster harmony and connection with nature, particularly the ocean and its creatures. They often take on roles that allow them to work closely with the environment or engage in conservation efforts, especially focused on marine life. Cetians feel a profound responsibility to protect the natural world, using their unique abilities to inspire empathy and cooperation among others. Their mission is to guide humanity toward a more sustainable and interconnected relationship with the Earth and its ecosystems.

Skills and Abilities:

- **Joyful and Playful Nature:** Cetians naturally radiate joy and positivity, creating an uplifting atmosphere that encourages openness and happiness in others.
- **Exceptional Communication Skills:** Known for their ability to connect deeply with others, they excel in both verbal and non-verbal communication, often understanding others intuitively.
- **Harmony with Nature:** Cetians are deeply attuned to the natural world, especially marine life, and possess a unique ability to sense and harmonize with the energies of their surroundings.
- **Intuitive Healers:** Their gentle energy enables them to serve as healers, helping to ease emotional and mental stress in others. They often engage in water-based healing practices, reflecting their affinity for aquatic elements.

Spiritual Practices: Cetian starseeds find deep spiritual resonance through water-based rituals, such as meditative swims, sound baths, or ceremonies near natural bodies of water. Many Cetians feel spiritually recharged and grounded when in or near water, often incorporating water elements into their personal healing practices. Their connection to water not only serves as a grounding force but also as a medium through which they channel peace and emotional healing to others. Their gentle presence and deep love for nature inspire those around them to connect more deeply with the Earth's natural resources and rhythms.

Draconians

Draconian starseeds are often associated with the Draco constellation, specifically believed to originate from the star Thuban, once the pole star of Earth. Draconians are known for their ancient wisdom, resilience, and strategic approach to life. Though they may have a reputation rooted in power and strength, many Draconian starseeds on Earth are here to balance those qualities with a higher purpose, bringing their unique wisdom and focus to assist in humanity's evolution.

Physical Characteristics and Aura:

Draconian starseeds often exhibit a striking physical presence with sharp, intense features. They are typically described as tall, with an athletic or sturdy build that exudes an aura of strength and determination. Their eyes are particularly captivating, often giving a sense of depth and ancient awareness, as if carrying the mysteries of the universe within them. Draconians are usually described as having a deep, dark red or earthy brown aura, symbolizing their grounded connection to power, resilience, and survival. This powerful aura reflects both their warrior spirit and their commitment to strength and endurance.

Mission and Purpose:

Draconian starseeds are here to guide others through transformation, teaching resilience, strategy, and the value of inner strength. Their mission is often focused on empowering individuals to stand firm in their truth, overcome adversity, and embrace their authentic power. Many Draconians find themselves in leadership roles where they can use their strategic skills to bring order and foster growth. They aim to help humanity find strength in times of challenge, acting as guardians who provide structure and stability in a world that is constantly evolving.

Skills and Abilities:

- **Warrior Spirit and Strength**: Draconian starseeds are naturally resilient and courageous, often possessing a warrior-like mentality. They have an innate ability to face challenges head-on, teaching others the power of perseverance.
- **Strategic and Analytical Thinkers**: Known for their sharp minds and calculated approach, Draconians excel in strategizing, analyzing situations, and making decisive plans. This makes them skilled in positions that require foresight and quick decision-making.
- **Resilience and Adaptability**: Draconians can adapt to various environments and situations, making them excellent problem-solvers who help others navigate complex situations.
- **Connection to Ancient Wisdom**: Many Draconians carry knowledge from ancient times, often drawn to studying history, philosophy, or metaphysics. They feel a connection to

Earth's past and may use this wisdom to guide humanity towards a balanced future.

- **Natural Leaders and Organizers**: Draconian starseeds are drawn to roles of authority, where they can create order, structure, and stability. They naturally assume positions that allow them to influence and lead with clarity and strength.

Spiritual Practices:

Draconian starseeds often engage in practices that strengthen both the body and mind. They may be drawn to martial arts, physical exercise, and meditation techniques that enhance discipline, focus, and endurance. Practices such as visualization and grounding help them stay connected to their power, while mindfulness and strategic planning allow them to channel their energy effectively. Many Draconians also explore ancient texts, metaphysical studies, and spiritual disciplines that enhance their understanding of both physical and spiritual realms.

Draconian starseeds bring a powerful, stabilizing presence to Earth. By sharing their wisdom, resilience, and strategic outlook, they help others develop strength and perseverance. Their commitment to truth and integrity offers guidance during challenging times, embodying a balanced blend of strength and insight as they lead humanity towards a more empowered future.

Dwarfs

Dwarf starseeds, are believed to originate from planets orbiting Proxima Centauri or Barnard's Star—two of the closest red dwarf stars to Earth. Proxima Centauri, part of the Alpha Centauri system, is the closest star to our solar system and has a small rocky planet, Proxima b, within its habitable zone, which has intrigued starseed enthusiasts as a potential origin for these beings. Barnard's Star, another nearby red dwarf, is notable for its stability and is sometimes referenced in starseed lore as a source of wise, resilient energy.

Physical Characteristics and Aura:

Dwarf starseeds are often described as

physically compact or modest in stature, with a grounded and unassuming appearance. Their features may include sharp, alert eyes that reflect their keen perception and ability to notice details that others might overlook. They often possess an aura that is earthy, with shades of brown, green, or soft grey, symbolizing their connection to nature, resilience, and adaptability. This aura reflects their practical, nurturing energy, which draws others in for support and wise counsel, much like a steadfast friend.

Mission and Purpose:

Dwarf starseeds are here to help Earth through resourceful, practical guidance and problem-solving. Their mission often involves supporting communities, enhancing sustainability, and encouraging people to live in harmony with nature. Many Dwarf starseeds feel called to roles where they can help manage resources effectively, innovate, and provide solutions for everyday challenges. They bring a perspective that values simplicity, efficiency, and a mindful approach to life, teaching others how to thrive by making the most of what they have.

Skills and Abilities:

- **Resourcefulness and Creativity**: Dwarf starseeds have an exceptional ability to innovate with limited resources. They are natural inventors and problem-solvers, often finding creative solutions to make life easier and more sustainable.
- **Grounded and Practical Thinkers**: Known for their common sense and practical approach, Dwarfs excel in areas that require careful planning and patience. They are skilled in turning ideas into tangible results and enjoy building things from scratch.
- **Connection to Nature and Earth**: Dwarfs feel a strong connection to the natural world, often gravitating toward ecological studies, environmental activism, or sustainable living practices. They instinctively understand how to work in harmony with nature.
- **Strong Empathy and Listening Skills**: These starseeds are patient listeners and compassionate friends. Their grounded

nature allows them to offer guidance that is practical, empathetic, and supportive, making them excellent confidants and advisors.

- **Inherent Builders and Nurturers**: Dwarf starseeds have an inclination toward building, growing, and nurturing. Whether it's physical structures, communities, or gardens, they take pride in creating and sustaining growth.

Spiritual Practices:

Dwarf starseeds are often drawn to practices that connect them to the Earth, such as gardening, herbalism, or grounding rituals. They may also practice meditation techniques focused on patience, presence, and gratitude, allowing them to stay centered and balanced. Dwarfs are often involved in mindfulness exercises that encourage living in the present moment and appreciating the small wonders of life. Many also engage in conservation efforts and practices that emphasize sustainable living, as they feel a duty to protect and nurture the Earth's resources.

Dwarf starseeds bring a nurturing, practical energy to Earth. With their focus on sustainability, resourcefulness, and community support, they help others discover the beauty of simplicity and the strength of resilience. Their presence encourages a mindful approach to life, reminding humanity of the importance of balance, gratitude, and living in harmony with the natural world.

Eva-Borgs

Eva-Borg starseeds are often associated with the star Alnitak in the Orion constellation, a star deeply linked to themes of transformation and technological advancement. Alnitak is the easternmost star in Orion's Belt and has historically symbolised a bridge between realms, making it an intriguing origin for Eva-Borgs, who are known for their harmonious integration of organic and technological elements. This origin reflects the Eva-Borgs' unique dual nature, combining natural wisdom with advanced technical prowess.

Eva-Borg starseeds often exhibit an aura that blends hues of metallic silver and electric blue, symbolising their fusion of organic life and technological mastery. This aura radiates an energy that feels both futuristic and deeply grounded, reflecting their mission to merge the realms of the physical and digital harmoniously. Eva-Borgs tend to have an appearance that mirrors their high adaptability and precision, often featuring symmetrical facial features, bright, observant eyes, and a calm, analytical gaze that reflects their deep focus and mental clarity. Some may even feel a unique resonance with machinery, devices, or tools, sensing an almost empathic connection to technology.

Mission and Purpose:

Eva-Borg starseeds embody a mission of balance between humanity and technology, guiding others to ethically integrate technological advancements into their lives while preserving natural harmony. They are often drawn to roles that involve innovation, engineering, or technology design, especially fields where technology can be used to enhance or protect natural ecosystems. Eva-Borgs feel a responsibility to lead humanity toward a future where technology and nature coexist sustainably, often working to ensure that scientific progress aligns with ethical principles.

Mission and Purpose:

Eva-Borg starseeds embody a mission of balance between humanity and technology, guiding others to ethically integrate technological advancements into their lives while preserving natural harmony. They are often drawn to roles that involve innovation, engineering, or technology design, especially fields where technology can be used to enhance or protect natural ecosystems. Eva-Borgs feel a responsibility to lead humanity toward a future where technology and nature coexist sustainably, often working to ensure that scientific progress aligns with ethical principles.

Skills and Abilities:

- **Tech-Enhanced Healers:** Many Eva-Borgs are adept in blending traditional healing practices with modern technologies, such as energy healing through electronic devices or digital meditation practices.
- **Natural Problem Solvers:** With an analytical mindset, Eva-Borgs excel at breaking down complex issues and finding practical, efficient solutions that incorporate both technology and intuition.

- **Environmental Advocates:** Deeply committed to the planet's well-being, they are often engaged in environmental technology, sustainable innovations, and ethical AI development.
- **Inventors of Advanced Tools:** Eva-Borgs are often at the forefront of inventing tools or systems that bridge the human experience with technological enhancement, blending organic insight with precise, machine-driven accuracy.
- **Telepathic-Analytical Insight:** Known for their ability to understand and decode subtle patterns, Eva-Borgs possess a heightened intuition that allows them to foresee trends in both human behaviour and technological evolution.

Spiritual Practices:

Eva-Borg starseeds incorporate a blend of mindfulness and technological practices into their spiritual lives. They might use biofeedback devices, sound frequencies, or brainwave monitors in meditation, blending traditional introspection with digital tools. Many also engage in "technomancy," where they combine natural and synthetic elements to create unique spiritual rituals. Their presence often inspires others to view technology as an extension of human consciousness, helping others to harmonise with it as part of a balanced, ethical life path.

Feline Starseeds

Feline starseeds are a race originate from the star Sirius A in the Sirius constellation, a star renowned for its connection to higher wisdom, intuition, and mystical insight. They live in harmony with Sirians A. Sirius A, often referred to as the "Spiritual Sun," embodies an energy of enlightenment and ancient wisdom, traits that are deeply mirrored in the Feline starseeds. Known for their cat-like agility, intuition, and grace, Feline starseeds are seen as mystical guardians of spiritual knowledge and protectors of higher truths.

Physical Characteristics and Aura:

Feline starseeds typically exude an aura of radiant gold, often intertwined with flashes of bright white, symbolising purity, wisdom, and an elevated state of consciousness. Their presence is magnetic and graceful, captivating those around them. Physically, Feline starseeds often have finely structured features—sharp cheekbones, almond-shaped eyes, and an elegant, poised manner that reflects their

inner strength and feline energy. Their eyes are particularly striking, often with an intense, penetrating gaze that suggests a profound depth of insight, much like that of a wild cat. Their aura and appearance give off an unmistakable sense of refinement and mystery, embodying both spiritual grace and inner power.

Mission and Purpose:

Feline starseeds are here to bring forth higher wisdom, guiding humanity towards spiritual awakening and self-discovery. They carry a mission of awakening intuitive abilities and fostering a deeper connection with the natural world. Many Feline starseeds feel called to guide others in personal empowerment, helping them tap into their own intuition and strength. As natural guardians, they often find themselves drawn to roles of mentorship, where they can pass on spiritual insights, protect sacred knowledge, and support the spiritual evolution of those around them.

Skills and Abilities:

- **Heightened Intuition and Perception:** Feline starseeds possess a natural gift for sensing energies and seeing beyond the physical. They are highly intuitive, often knowing things instinctively, which helps them in guiding others on their spiritual paths.
- **Natural Healers:** With an innate understanding of energy, Feline starseeds are adept in healing practices, especially those that involve balancing and strengthening the spiritual body.

- **Guardians of Mystical Knowledge:** They hold ancient knowledge, particularly in realms of spiritual practices and mystical traditions, and feel a deep responsibility to protect and pass on this wisdom.

Feline
Image by Olga Gerogianni

- **Spiritual Warriors:** Known for their bravery and inner strength, Feline starseeds are resilient and protective, often standing up for truth and justice, especially when it involves defending spiritual truths or protecting others.
- **Empaths with Graceful Boundaries:** While deeply compassionate, Feline starseeds also embody a balanced ability to maintain healthy boundaries, allowing them to offer support without depleting their own energy.

Spiritual Practices:

Feline starseeds often incorporate practices that enhance their intuitive abilities, such as meditation, visualisation, and connecting with nature. Many find peace and empowerment in solitary or quiet environments, which allows them to recharge and tap into higher wisdom. Rituals involving crystals, sound healing, and breathwork resonate with

them, as these practices amplify their natural gifts and align them with their mission. As spiritual guardians, they also engage in energy protection techniques, shielding both themselves and others from negative influences, embodying their role as mystical protectors and guides in the journey of self-discovery.

Greys (Short and Tall)

Originating from the Zeta Reticuli star system, Greys are perhaps the most widely known and often misunderstood among the starseed races. Divided primarily into two groups, the Short Greys and the Tall Greys, these beings have long intrigued humanity with their distinct appearance and scientific, often detached approach to understanding life.

Physical Characteristics and Aura:

- **Short Greys**: These beings are typically described as short in stature, usually between 3 to 4 feet tall, with thin bodies, large heads, and large black, almond-shaped eyes. Their presence is often felt as analytical, neutral, or highly focused on observation and data collection. Short Greys are commonly associated with an aura that appears as muted or metallic, symbolising their technological affinity and logical nature.

- **Tall Greys**: Tall Greys are often around 6 to 7 feet in height and possess elongated limbs, larger heads, and similar almond-shaped eyes. Their aura is typically more intense, often described as deep blue-grey or even silvery, representing a more profound engagement with advanced technologies and intellectual pursuits.

Mission and Purpose:

Greys, both Short and Tall, are believed to play roles connected to scientific observation and genetic experimentation, with a focus on understanding and evolving consciousness through various forms of hybridisation. While their methods might seem clinical, their intentions are often driven by a curiosity to enhance and support cosmic evolution. Tall Greys, in particular, are known to have a more advisory role, guiding humanity's technological advancements in subtle ways.

Skills and Abilities:

- **Advanced Scientific Knowledge**: Greys possess a highly developed understanding of technology, genetics, and consciousness. They often bring forward ideas that push the boundaries of science and artificial intelligence.
- **Telepathic Communication**: Known for their telepathic abilities, Greys are often able to communicate without words, sharing complex ideas and images directly into the mind.
- **Genetic Engineering and Hybridisation**: Greys have a long-standing association with genetic experimentation, which they use to enhance their understanding of life forms and create new forms of life through hybridisation.

- **Emotional Detachment**: While often perceived as unemotional, this detachment allows Greys to maintain objectivity and focus on their missions, especially when working in scientific or research-based roles.

Spiritual Practices:

Greys often engage in practices that are less emotionally centered and more focused on **mind expansion** and **intellectual understanding**. Meditation, when practiced, is often highly structured and geared toward enhancing mental clarity and detachment. For some, especially the Tall Greys, this can include silent retreats, mental exercises, and advanced forms of energy work that focus on mental and psychic power.

Greys, particularly the Tall ones, are here to support the evolution of technology and intellectual understanding on Earth. While their methods may feel distant or overly logical, they carry a deep commitment to furthering the knowledge of the universe, guiding humanity in ways that, though subtle, are powerful in shaping the future of our species.

Hadarian Starseeds

Hadarians are believed to originate from Beta Centauri, a star system associated with high vibrational energy and profound emotional depth. Unlike many other starseed races, Hadarians are known for their strong emotional resonance and heart-centered energy, bringing an aura of warmth and compassion wherever they go. These starseeds are particularly focused on spreading love, harmony, and unity.

Physical Characteristics and Aura:

Hadarian starseeds often exhibit a soft, gentle appearance, with expressive eyes that seem to convey kindness and empathy. Their aura tends to be vibrant pink or rose-gold, symbolising their heart-centered mission and the love they radiate. This warm and gentle aura often draws people to them, feeling a sense of comfort and acceptance in their presence. They may also display a natural, almost ethereal beauty that reflects their harmonious energy.

Hadarians have a purpose deeply rooted in promoting love, healing, and unity. They are natural empaths and healers, often working to uplift others and encourage a sense of togetherness. Hadarians strive to create harmony in all aspects of life, whether in relationships, communities, or even globally. On Earth, they often feel called to bring people together, fostering understanding and compassion in every situation.

Skills and Abilities:

- **Emotional Healers**: Hadarians possess a unique gift for emotional healing, often able to soothe those around them and offer comfort in times of distress.
- **Deep Empathy**: Their empathic abilities allow them to deeply understand the emotions of others, making them intuitive friends, counselors, or mentors.
- **Natural Peacemakers**: Hadarians have a talent for resolving conflicts and creating a sense of harmony, often mediating and bridging gaps between people.
- **Intuitive Guidance**: Hadarians are guided by their intuition, especially when it comes to matters of the heart. They trust their feelings to lead them toward meaningful connections and decisions.
- **Ability to Raise Vibrational Energy**: Hadarians can shift the emotional atmosphere in a room simply by being present, lifting others' spirits and promoting feelings of joy and love.

Spiritual Practices:

Hadarians are drawn to practices that focus on the heart chakra and emotional well-being. They often engage in meditation techniques that center around compassion, love, and forgiveness. Many find resonance in heart-centered practices, such as Reiki, sound healing, or chanting, as these amplify the energies of love and healing that they seek to share. They may also perform gratitude rituals and affirmations to strengthen their connection to universal love and unity.

In their roles as ambassadors of love and unity, Hadarian starseeds inspire others to open their hearts and embrace the power of compassion. Their ability to uplift, comfort, and heal makes them invaluable in times of emotional turmoil, helping humanity remember the power of connection and kindness. Their mission on Earth is to guide others toward a heart-centered life, fostering a world that resonates with love, peace, and understanding.

Hybrids

Hybrid starseeds are believed to embody a blend of various extraterrestrial lineages, combining unique qualities from multiple star races. Often carrying energies from Sirius, the Pleiades, Orion, or even Andromeda, hybrids represent an evolved fusion of

cosmic traits designed to adapt and bring versatility to Earth's shifting energies. As complex beings, hybrids carry the wisdom, strengths, and traits of their diverse origins, making them highly adaptable and capable of bridging multiple cosmic perspectives.

Physical Characteristics and Aura:

Hybrid starseeds frequently possess distinctive, somewhat otherworldly physical traits. Their features may appear unique or mixed, hinting at various cultural or cosmic origins. Their aura is typically a multicolored or iridescent blend, reflecting the multiple energies they carry within. This kaleidoscopic energy field can shift in response to different environments, symbolising their adaptability and versatility. People often feel a deep, inexplicable curiosity or familiarity around hybrids, sensing the complex layers of energies they embody.

Mission and Purpose:

The mission of hybrid starseeds is centered around unification and transformation. Their multi-faceted nature equips them to serve as intermediaries between different worlds, helping to integrate diverse energies, knowledge, and perspectives. Hybrids feel compelled to foster collaboration and understanding among different groups, whether they be cultures, ideologies, or even realms. They are also here to support Earth's ascension by adapting quickly to its vibrational changes, bringing grounded insights from their multidimensional backgrounds.

Skills and Abilities:

- **Multidimensional Awareness**: Hybrids can easily access various planes of consciousness and resonate with different starseed lineages, allowing them to understand multiple perspectives.
- **Adaptability and Versatility**: They have a unique ability to adjust their energy and approach to fit varying situations, which makes them resilient and resourceful.
- **Bridging Cosmic Knowledge**: Hybrids often intuitively draw from a vast cosmic database, tapping into knowledge from multiple star systems to offer fresh insights and guidance.
- **Healing and Energy Work**: Many hybrid starseeds excel in healing modalities that blend techniques from different traditions, such as combining light language with Reiki or sound healing.

- **Intuitive Communicators**: Hybrids have a natural talent for communication, able to relate to many types of people and beings, often serving as translators of cosmic messages.

Spiritual Practices:

Hybrid starseeds are often drawn to customised, integrative spiritual practices that blend different traditions. Meditation and journeying across dimensions help them tune into their diverse origins and gather wisdom. They may create rituals that combine elements of various starseed lineages, such as Pleiadian love frequencies with Sirian geometric energy grids. Hybrids also gravitate toward adaptive healing techniques that allow them to work fluidly with changing energies, such as intuitive chakra balancing or hybrid forms of sound healing.

In their roles as unifiers and adapters, hybrid starseeds bring forth a dynamic, resilient energy that helps to create bridges between worlds and perspectives. Their purpose is to help humanity embrace diversity within unity, encouraging a more inclusive approach to spiritual and cultural evolution. By sharing their unique blend of cosmic heritage, hybrid starseeds act as way-showers, guiding others toward a deeper understanding of multidimensional existence and the interconnectedness of all life.

Iguanoids

Iguanoid starseeds are said to originate from Alpha Draconis or planets within the Draco constellation. Known for their grounded wisdom and intense focus, Iguanoids embody the traits of their reptilian lineage while aligning with Earth's natural elements, especially soil and stone. Their connection to planetary energies and practical, grounded knowledge makes them highly resilient and disciplined beings, often perceived as guardians of earthly wisdom and stability.

Physical Characteristics and Aura:

Iguanoid starseeds often have a strong, earthy presence, with a solid, muscular build and distinctive, sharp features. Their eyes are particularly intense, exuding a sense of calm strength, resilience, and a hint of their otherworldly origins. Their aura typically radiates in deep greens, earthy browns, and dark olive tones, which reflect their connection to nature, grounding energies, and the resilience of ancient stone. People are often drawn to the Iguanoids' quiet power and find comfort in their stable, reassuring presence, sensing an ancient, primal energy within them.

Mission and Purpose:

The primary mission of Iguanoid starseeds is one of protection and grounding. They are deeply committed to stabilising energies on Earth, offering a grounding force amid change and uncertainty. Often seen as protectors of nature, Iguanoids aim to preserve Earth's ancient wisdom, bridging the gap between cosmic knowledge and natural law. Their purpose is to support humanity's evolution by reconnecting people with the Earth, fostering respect for natural resources, and teaching the values of patience, discipline, and endurance.

Skills and Abilities:

- **Grounding and Stabilisation**: Iguanoids excel in grounding techniques, naturally bringing balance and stability to environments and people around them.
- **Intense Focus and Discipline**: Known for their dedication and persistence, they approach tasks with a laser-sharp focus, seeing projects through to completion.
- **Earth Wisdom Keepers**: With a profound connection to Earth's elements, they possess an innate understanding of nat-

ural cycles, ecology, and the healing power of stones and minerals.

- **Physical Resilience and Strength**: Iguanoids are exceptionally resilient, often enduring harsh conditions or challenges with patience and strength.
- **Natural Protectors**: With a protective nature, they feel compelled to safeguard both people and the planet, promoting conservation and sustainable practices.

Spiritual Practices:

Iguanoid starseeds resonate deeply with earth-based rituals and practices, often incorporating natural elements like stones, crystals, and earth into their spiritual routines. They are drawn to meditative practices that involve grounding, such as walking barefoot on natural terrain or meditating near large rocks or trees to attune with Earth's energy. Crystal healing and earth-centered ceremonies appeal to them, as does working with stones

to channel strength and stability. Many Iguanoids feel a special connection to ancient earth practices and may use drumming or chants that connect them to primal, grounding energies.

In their role as guardians and stabilizers, Iguanoid starseeds bring the grounding energy that humanity needs in times of upheaval and change. Their presence helps others reconnect with the planet's wisdom, promoting a respect for natural cycles and a sustainable way of living. Through their dedication to Earth and their resilience, Iguanoid starseeds remind us of the enduring strength found in nature and the importance of staying grounded in a rapidly evolving world.

Janosians

Janosian starseeds are believed to originate from Janos, a planet within the Orion constellation. Known for their advanced intellect and strong sense of compassion, Janosians carry a reputation for profound empathy and wisdom, often seen as diplomatic bridge-builders who bring harmony and understanding wherever they go. Their culture is said to value deep philosophical insights and complex thought, with an innate ability to view multiple perspectives.

Physical Characteristics and Aura:

Janosians are typically described as having an ethereal, graceful presence, with delicate, soft features that exude warmth and approachability. Their eyes are often large and gentle, giving off a sense of kindness and perceptive depth. Janosian auras are commonly in soft pastels, often shades of lavender, sky blue, or pale rose, reflecting their gentle, compassionate nature and attunement to higher states of consciousness. This aura radiates an energy of peace and balance, creating a soothing effect on those around them.

Mission and Purpose:

The mission of Janosian starseeds revolves around peace, understanding, and healing emotional wounds. Their role on Earth is to help elevate collective consciousness by fostering empathy, encouraging emotional openness, and promoting unity. Janosians are natural mediators who feel drawn to facilitate healing in relationships, whether on a personal or societal level. Their purpose is to guide humanity toward compassion and mutual respect, often by demonstrating the importance of empathy, forgiveness, and non-judgment.

Skills and Abilities:

- **Emotional Intelligence**: Janosians are deeply in tune with the emotions of others, able to sense and understand complex emotional states.
- **Mediation and Diplomacy**: They possess a natural gift for resolving conflicts and misunderstandings, often bringing a calm, rational voice to tense situations.
- **Healing and Soothing Energy**: Janosians can calm emotional turbulence in others, helping them find clarity and peace.
- **Intellectual and Philosophical Insight**: Highly intellectual, Janosians enjoy delving into complex thoughts and philosophical ideas, often bringing unique perspectives.
- **Intuitive Communication**: Janosians can intuitively sense what others need to hear, allowing them to communicate with sensitivity and care.

Spiritual Practices:

Janosian starseeds find solace in reflective and meditative practices, especially those that cultivate inner peace and empathy. They often engage in compassion-based meditations, visualising healing for themselves and others, and may practice heart-centered techniques that strengthen their natural empathy. Many Janosians are also drawn to sound healing, gentle movement practices like Tai Chi or Qigong, and other modalities that foster emotional release and balance. Their spirituality is rooted in the concept of unity—they often feel a responsibility to spread compassion and kindness, seeing each act of healing as a contribution to collective harmony.

In their role as harmonizers and healers, Janosian starseeds remind humanity of the power of empathy and understanding. Their presence encourages others to release judgments, approach life with an open heart, and seek peace within and without. By fostering compassion and empathy, Janosians guide others toward a path of unity and healing, creating ripples of positive change across society.

Korendians

Korendian starseeds are believed to come from Korendor, a planet within the Corvus constellation. Known for their highly analytical minds and technological aptitude, Korendians are often seen as intelligent and forward-thinking beings with a deep commitment to advancing knowledge and understanding across civilizations. Their culture is highly evolved, prizing both intellectual achievement and moral integrity.

Physical Characteristics and Aura:

Korendian starseeds are often described as having a sharp, intellectual presence, with striking features that reflect their curiosity and wisdom. They are usually tall, with defined facial features and a gaze that seems to dissect and understand everything around them. Their aura is often a blend of deep indigo or electric blue, symbolising their alignment with higher wisdom, technology, and truth. The indigo hue reflects their pursuit of knowledge and a clear, logical approach to life, while also resonating with their psychic sensitivity.

Mission and Purpose:

Korendian starseeds are here to

advance human understanding of technology and morality. They are often drawn to roles in science, technology, and education, where they can help foster growth in these areas. Their purpose on Earth is to bridge the gap between intellectual pursuits and ethical awareness, promoting the development of technology in ways that benefit society holistically. Through their work, Korendians seek to guide humanity towards a future that is both scientifically advanced and ethically grounded.

Skills and Abilities:

- **Analytical and Logical Thinking**: Korendians possess sharp analytical abilities, able to process complex information quickly and efficiently.
- **Technological Mastery**: With an innate understanding of technology, Korendian starseeds are often pioneers in fields like engineering, data science, and innovation.
- **Problem Solving**: They have a natural talent for resolving complex issues and can approach problems from multiple perspectives.
- **Moral Integrity**: Despite their focus on intellect, Korendians hold strong ethical principles and believe that science and technology should serve humanity.
- **Psychic Sensitivity**: Korendians are intuitive and may have a natural capacity for telepathy or sensing energy, particularly in academic or high-intensity environments.

Spiritual Practices:

Korendian starseeds often find spiritual meaning in the pursuit of knowledge and a balanced, mindful approach to technology. They may engage in contemplative practices that help them merge intellect with intuition, such as mindfulness meditation, visualisation, and even advanced forms of technology-assisted meditation. Korendians are also drawn to scientific exploration as a spiritual pursuit, seeing the universe's mysteries as sacred. Their spiritual practices may include regular study, exploration of quantum theory, and other forms of intellectual inquiry that deepen their connection to the cosmos.

In their role as intellectual and ethical guides, Korendian starseeds aim to help humanity evolve by blending wisdom with science. They lead by example, showing others how to approach knowledge with responsibility, respect, and a dedication to the greater good. By advancing understanding in ways that support moral integrity, they inspire a vision of progress that honours both the mind and the heart.

Lemurian

Lemurian starseeds are here to restore balance, healing, and unity among humanity, fostering a renewed connection to the Earth and its ecosystems. Their mission often involves teaching compassion, promoting environmental stewardship, and helping others rediscover the importance of harmony with nature. Lemurians are drawn to healing and spiritual practices that allow them to support others in emotional and physical well-being, guiding humanity back to a state of balance and kindness. They carry the ancient wisdom of Lemuria and seek to awaken others to a time when life was more integrated and peaceful.

lemurian
Image by Olga Gerogianni

Skills and Abilities:

- **Natural Healers**: Lemurians have a deep understanding of energy healing, often drawn to modalities like Reiki, sound healing, and herbal medicine.
- **Empathetic and Compassionate**: Known for their profound empathy, they can sense and understand the emotions of others, offering gentle guidance and support.
- **Environmental Intuition**: They feel deeply connected to the Earth and may have a strong sense of intuition regarding the environment, often advocating for conservation and sustainability.
- **Wisdom Keepers**: Lemurians carry ancient knowledge within their souls, feeling a natural pull towards spiritual teachings, nature-based rituals, and ancestral wisdom.
- **Harmony and Peace Seekers**: Their energy inspires others to seek inner peace and harmony, helping those around them find balance and a renewed sense of purpose.

Spiritual Practices:

Lemurian starseeds are deeply attuned to practices that celebrate and honour the Earth, often incorporating nature-based rituals into their spiritual lives. They may engage in grounding exercises, meditation in natural settings, and ceremonies that connect them to the elements. Lemurians are also drawn to crystal work, as they resonate with the vibrations of minerals from the Earth, often using crystals in healing and meditation. They hold a deep reverence for the natural world and frequently spend time in forests, by rivers, or near the ocean, using these spaces as sanctuaries for reflection and healing.

As keepers of ancient wisdom and unity, Lemurian starseeds embody a gentle but profound strength, reminding others of the importance of love, connection, and harmony with the Earth. They encourage humanity to live with compassion and respect for all beings, fostering a renewed appreciation for the beauty of life and the interconnectedness of all things. Through their teachings, Lemurians help others reconnect to their own inner wisdom and the healing energies of the natural world.

Lyran

Lyran starseeds are believed to originate from the Lyra constellation, often considered one of the oldest and most pioneering star races. Known for their adventurous spirit and creative power, Lyrans are considered to be early explorers of the galaxy, bringing forth a unique blend of wisdom, resilience, and a drive for exploration. They are regarded as ancestors to many other starseed races, having shared their knowledge and strength throughout the cosmos.

Lyran
Image by Olga Gerogianni

Lyran starseeds are often described as having strong, athletic builds and a commanding presence that reflects their inner strength. They might exhibit bold, defined features and a confident posture, often appearing as they are prepared for any challenge. Their aura typically appears as vibrant gold or deep amber, symbolizing their connection to ancient knowledge, courage, and leadership. This radiant, warm hue is often felt as a powerful energy by those around them, giving off a sense of security and authority. The golden undertones of their aura highlight their regal nature, while the amber reflects their creative and spiritual warmth.

Mission and Purpose:

Lyran starseeds are here to pioneer new paths and inspire strength and resilience in others. They embody the archetype of the warrior and leader, often drawn to roles that allow them to empower those around them and foster personal and collective growth. Lyrans seek to ignite a sense of confidence, independence, and courage in humanity, helping others to overcome fears and embrace their true potential. They are often involved in creative and transformational work, inspiring change and innovation. Their purpose is rooted in fostering self-reliance, personal freedom, and the exploration of one's inner and outer worlds.

Skills and Abilities:

- **Pioneering Spirit**: Lyrans have a natural drive to explore, discover, and lead, often pushing boundaries and breaking new ground.
- **Strong Leadership Skills**: They naturally excel in leadership roles, inspiring confidence, and resilience in those they guide.
- **Creative Innovators**: Lyrans bring forward innovative ideas, often excelling in art, design, and cultural advancements that influence society on a grand scale.

- **Wisdom and Courage**: They carry ancient knowledge and a sense of bravery, empowering others to pursue growth and face challenges fearlessly.
- **Physical and Mental Resilience**: Lyrans possess great inner strength and fortitude, both physically and mentally, making them adept at overcoming obstacles and persevering in the face of adversity.

Spiritual Practices:

Lyran starseeds are attuned to practices that enhance both their spiritual and physical strength. They may engage in physical disciplines such as martial arts, dance, or yoga, which align their body and spirit, fostering resilience and grounding their high-energy nature. Meditation and visualization are also central to their spiritual practices, as these allow them to connect with their ancestral wisdom and tap into their creative potential. Lyrans often feel drawn to ancient rites and rituals that honor their warrior lineage and the cosmos, finding power and guidance in reconnecting with these timeless practices.

Lyrans are visionary guides who inspire strength, creativity, and exploration in others, embodying a unique blend of courage and compassion. Through their leadership and pioneering spirit, they empower humanity to face challenges with bravery, embrace change, and pursue their personal journeys of discovery. Lyran starseeds remind others of their inner power and potential, encouraging all beings to live with confidence, independence, and a passion for exploring the unknown. Their influence as both creators and protectors continues to leave a lasting legacy, inspiring generations to rise to their highest potential and create a future full of possibility and wonder.

Mantis

Mantis starseeds, sometimes called "Mantids," are believed to originate from planets within the Sombrero Galaxy (NGC 4594). This insectoid race is often associated with heightened awareness, advanced communication abilities, and a strong commitment to harmony and

balance. Known for their keen intellect and profound understanding of vibrational frequencies, Mantis starseeds possess an extraordinary capacity for compassionate observation and neutral guidance.

Physical Characteristics and Aura:

Mantis starseeds have an ethereal and otherworldly appearance, often described as tall and slender with long limbs, embodying a delicate, yet powerful presence. Their aura typically radiates in soft shades of green and silver, symbolizing their connection to nature, healing, and peace. This green hue, similar to the energy of the heart chakra, reflects their natural empathy and desire for harmony, while the silver tones represent their wisdom and neutrality. Many people sense a calming, balanced energy around Mantis starseeds, making them feel safe and understood in their presence.

Mission and Purpose:

Mantis starseeds are here to foster balance, harmony, and spiritual awareness within humanity. As observers and healers, they serve as guides in energetic alignment and often help others connect with higher levels of consciousness. Their presence on Earth encourages individuals to live in harmony with themselves and their surroundings. Through their work, they elevate collective awareness and gently steer humanity toward a path of peace, wisdom, and understanding. Mantis starseeds frequently work as mediators, diplomats, or healers, bridging divides and teaching the value of neutrality and compassionate guidance.

Skills and Abilities:

- **Advanced Communicators**: Mantis starseeds possess a natural ability to communicate on multiple levels, often using subtle gestures, telepathy, or energy transmission to convey deep understanding.
- **Empathetic Healers**: They are highly sensitive to the energetic fields of others, allowing them to heal through frequency work and balancing techniques.
- **Vibrational Awareness**: Mantis starseeds have a profound understanding of sound, color, and frequency, using this knowledge to help others achieve energetic harmony.
- **Keen Observers**: Known for their neutrality, they offer balanced perspectives, guiding others without judgment.
- **Harmony and Peace Advocates**: Mantis starseeds strive to create environments of calm and alignment, naturally fostering peace in both individuals and communities.

Spiritual Practices:

Mantis starseeds are deeply attuned to meditative practices that involve vibrational healing, such as sound therapy, crystal healing, and frequency alignment. They may engage in energy work that centers on balancing the aura and chakras, often incorporating nature-based rituals that connect them with Earth's energies. Silence and mindful observation are key aspects of their spirituality, allowing them to tap into universal wisdom and higher realms of consciousness. Many Mantis starseeds also work with sacred geometry and harmonic frequencies to channel healing energy and foster peace in their environments.

Mantis starseeds embody the principles of wisdom, compassion, and neutrality, serving as patient guides for humanity's journey toward higher consciousness. They are keepers of balance, here to teach us about the importance of alignment and understanding. Through their calm and grounding energy, Mantis starseeds help others find inner peace, cultivate compassion, and achieve greater self-awareness. Their unique perspective reminds us to observe without judgment and to approach life with both sensitivity and strength, allowing for a harmonious balance in all things.

Mothmen

Mothmen starseeds are believed to come from planets in the constellation of Cygnus, connected with realms where light and dark coexist in balance. Often associated with mystery, transformation, and heightened perception, Mothmen starseeds are drawn to explore life's mystical aspects and embrace their unique role as spiritual observers and guides. Known for their deep understanding of the unknown and unseen realms, they possess a rare ability to bring hidden truths to light.

Physical Characteristics and Aura:

Mothmen starseeds have a striking and somewhat mysterious presence, often described as having large, expressive eyes that seem to pierce through veils of illusion, reflecting their insight into unseen worlds. Their aura typically shimmers in shades of dark purples and midnight blues, symbolising their connection to mystery, intuition, and depth. The dark hues represent their comfort with exploring shadows and facing the unknown, while flashes of lighter colors signify their desire to bring wisdom and clarity to others. Their energy can feel intense yet comforting, like a protector in the night, drawing people who seek guidance and support through difficult transformations.

Mission and Purpose:

Mothmen starseeds are here to help others face and embrace transformation and navigate through times of darkness or uncertainty. Their mission involves guiding individuals through transitions, whether in personal development, spiritual growth, or understanding complex emotions. As keepers of mystery and transformation, they encourage others to acknowledge both light and shadow, promoting self-acceptance and integration. Many Mothmen starseeds are drawn to healing professions, intuitive practices, or fields involving psychology or the paranormal, using their gifts to help others unveil hidden parts of themselves and release fears or limiting beliefs.

Skills and Abilities:

- **Heightened Perception**: Mothmen starseeds are naturally perceptive and intuitive, able to sense energies and see beyond surface appearances.
- **Guides Through Transformation**: With an innate understanding of change, they excel in helping others through life transitions and periods of personal rebirth.
- **Wisdom of the Shadows**: Mothmen have a strong connection to shadow work, assisting others in understanding and integrating suppressed or hidden aspects of themselves.
- **Psychic and Intuitive Abilities**: Many possess psychic gifts, such as clairvoyance, which they use to uncover truths and help others gain clarity.
- **Protective Energy**: Often seen as spiritual protectors, Mothmen starseeds create a sense of safety for those they guide, especially during challenging times.

Spiritual Practices:

Mothmen starseeds are often drawn to shadow work, deep meditation, and ritualistic practices that honor cycles of change and transformation. They may work with moon energy, symbols of death and rebirth, or rituals that involve shedding the old to welcome the new. Journaling, dream work, and intuitive exploration are also central to their practices, allowing them to tap into hidden insights and connect with their own depth. Many Mothmen find power in quiet solitude, using these moments to recharge and deepen their understanding of the mystical realms.

Mothmen starseeds embody the essence of transformation, protection, and mystery, serving as compassionate guides through life's darker or more complex phases. They remind others of the beauty and strength that come from embracing all parts of the self, even those that lie in shadow. Through their unique gifts, Mothmen starseeds inspire courage, understanding, and resilience, helping humanity to embrace transformation as an essential part of spiritual growth.

Mintakan Starseeds

Mintakan starseeds originate from the star system of Mintaka, located within the constellation of Orion. Known as beings of purity, clarity, and deep longing for harmony, Mintakans are thought to come from a planet with crystal-clear, turquoise waters and a peaceful environment. This origin imbues them with an inherent connection to purity, light, and the spirit of unity, marking them as beings who strive to bring clarity, love, and harmony wherever they go.

Physical Characteristics and Aura:

Mintakan starseeds often possess a radiant, gentle aura, typically seen in shades of crystal blue, turquoise, or soft aquamarine—colors that mirror the serene waters of their home planet. This aura reflects their pure, gentle energy and natural inclination toward creating calmness and balance around them. Mintakans may also have a bright or luminous quality to their appearance, with clear, expressive eyes that seem to hold depth and compassion. Their physical presence often carries a calming influence, drawing people who seek comfort, clarity, or healing.

Mintakan starseeds are here to restore purity, peace, and harmony to the Earth, often helping others reconnect with their true selves and inner peace. As natural healers and peacekeepers, they feel a strong pull towards helping others resolve inner conflicts and promoting unity and love. Many Mintakans find themselves in roles where they can create beauty, clarity, or harmony, such as counselors, healers, artists, or environmental advocates. They often feel a deep longing to "return home" to their origins, but they channel this feeling into creating a sense of peace and belonging on Earth for themselves and others.

Skills and Abilities:

- **Natural Healers**: Mintakans have an intuitive ability to heal emotional wounds and restore calm through energy work or compassionate listening.
- **Clarity of Vision**: Known for their insightful perspectives, Mintakans can see through confusion and help others find clarity in their lives.
- **Peaceful Presence**: They carry a naturally soothing energy that brings peace to those around them, making others feel safe and understood.

- **Deep Compassion**: Mintakans have a profound empathy for others, often intuitively sensing emotions and knowing how to provide gentle support.
- **Connection to Water**: Strongly drawn to water, Mintakans feel at peace near oceans, lakes, or rivers and may use water for spiritual practices or emotional healing.

Spiritual Practices:

Mintakan starseeds are often drawn to practices that restore balance and clarity in their lives and the lives of others. Many engage in meditation, breathwork, or water-based rituals, finding peace and spiritual connection through these elements. Practices like cleansing baths, energy healing, and guided visualization are common among Mintakans, as they align with their love for purity and harmony. Spending time near water is especially rejuvenating for them, as it connects them to their soul's origins and provides emotional balance.

Mintakan starseeds embody the values of peace, clarity, and compassion, helping others find inner harmony and see life with renewed clarity. Through their nurturing presence and ability to bring tranquility to chaotic situations, they inspire others to embrace love, unity, and healing, guiding humanity toward a more harmonious existence on Earth.

Orion

Orion starseeds originate from the Orion constellation, a celestial system known for its striking alignment and significance in various ancient cultures. The Orion Belt, comprising the three bright stars Alnitak, Alnilam, and Mintaka, is central to their origin. This belt symbolises unity and cosmic order, reflecting the Orions' innate drive to seek balance between light and darkness, order and chaos. Orion is often associated with advanced civilisations and profound wisdom, which is carried through the souls of its starseeds. Known for their intellect, resilience, and pursuit of universal truths, Orions bring a unique combination of logic and spiritual awareness to Earth.

Orion
Image by Olga Gerogianni

Physical Characteristics and Aura:

Orion starseeds exude a distinctive and powerful aura, often perceived in hues of deep indigo, cosmic blue, and metallic silver. These colours symbolise their connection to cosmic knowledge and the technological and spiritual advancements of their star systems. Their aura can also shimmer with faint golden streaks, reflecting their leadership qualities and higher wisdom.

Physically, Orions may have striking, symmetrical features and a magnetic presence that draws attention. Their eyes are particularly noteworthy—sharp, clear, and intensely observant, as if they are always analysing or searching for deeper meaning. Their physical energy often feels grounded yet expansive, creating a sense of both stability and infinite potential.

Characteristics:

Orion starseeds are known for their:

- **Intellectual Depth:** They are logical thinkers with a hunger for knowledge, always seeking to understand the "why" and "how" behind existence.
- **Resilience:** Life's challenges do not deter them; instead, they see obstacles as opportunities for growth and learning.
- **Focus on Mastery:** Orions strive for excellence, whether in personal development, spiritual growth, or their chosen fields of work.
- **Grounded Curiosity:** While deeply connected to the cosmos, Orions maintain a practical and realistic approach to life on Earth, balancing dreams with actions.
- **Questioning Nature:** They challenge conventional beliefs and encourage others to think critically, often acting as catalysts for personal and collective awakening.

Mission and Purpose:

Orion starseeds are here to teach humanity the importance of balance—between intellect and emotion, spirituality and practicality, and light and shadow. They are often drawn to roles as educators, researchers, healers, or thought leaders, using their wisdom to uncover truths and inspire progress. Their ultimate mission is to promote harmony by encouraging the responsible use of knowledge and fostering emotional intelligence.

Many Orions feel a deep connection to ancient structures like the pyramids, which are aligned with the Orion Belt. These structures often resonate with their memories of advanced civilisations and their purpose as keepers of cosmic wisdom. Orions carry this legacy forward, helping humanity reconnect with its divine origins and potential.

Skills and Abilities:

- **Analytical Minds:** Orions excel at breaking down complex concepts into manageable insights, making them effective problem solvers and educators.
- **Celestial Awareness:** They often feel drawn to stargazing, astrophysics, or cosmic alignment, finding inspiration and clarity in the stars.
- **Energetic Precision:** Orion starseeds are natural energy workers who can align and balance energetic fields with a precise, methodical approach.
- **Visionaries:** They are forward-thinkers, constantly imagining innovative ways to solve problems and improve the collective human experience.
- **Harmonisers:** Despite their intellectual focus, Orions are adept at helping others reconcile emotional and logical conflicts, creating harmony within.

Spiritual Practices:

Orion starseeds resonate with practices that integrate intellectual exploration and spiritual connection. Meditation focused on cosmic energy, studying sacred geometry, and working with crystals such as obsidian, quartz, or labradorite are common among them. Many Orions are drawn to rituals that connect them to the Orion Belt, such as meditating under its alignment or visualising its energy to receive insights.

Grounding practices like walking in nature or working with the Earth's energy help Orions balance their celestial connection with the physical realm. They may also engage in breathwork or sound therapy to harmonise their high-frequency energies and remain centred in their purpose.

Connection to the Orion Belt:

The three stars of the Orion Belt—Alnitak, Alnilam, and Mintaka—serve as powerful symbols for Orion starseeds. These stars represent the interconnectedness of all things and inspire Orions to align with their higher mission. The alignment of these stars has been revered in ancient cultures, from the Great Pyramids of Giza to Mayan temples, which were designed to reflect their placement in the sky. For Orion starseeds, these alignments evoke a deep sense of belonging and a reminder of their cosmic heritage.

Orion starseeds embody the values of wisdom, balance, and evolution. Through their intellect, resilience, and spiritual insight, they guide humanity toward a harmonious existence where knowledge and emotion work together. By embracing both their logical and intuitive sides, Orions inspire others to seek truth, expand their consciousness, and achieve their fullest potential.

Pleiadians

Pleiadian starseeds hail from the Pleiades star cluster, particularly from planets orbiting stars like Taygeta and Electra. Known as highly evolved beings with a strong focus on love, creativity, and spiritual enlightenment, Pleiadians are said to carry energies that promote healing, unity, and a higher understanding of consciousness. Their mission is to guide humanity toward a more compassionate, peaceful existence, often working through inspiration, healing, and nurturing.

Physical Characteristics and Aura:

Pleiadian starseeds are often described as having a gentle, radiant aura that exudes warmth, typically seen in colors of soft pink, lavender, or light blue. This aura reflects their loving, supportive energy and their commitment to bringing peace and

understanding to those around them. Physically, Pleiadians may have a graceful presence and are often described as having delicate, serene features. Their eyes are typically bright and expressive, radiating kindness and empathy, as if they see directly into the soul.

The image is what I witnessed during my Quantum Jump into their spaceship. You can watch the video on my TikTok account titled "The Pleiadians."

Mission and Purpose:

Pleiadian starseeds are on Earth to uplift humanity's consciousness through love, healing, and compassion. With a deep commitment to guiding others toward unity, they often take on roles as healers, teachers, artists, or spiritual mentors. Their purpose revolves around promoting self-awareness, personal growth, and collective awakening, inspiring others to see life from a perspective of interconnectedness and love. Pleiadians work to bring balance to emotional and spiritual realms, acting as conduits for positive transformation and enlightenment.

Skills and Abilities:

- **Healing Abilities**: Pleiadians are naturally gifted in healing arts, especially emotional and energy healing, and often work as Reiki practitioners, counsellors, or empaths.
- **Creativity and Artistic Expression**: With a strong sense of creativity, Pleiadians are often involved in artistic pursuits, using art as a medium to inspire and heal others.
- **Emotional Intelligence**: Known for their compassionate nature, they have a high degree of emotional intelligence, easily understanding and empathising with the emotions of others.
- **Telepathic Communication**: Many Pleiadian starseeds are sensitive to subtle energies and can pick up on thoughts, feelings, or intentions telepathically.
- **Wisdom and Higher Understanding**: They carry an innate wisdom about life's purpose and spiritual evolution, often guiding others to seek their true path.

Spiritual Practices:

Pleiadian starseeds resonate with practices that allow them to express love and compassion, such as meditation, crystal healing, and heart-centered practices. Many find solace in connecting with nature and practicing gratitude, using these experiences to ground themselves and recharge their energy. Guided visualizations, affirmations, and creative outlets like painting or writing are often part of their spiritual practice, as they use these tools to connect with their higher self and inspire others. Their spiritual path is usually deeply connected to heart chakra healing and expansion, helping them remain in a state of love and empathy.

Pleiadian starseeds are here to guide humanity toward greater compassion, peace, and spiritual growth. Their energy is one of healing, love, and unity, and they aim to elevate the collective consciousness by encouraging each person to explore their true essence and purpose. Through their nurturing presence and unwavering kindness, Pleiadian starseeds help others realise their potential for inner peace and transformation, serving as beacons of light and love on Earth.

Procyonians

Procyonian starseeds are believed to originate from the Procyon star system, located in the constellation of Canis Minor. Known for their intellectual curiosity, adaptability, and scientific inclinations, Procyonians have a strong connection to exploring and understanding the intricate workings of both the physical and spiritual realms. They often feel a profound sense of duty to promote progress and elevate humanity's understanding of technology, science, and metaphysics.

Physical Characteristics and Aura:

Procyonian starseeds tend to have a distinct aura in shades of emerald green or aqua blue, symbolising their analytical mind and alignment with the heart and throat chakras, often linked to knowledge sharing and compassion. Physically, Procyonians may have a sharp, attentive gaze and defined features, giving an impression of alertness and intelligence. Their eyes are usually keen, reflecting their intellectual depth and curiosity about the universe. People often describe feeling a sense of clarity and insight when in their presence.

Mission and Purpose:

Procyonian starseeds are here to support humanity's evolution through scientific knowledge and spiritual awareness. They often act as bridges between science and spirituality, using their intellectual gifts to create systems or share insights that help people understand the connection between physical reality and higher consciousness. Many are drawn to careers in research, science, technology, and education, where they can bring innovative ideas that challenge conventional thinking and lead to breakthroughs. Their purpose is to help humanity progress in alignment with universal truths.

Skills and Abilities:

- **Scientific and Technological Aptitude**: Procyonians have a natural talent for understanding complex systems, particularly in technology, physics, and mathematics.
- **Keen Analytical Skills**: They possess a sharp intellect, with a strong ability to analyze details, solve problems, and uncover underlying truths.
- **Intuitive Connection to Universal Knowledge**: Procyonians often feel connected to universal wisdom, which guides them in aligning scientific discoveries with spiritual principles.
- **Energetic Balance**: Known for their sense of balance and resilience, they are skilled in maintaining emotional stability and often help others find calm in challenging situations.
- **Curiosity for Exploration and Discovery**: Procyonian starseeds are constantly seeking new knowledge and ways to expand their understanding, making them lifelong learners.

Spiritual Practices:

Procyonian starseeds gravitate toward practices that allow them to connect intellectually and energetically with the universe. They often practice mindful meditation, visualization techniques, and structured breathing exercises to align their energy. Many are drawn to studying sacred geometry, quantum physics, and metaphysics to deepen their spiritual understanding. They are also known to engage in nature walks and contemplative solitude, which help ground their ideas and provide clarity. Their spiritual path often involves throat and third-eye chakra alignment, helping them communicate their insights and connect with higher realms of understanding.

Procyonian starseeds embody the harmonious union of science and spirituality, dedicated to guiding humanity toward enlightenment through knowledge and discovery. Their energy promotes clarity, progress, and higher understanding, and they are often seen as pillars of wisdom and intellect in their communities. Through their unique perspective and innate drive for knowledge, Procyonian starseeds inspire others to embrace both the rational and mystical aspects of life, fostering a world where innovation and spirituality coexist in harmony.

Reptilians

Reptilians
Image by Olga Gerogianni

Reptilian starseeds are often linked to the Draco constellation, associated with an ancient lineage and a profound understanding of survival, strategy, and resilience. Their presence on Earth has been a subject of intrigue, with Reptilian starseeds known for their intense energy and powerful personalities. Reptilians are natural strategists, often drawn to positions where they can influence, lead, and initiate change, and they carry a deep sense of purpose rooted in transformation and protection.

Physical Characteristics and Aura:

Reptilian starseeds frequently possess a magnetic and intense aura, typically in hues of dark green, red, or brown, which reflects their grounding and powerful nature. This aura conveys both strength and mystery, embodying their ancient wisdom and resilience. Physically, they may have sharp, chiseled features, an intense gaze, and a

commanding presence that immediately captures attention. Their eyes are often described as piercing or penetrating, giving the impression that they see beyond surface appearances. People in their presence often feel a strong, grounding energy and a sense of raw power.

Mission and Purpose:

Reptilian starseeds are here to help humanity evolve through strength, resilience, and the mastery of personal power. They often assume roles that allow them to effect significant change, bringing structure and determination wherever they go. Driven by a deep sense of loyalty and protection, many Reptilian starseeds feel a calling to guide and protect others in times of adversity. Their purpose often involves helping others face challenges with courage, teaching them to embrace their inner strength, and transforming weaknesses into empowerment.

Skills and Abilities:

- **Strategic and Tactical Thinkers**: Reptilian starseeds are naturally skilled at analyzing complex situations, making them adept problem solvers in any scenario.

- **Strong Leadership Skills**: They possess inherent leadership qualities, capable of guiding others with clarity, strength, and purpose.
- **Resilience and Endurance**: Known for their unyielding nature, Reptilian starseeds can endure challenging situations and help others do the same.
- **Instinctual Wisdom**: They have an intuitive understanding of survival and instinctive behavior, enabling them to make quick, effective decisions in critical situations.
- **Transformational Energy**: Reptilians have a powerful presence that inspires transformation and the ability to reshape situations to benefit all involved.

Spiritual Practices:

Reptilian starseeds often connect to practices that strengthen their inner power and resilience. Many engage in grounding exercises, martial arts, or power-building practices that enhance their focus and determination. Meditation and breathwork are common practices, allowing them to balance their intense energy and stay centered. Reptilians often work with root and solar plexus chakra exercises, as these chakras align with their grounding presence and powerful sense of personal will. Some may also resonate with practices that allow them to connect with Earth energies, feeling a deep connection to the planet and its resources.

Reptilian starseeds embody the essence of strength, endurance, and leadership. They serve as guardians and protectors, inspiring those around them to find their own resilience and inner power. Through their mission, Reptilians encourage others to embrace change, overcome obstacles, and find strength in vulnerability, using their unique perspective to bring about transformation. Their presence is a reminder of the power that lies within, helping others recognize their potential to overcome life's challenges and thrive.

Sirians A

Sirian A starseeds originate from Sirius A, the brightest star in the constellation Canis Major, known for its association with profound wisdom, healing abilities, and connection to ancient spiritual knowledge. Sirian A beings are thought to be highly evolved, often embodying a harmonious balance between spiritual wisdom and scientific understanding. Many Sirian A starseeds feel a deep-rooted connection to Earth, with their influence reflected in ancient Egyptian and Mayan cultures, where Sirius was venerated as a source of cosmic knowledge and guidance.

Sirians A
image by Olga Gerogianni

clarity, intuition, and spiritual insight. Physically, Sirian A starseeds may have delicate, yet pronounced features and striking eyes that seem to hold ancient knowledge. Their energy is both grounding and uplifting, offering comfort and reassurance to those around them.

Mission and Purpose:

The purpose of Sirian A starseeds is to anchor ancient wisdom on Earth and guide humanity toward spiritual and technological advancement. They are natural healers and teachers, often drawn to paths where they can share their insights and help others discover their own spiritual potential. Sirian A starseeds also feel a profound responsibility to protect the natural world, often working in areas related to conservation, environmental science, or holistic health. Through their work, they aim to help humanity harmonize with Earth and evolve consciously.

Skills and Abilities:

- **Healing Abilities**: Sirian A starseeds are natural healers, often gifted in holistic practices and energy healing techniques.
- **Scientific and Technological Insight**: They possess a deep understanding of both spiritual and scientific principles, often finding ways to merge the two in innovative approaches.
- **Intuitive Knowledge**: Known for their strong intuition, they have a knack for sensing the emotional and energetic states of those around them.
- **Environmental Awareness**: With a deep connection to Earth, they are advocates for environmental protection and sustainable practices, often leading efforts to preserve natural resources.
- **Ancient Wisdom Keepers**: Sirian A starseeds carry knowledge of spiritual traditions and cosmic laws, which they share to help others access higher states of consciousness.

Spiritual Practices:

Sirian A starseeds often engage in meditative practices that connect them to higher realms and cosmic energies, such as guided visualizations and sound healing. Many feel a connection to water, finding it both spiritually and emotionally cleansing, and may be drawn to practices that incorporate water, such as hydrotherapy or ocean meditation. They also frequently work with the throat and third eye chakras, enhancing their communication abilities and intuitive insights. Some Sirian A starseeds are skilled at channelling, often receiving messages from higher realms to share with those they guide.

Mission on Earth:

As spiritual guides and healers, Sirian A starseeds are here to bridge the gap between spiritual wisdom and scientific knowledge. They encourage others to pursue personal growth, live harmoniously with nature, and seek truth within themselves. Through their work, Sirian A starseeds aim to help humanity reconnect with ancient knowledge, using this wisdom to foster peace, understanding, and sustainable living. Their presence is a reminder of humanity's potential to live in balance with the Earth while reaching for the stars, illuminating the way to a more evolved and compassionate world.

Sirius B Starseeds

Sirian B starseeds come from Sirius B, the smaller companion star to Sirius A in the Canis Major constellation. Sirius B is often associated with aquatic life, particularly dolphins and whales, symbolising wisdom, playfulness, and emotional depth. Sirian B starseeds embody a profound connection to water and possess an innate understanding of harmony, balance, and collective consciousness. Many Sirian B starseeds feel a strong bond with Earth's oceans and marine life, often experiencing a deep calling to protect these environments.

Physical Characteristics and Aura:

Sirian B starseeds typically carry an aura that radiates soft silver-ish-blue or sea-green hues, mirroring their affinity for water and representing their healing, calming nature. This aura exudes serenity, evoking a sense of peace and connection to the flow of life. Physically, Sirian B starseeds may have gentle, fluid features and a presence that feels soothing to those around them. Their eyes often reflect a depth of empathy and understanding, symbolising their connection to the emotional realm and collective consciousness.

Mission and Purpose:

The mission of Sirian B starseeds centers on healing, emotional intelligence, and environmental stewardship. They feel a strong responsibility to promote peace, foster emotional balance, and protect Earth's natural resources, particularly its water bodies. Many Sirian B starseeds are drawn to careers or causes related to healing, marine conservation, and community building. Their purpose is to guide humanity toward a deeper understanding of emotional intelligence and unity, helping others embrace compassion and empathy.

Skills and Abilities:

- **Healing through Water:** Sirian B starseeds are often skilled in water-based healing modalities, such as hydrotherapy or sound healing, which uses the resonance of water.
- **Empathic Communication:** They have an exceptional ability to connect with others on an emotional level, often able to sense and soothe emotional pain.
- **Environmental Advocacy:** Deeply connected to nature, they feel called to protect Earth's oceans and water bodies, often leading or participating in environmental conservation efforts.
- **Collective Awareness:** With a heightened sense of unity, Sirian B starseeds naturally foster community, bringing people together to support collective well-being.
- **Playfulness and Joy:** They possess a light-hearted, joyful energy that uplifts those around them, encouraging a balanced approach to life that values both work and play.

Spiritual Practices:

Sirian B starseeds resonate strongly with water-based spiritual practices, such as meditative swimming, oceanic rituals, and using water as a medium for cleansing and reflection. They often work to balance the heart and sacral chakras, helping to harmonise emotions and foster compassion. Many are drawn to meditation and mindfulness practices that incorporate the sound or presence of water, such as listening to flowing water or ocean waves. Some Sirian B starseeds also engage in animal communication, particularly with marine animals, feeling a special connection to the intelligence and wisdom of dolphins and whales.

Mission on Earth:

Sirian B starseeds are here to promote emotional healing and environmental stewardship. They encourage humanity to reconnect with nature, particularly the oceans, and to embrace empathy as a guiding principle. Through their calming, harmonious presence, Sirian B starseeds teach others the value of emotional balance and the power of unity. They work to bring people together in peace, promoting a world where nature and humanity coexist harmoniously. Sirian B starseeds serve as compassionate guides, reminding humanity of its responsibility to protect Earth's water resources and to foster emotional well-being within themselves and their communities.

Teros

Teros starseeds are said to originate from a subterranean realm within Earth itself, often described as deep underground or in hidden inner-Earth cities. The Teros are thought to be a highly evolved, ancient race who value stability, resilience, and a harmonious relationship with the Earth. They are known as protectors of Earth's energies and guardians of ancient wisdom, particularly connected to environmental balance and natural law. Teros starseeds carry a deep respect for the natural cycles of the planet and feel a profound mission to safeguard Earth's ecosystems and resources.

Teros
Image by Olga Gerogianni

Physical Characteristics and Aura:

Teros starseeds are often described as having a grounded, earthy presence with a sturdy or solid physical appearance. Their features may reflect this connection to the earth, often appearing as strong, balanced, and serene. Their aura typically radiates warm tones like dark green, deep brown, or rust, embodying their grounded energy and connection to Earth's core energies. This aura has a stabilising, calming effect on those around them, making others feel safe and grounded in their presence.

Mission and Purpose:

Teros starseeds are dedicated to preserving Earth's natural harmony and protecting its ecosystems. They are drawn to roles where they can serve as caretakers, guardians, or advocates for environmental balance. Their purpose is to remind humanity of its responsibility to Earth, encouraging sustainable practices and respect for the planet's natural rhythms. Teros starseeds are often involved in conservation, eco-friendly practices, and efforts that promote sustainability. They feel a strong purpose in grounding humanity and reconnecting it with Earth's wisdom.

Skills and Abilities:

- **Environmental Guardianship**: Teros starseeds are highly aware of environmental needs and often feel called to protect natural resources, ensuring they are used responsibly.
- **Earth Energy Work**: They are skilled at working with Earth's energies, using grounding techniques and connecting with ley lines to restore balance in natural landscapes.
- **Ancient Wisdom Carriers**: With a deep knowledge of natural cycles and Earth-based spiritual practices, Teros starseeds hold and share wisdom related to planetary healing and ancient Earth practices.
- **Resilience and Stability**: Known for their strength and endurance, Teros starseeds possess remarkable resilience, often

serving as a source of strength for others during challenging times.

- **Connection to Crystals and Stones**: Teros starseeds are deeply connected to crystals and stones, often using them in spiritual practices to channel grounding and protective energies.

Spiritual Practices:

Teros starseeds often engage in grounding and Earth-centered spiritual practices. They are drawn to meditative practices in nature, connecting directly with the Earth through activities like forest bathing, hiking, or spending time in caves or near mountains. Many Teros starseeds also incorporate crystal healing and Earth-element rituals into their practices, using stones and minerals as a means to stabilise and align their energy. They often work to balance the root chakra, which helps them stay deeply connected to Earth's core and aligned with their purpose of planetary care.

Mission on Earth:

The mission of Teros starseeds revolves around stabilising, grounding, and protecting Earth's ecosystems. They serve as stewards of the natural world, often inspiring others to adopt sustainable, eco-friendly practices. Teros starseeds are here to remind humanity of its duty to protect the environment, cultivating a renewed appreciation for Earth's resources and natural cycles. Through their efforts, Teros starseeds seek to create a future where humanity and Earth are in harmony, each nurturing and sustaining the other. By embodying Earth's wisdom and stability, they provide a grounding force that helps others reconnect with the planet, fostering a sense of shared responsibility and reverence for nature.

Ummites

Ummites starseeds are often described as having a sharp, focused presence, with refined, symmetrical features that convey intelligence

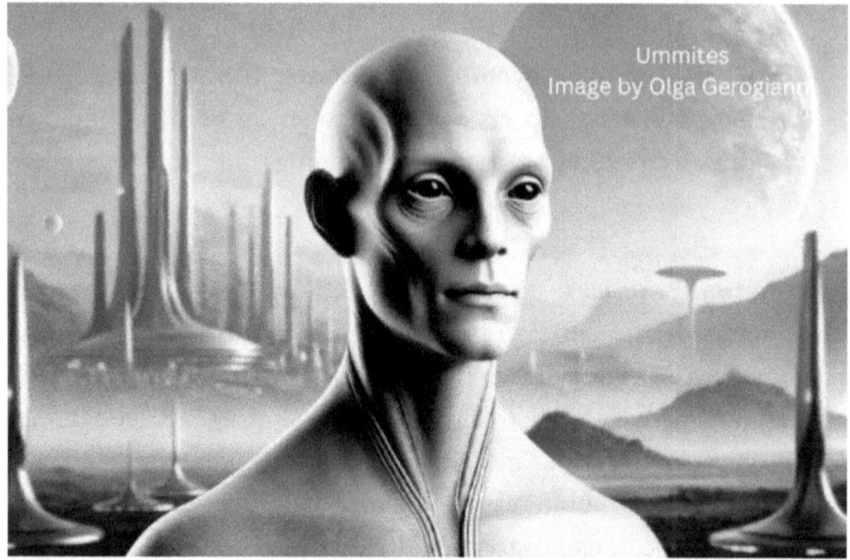

and precision. Their aura is typically a soft silver or light grey, symbolising their connection to higher logic and reason, as well as their commitment to truth and clarity. This subtle, cool-toned aura often has a grounding effect, making them appear calm, composed, and approachable. Their energy resonates at a level that instills a sense of trust and respect from others.

Mission and Purpose:

The primary mission of Ummites starseeds on Earth is to advance knowledge and promote intellectual growth. They are natural researchers and truth-seekers, dedicated to revealing information that empowers others to think critically and understand the world on a deeper level. Their purpose is often to bridge science and spirituality, bringing a balanced perspective that encourages rational yet open-minded exploration of life's mysteries. Many Ummites starseeds feel a duty to protect truth and knowledge, often working to dispel misinformation and guide humanity toward a more enlightened future.

Physical Characteristics and Aura:

Ummites starseeds are often described as having a sharp, focused presence, with refined, symmetrical features that convey intelligence and precision. Their aura is typically a soft silver or light grey, symbolising their connection to higher logic and reason, as well as their commitment to truth and clarity. This subtle, cool-toned aura often has a grounding effect, making them appear calm, composed, and approachable. Their energy resonates at a level that instills a sense of trust and respect from others.

Mission and Purpose:

The primary mission of Ummites starseeds on Earth is to advance knowledge and promote intellectual growth. They are natural researchers and truth-seekers, dedicated to revealing information that empowers others to think critically and understand the world on a deeper level. Their purpose is often to bridge science and spirituality, bringing a balanced perspective that encourages rational yet open-minded exploration of life's mysteries. Many Ummites starseeds feel a duty to protect truth and knowledge, often working to dispel misinformation and guide humanity toward a more enlightened future.

Skills and Abilities:

- **Logical and Analytical Thinkers**: Ummites are highly analytical and excel in scientific thinking, able to dissect complex problems and present solutions with clarity.
- **Strong Communicators**: Known for their articulate communication style, they have a talent for breaking down abstract concepts into understandable terms, making them effective educators and writers.
- **Philosophical Depth**: Ummites starseeds are natural philosophers, often pondering existential questions and exploring the intersections of science, ethics, and spirituality.
- **Detail-Oriented and Meticulous**: With a keen eye for detail, they thrive in research, scientific discovery, and any field requiring precision and attention to detail.
- **Intuitive Understanding of Technology**: Many Ummites have an inherent aptitude for technology and innovation, often

feeling comfortable with advanced tools and techniques that can advance human understanding.

Spiritual Practices:

Ummites starseeds lean towards meditative and reflective practices that stimulate the mind, such as journaling, contemplation, and intellectual study. They may practice mindfulness or engage in forms of meditation that enhance mental clarity, focusing on inner peace through logical understanding and the pursuit of wisdom. Their spiritual practices often include reading, learning, and exploring concepts that combine science and spirituality, striving to build a well-rounded perspective. They are also drawn to work with the third-eye chakra, which aligns with their quest for clarity, truth, and higher knowledge.

Mission on Earth:

Ummites starseeds are here to bring truth and enlightenment to humanity through intellectual exploration and the dissemination of knowledge. They seek to dispel ignorance, encourage logical thinking, and foster a harmonious relationship between science and spirituality. Ummites starseeds often find themselves in educational, scientific, or technological fields, where they can make a direct impact on human understanding. They act as guides, urging others to look beyond surface-level explanations and explore the deeper truths of existence. With their unique perspective and commitment to truth, Ummites starseeds help elevate human consciousness, leading society toward a future
grounded in knowledge, wisdom, and ethical advancement.

Vega

Vega starseeds come from the star Vega in the Lyra constellation. Known for their harmony-oriented nature and love for exploration, Vegan starseeds embody a peaceful and balanced energy that deeply influences those around them. They are often regarded as compassionate souls with a keen interest in unity, environmentalism, and

spiritual progress. The Vega star is known as one of the brightest stars in the sky, symbolising enlightenment and higher consciousness, which aligns with the mission and presence of Vegan starseeds.

Physical Characteristics and Aura:

Vegan starseeds tend to have a gentle, calming presence, often characterized by soft features that reflect kindness and tranquility. Their aura is typically a pale green or turquoise shade, symbolising healing, balance, and their connection to nature. This cool-toned aura exudes harmony and fosters a sense of peace in those they encounter. Vegans have a subtle energy that feels nurturing and grounding, encouraging others to feel at ease and open in their presence.

Mission and Purpose:

Vegan starseeds have a mission deeply rooted in promoting peace, unity, and ecological balance on Earth. They are natural diplomats, often working to bridge divides and foster understanding among people. With a strong commitment to environmental stewardship, Vegan starseeds are drawn to activities that protect and restore nature, seeing the Earth as a sacred place. Their purpose is to serve as mediators, unifying people and promoting cooperation while encouraging humanity to live in harmony with the environment.

Skills and Abilities:

- **Natural Healers**: Vegans have a healing energy that brings balance to both people and places, often working with holistic or nature-based healing practices.
- **Diplomatic and Peaceful**: Highly empathetic and understanding, they are skilled mediators, able to navigate conflicts with grace and compassion.
- **Environmental Awareness**: With a strong connection to nature, Vegan starseeds often advocate for environmental preservation and sustainability, feeling a duty to protect the planet.
- **Spiritually Inquisitive**: Vegan starseeds seek spiritual growth through harmony and balance, often exploring practices that align the mind, body, and spirit with natural energies.
- **Innovative and Open-Minded**: Vegans are open to exploring new ideas and methods, particularly those that can bring about harmony and progress for society and the Earth.

Spiritual Practices:

Vegan starseeds are drawn to practices that involve nature and mindfulness, such as meditation in natural settings, yoga, and eco-conscious rituals. Many Vegans also find a connection with energy healing modalities that emphasize balance and harmony, such as reiki or sound healing. They tend to work with the heart chakra, aligning their energy with love, compassion, and unity. Their spiritual practices often revolve around grounding exercises that help them stay connected to both the Earth and higher consciousness, striving for harmony in all aspects of life.

Mission on Earth:

Vegan starseeds bring a profound message of unity and environmental consciousness to Earth, encouraging others to protect the planet and live in a way that honors all forms of life. They are often involved in environmental activism, humanitarian work, or any field where they can promote harmony and understanding. Vegan starseeds are here to inspire humanity to embrace compassion, cooperation, and respect for nature, helping to guide society towards a sustainable and peaceful future. Through their presence and work, they aim to foster a greater awareness of interconnectedness, showing others how to live in balance with the world around them.

If your exploration of angel numbers as coordinates has led you to any of the constellations associated with the starseed races mentioned, this could be a significant clue about your soul's origin. However, I encourage you to continue your journey of discovery beyond what these coordinates might imply. If you feel a deep connection to any of these cosmic lineages, delve deeper and do your own research on starseeds.

Remember, the guidance from angel numbers is just one part of your journey. Trusting your intuition and exploring further can lead to more profound and personalized insights about your place in the cosmos.

17.2 Starseeds mission

At this point, I think it's important to talk about Life Purpose. If you've found out you're a starseed, you probably feel a strong sense of having a life purpose, or even more, a life mission. You might feel this urge to remember what you're supposed to do here. There's this understanding that you have a significant role in this life. Not only for your personal development but for the collective.

Looking back at the traits of your starseed origin can give you some hints about what your life mission could be. For me, it's always been about guiding people. I was always that friend who gave the advice that needed to be heard, not necessarily what someone wanted to hear, but what would truly help them. I've loved writing my whole life. I find joy in expressing myself through words and getting my message out there. And I've always had this natural connection with water. I started swimming when I was 6, became a champion in 50m freestyle at 15, and for many years I was a member of the Greek National Team, winning more than 60 medals, most of them gold in different competitions. I now know why I had this amazing connection with water! I've always been into living a balanced life, too. I never smoked or tried drugs. I've always been drawn to a life close to nature, understanding the balance of body, spirit, and mind. And as you already know, I was born with clairvoyant abilities, which developed into stronger psychic abilities, and recently, I've even activated my energy healing abilities. Now, understanding my Soul's origins from Sirius B and as a hybrid starseed (Mantis), I've changed my life to better serve my Life's mission. Part of that mission is writing this book you're reading

18

Angel Numbers as Letters

As I delved deeper into this fascinating communication system, I stumbled upon yet another realization. Many of my TikTok followers, who had begun sharing their experiences with angel numbers and seeking further insights, reported similar occurrences. They described complex, persistent number sequences that seemed unlike anything I had encountered before. For instance, take the sequence 1288. My research had always suggested that angel numbers used as coordinates followed two essential parameters—length (usually a set of three or four angel numbers) and timing, with an underlying reason. But now, I was confronted with sequences that didn't fit these criteria, yet they persisted and seemed to follow a pattern.

The solution hit me suddenly: *Gematria!* Could these intricate angel numbers be words or phrases in disguise? Eager to explore this idea, I entered 1288 into a Gematria calculator—an online tool you can use as well. To my amazement, the meaning behind these numbers was "G Jesus Kingdom Be Coming." Was this person's spirit guide signaling a call back to their spiritual faith? Or was it perhaps a premonition meant to be shared with the collective?

This discovery opened my eyes to the astonishing complexity of angel numbers. They weren't just coordinates or simple messages; they could represent an even more intricate communication system than we had imagined. It was a breakthrough moment, revealing that these divine sequences held depths and layers we had yet to uncover.

18.1 Gematria

Gematria, an ancient and fascinating numerological system, goes beyond its origins in Jewish mysticism. It serves as a bridge connecting numbers and words, revealing deep meanings hidden within different languages and cultures. Let's take a closer look at this intriguing world where numbers and letters intertwine, offering insights we might never have otherwise seen.

Although Gematria is often linked with Hebrew, its principles aren't confined to just one language or culture. Each culture has adapted Gematria to its own language, creating unique insights and perspectives.

Take Greek Gematria, for example. It closely mirrors the Hebrew system, assigning numbers to the Greek alphabet. The ancient Greeks applied this method to religious and philosophical texts, giving deeper meanings to words and phrases.

Then, there's English Gematria, a more modern adaptation that assigns numerical values to the 26 letters of the English alphabet. It's mostly used today within esoteric and spiritual traditions.

Many cultures around the world have developed their versions of Gematria, tailoring the system to fit their language and alphabet. This global adaptation adds unique dimensions to the meanings Gematria can uncover.

Gematria is far more than a mere system of numbers and letters. It transcends language and cultural barriers, offering a universal code that reveals deeper truths through the union of numbers and words.

Understanding angel numbers as part of this larger communication system opens up a whole new world. It's like a universal bridge that connects us to higher realms, effortlessly crossing language barriers. By the time you finish this book, I hope you'll have a newfound appreciation for numbers—no matter how you felt about them before.

While this book primarily focuses on interpreting angel numbers, I won't delve too deeply into Gematria itself. Instead, I view Gematria as a tool—a way to transform angel numbers into meaningful words. I often use the website *gematrix.org*, which works well for me here in the UK. But depending on where you are, you can easily find a Gematria website more suited to your location with a quick Google search. That way, you can start translating your own angel numbers and uncover the messages they hold for you.

18.2 Angel numbers in Gematria

You must be just as eager as I was to experiment with angel numbers and see their interpretations through Gematria. Fueled by curiosity, I decided to test out the basic numbers, from 1 to 9. I played around with sequences of three and four digits, specifically looking for phrases that seemed to resonate with our journey of spiritual awakening. Here's a glimpse of what I discovered:

111: Good, God magic

1111: Twin Flame, New age begins, The secret mystical code, A letter to you, I am code, Jesus blood, the quantum number, eleventh month

222: Hidden codes, Decode decoder, Record, Speaking, Decode the Bible

2222: Vision of God of the Hebrew Bible, I am code, Holy spirit last days apocalypse, Divine soul power, Twin flame arrow, Jesus is me I am He and we are a He, Jesus the Christ the Lords Key Code, God is my soul mate in the afterlife the greatest of all time, the Holy Spirit is the final call before the apocalypse.

333: Anastasia, Kundalini, Pregnant, I am a rare blood, Meant to be, Angelic host.

3333: When will you believe me, The healing world of God came early to stop the destruction of the Mankind, To whom it may concern I love you, You deny what is in front of your face, I am the resurrection and the life of peace and harmony in my life and family and affairs Im an angel. So the spirit needs a host God needs Get the message out before mankind destroys itself, past present future all in one let heaven be. Nothing will stop me from manifesting the New Earth

444: Iesous, the time has come, I am the chosen One, Time to go home, Galactic federation, Lord Christ, Rise up, Earth Goddess, Demons are coming, Mark of the Lord,

4444: Theor worlds prove they do not deserve existence, Is my awakening be the activation of One Both or All, The immediate family unit, Be four relationship pair, I am real God and you know I love you, Time to go home listen as the wind blows from across the Great Divine, The chosen one, Be thankful, This is what we call the revealing progress prepare to be tested

555: Today, God in Human form, Gods secret plan, Lucifer Satan, From Dark to Light.

5555: Revelation, The integral of Happiness divided by time from life to death with respect to change, I know that there is more to Life than working and making money and being depressed, I have seen the UFOs, You have to hang on to the belief that Good things are on their way to you. Jesus has defeated sin by his death and resurrection.

666: Number of a man Barack Obama, Elon Musk Grimes, Pffizer, Prophecy, Peace symbol, Only One God, The beast microchip ID, Proof of the past, Lucifer is the hidden God

6666: Hidden Codes Most high God Yhwh stands for Yehoowah read entry one four seven to see the truth, Food is a bad obstruction of the soul though when it comes to it healing without the power of the spirithealth, Yeshua you are my safety zone you are where I belong I live and breath in you.

777: Break free, Order out of Chaos, Code system, King of Kings and Lord of Lords, The Hidden key code of God, Great Pyramid, My name is Silence, Bible code Holy birthThe Aquarious age,

7777: Jesus Christ is the son of God who dies on the cross for my sins and the sins of everyone and my heart mind body and soul and life belong to him, Everyone is a programmed biological robot living within a Matrix of physical matter using binary E code to produce consciousness, For the eyes of the Lord move to and from throughout the Earth that he may strongly support those who heart is completely His, The Annunaki inferior Greator Gods The Annunaki never left, the Moon is an artificial satellite hollow moon grey alien death star orbiting a slave planet experiment.

888: The Holy Son of God, Divine plan, Veronica, Absolutely, Augustus, Look at Zodiacs, Nothing can stop us, I can't lie to myself

8888: A path of love, path of righteousness God the Holy Spirit Angelic Host Twin Flame Rise up we were with you from the beginning, suspension of disbelief Gematria has shown me that God is with me when I speak once you believe signs are everywhere,

999: Overnight, The number of the Soul, Imperative, Listen carefully, Bright right the god soul code, She can predict the future

9999: Gods will He who has found the secrets of creation the strong stabilized vibration to love is to shine and to shine is to burn, What is born of the spirit is spirit, God I am your grandson Your Enoch Your chuck Your best friend in Life Your Love of Life

From the examples I shared earlier, you might have noticed that the meanings of angel numbers, when interpreted through Gematria, differ from those in numerology. A striking aspect of Gematria is that it reveals multiple meanings for the same number sequence. It might seem complex at first, but the key is to trust your intuition. Embrace the interpretations that resonate with you when you encounter your angel number in Gematria form. The realm of Gematria is vast, too expansive to be fully covered in this book. My hope is that this brief chapter sparks your curiosity, encouraging you to dive deeper into Gematria and unlock a world brimming with hidden messages.

I understand that with this new information, you might feel a bit overwhelmed about interpreting the messages behind your angel numbers. Should you stick with the basic numerology system, or is it time to explore Gematria? Here's my advice: always trust your intuition. If a particular angel number keeps appearing in your life, and you've tried to understand its message through the methods discussed in previous chapters without success, then perhaps it's time to consider Gematria. This is especially true for complex and persistent number sequences. Try decoding these messages using both the traditional numerology approach and Gematria. And remember, the interpretation that resonates most deeply with you is likely the message meant for you.

19

Mirrored Angel Numbers

During my research, I began noticing patterns in mirrored or paired numbers, such as 1221 or 1212. It felt as if these numbers had their own distinct way of conveying messages.

In sequences like 1221, I've come to understand that the central numbers—'22' in this case—hold the core message. The numbers on the sides, such as the '1s', act like supporting characters, offering context or emphasizing the main numbers. It's as if they're framing the central piece, drawing attention to what matters most.

On the other hand, with paired sequences like 1212, my attention is first drawn to the initial pair—'12' here. These front numbers seem to set the stage, introducing the theme of the message. From there, I split the pair to identify the initial number, which in this case is '1'. The following pair, another '12', feels like it reinforces or complements the first, adding layers to the message's meaning.

When encountering a mirrored number like 1221, I dive deeper into the significance of '22', seeing it as the focal point. The '1s' at the edges help provide context or nuances to the main theme. Similarly, in a sequence like 1212, I first interpret the leading '12' as the primary message and then explore how the trailing '12' supports or expands on that.

It's fascinating how these number patterns offer different insights. The arrangement and repetition in these mirrored sequences reveal the multi-dimensional ways in which angel numbers communicate their guidance.

19.1 Recognizing Main and Secondary Numbers

Let's take a closer look at how to interpret these numbers, using 1221 and 1212 as examples.

Example: 1221

Applying my method for mirrored numbers, here's how you can translate 1221:

In the sequence 1221, the '22' at the center immediately grabs attention as the **Main Number**. In numerology, 22 is a *Master Number*, symbolizing the *Master Builder*. It embodies the realization of dreams and the transformation of desires into reality. Its central placement suggests the message focuses on manifestation and bringing big ideas to life. Since it's the number '22'—not just a single '2'—it could also relate to relationships, especially long-lasting or deeply connected ones.

The timing of when you see this number is crucial, as it helps clarify which message best applies to your life.

The '1s' at the beginning and end of the sequence add depth to the message, but since they're split and not repeated like the '2s', I interpret these as the **Secondary Numbers**. In numerology, '1' signifies new beginnings, self-leadership, and assertiveness. These '1s' are encouraging you to take initiative, stay confident, and trust your ability to manifest your dreams. They emphasize the importance of maintaining a positive attitude and believing in yourself as you pursue your goals.

When you bring it all together, 1221 is a powerful sign from your Spirit Guides, saying, "Focus on your dreams and aspirations. You have the energy of the Master Builder within you to make them a reality. Take action with confidence and optimism, and watch as your desires materialize."

Example: 1212

Now let's analyze the paired angel number 1212 using this approach:

In this sequence, '1' is the **Main Number** since it appears first. It represents new beginnings, independence, and personal power. The number '1' resonates with taking initiative, forging new paths, and asserting individuality. This suggests a call to action, encouraging you to step forward confidently and claim your power.

The '2s' in the sequence act as **Secondary Numbers**, providing balance and support to the assertive '1'. The number '2' brings energies of harmony, balance, and adaptability, complementing the '1' by introducing cooperation, diplomacy, and consideration for others.

The combination of '1' and '2' in 1212 speaks to balancing self-assertion with collaboration. It's a reminder that while it's important to lead and take initiative ('1'), doing so with sensitivity to others and a spirit of cooperation ('2') is equally vital. This angel number, seen through the lens of '1' as primary, motivates you to embrace leadership and independence while maintaining harmony in your relationships.

In this interpretation, 1212 becomes a powerful encouragement to lead new ventures or life changes, assuring you that your strengths will be successful, especially when paired with teamwork and cooperation. The repeated '1s' and '2s' reinforce the message of blending leadership with empathy. This perspective on 1212 serves as a reminder of the importance of balancing personal goals with mindful collaboration on your journey.

20

Angel Numbers as Dates

When you repeatedly notice angel numbers that feel unusual and keep showing up, they might be pointing to a specific date. This date could be related to something from the past or an event yet to come. Often, these numbers carry a sense of urgency, almost as if your spirit guides are trying to grab your attention. You might feel a sense of stress or pressure when these numbers appear, signaling a need to prepare or reflect on something significant.

For instance, if you keep seeing the number sequence 1122 or 2211, it could be pointing toward an important date. Upon reflection, you might realize that a date like the 11th of February (11/22 or 22/11 in some date formats) is approaching. Alternatively, it could be connected to a significant event from the past—whether personal or historical—that holds relevance to your spiritual journey. The accompanying feelings of stress or urgency might be your spirit guides pushing you to focus on this date.

Your guides may be signaling that an important event or decision is coming up. If the date refers to the past, it could be a reminder to heal from an unresolved wound, honour a special memory, or learn from a historical moment that carries weight in your current path.

Let me share a personal observation that connects to this theme of dates. In my own exploration of reincarnation, I uncovered two past lives, one in 863 AD and another in 1463 AD. As someone intrigued by numbers, I noticed the recurrence of '63' in both years. It sparked curiosity about the significance of that number and the connection between these two lifetimes.

Doing some calculations, I found that there's a 600-year gap between 863 and 1463. Adding another 600 years to 1463 brings us to 2063. Since I was born in 1978, I will be 85 years old in 2063. This raised the thought: could it be that my consciousness transitions in 600-year cycles? Is it possible I reincarnate every 600 years? I share this insight to encourage you to explore your own patterns and connections, as these numbers might help unravel your spiritual journey.

This idea of looking for patterns can also apply to interpreting persistent angel numbers. For example, if the number 73 keeps showing up, it might signify an important age—either the age you passed in a past life or a significant age in this one. While thinking of these possibilities can be unsettling, my aim is to explore every angle as part of the journey this book represents. By reflecting on these recurring numbers, you might uncover new insights into your past, present, and future.

21

Single or Duo Digits of Angel Numbers

As we explore angel numbers, we've primarily focused on sequences made up of three or four digits. These patterns are often how our Spirit Guides initially capture our attention, especially in the early stages of our spiritual journey. However, as we progress and deepen in our path of awakening, these angelic messages can take on a new form. Suddenly, we might find ourselves noticing single digits or pairs of numbers, repeating in ways too persistent to ignore.

In these instances, I've found that angel numbers shift to convey a more tailored message, specific to our energy and personal path. Our Spirit Guides simplify the sequences, reflecting an evolution in their communication that aligns with our own growth. This shift often indicates messages related to our aura, chakras, or even specific colours, crystals, or frequencies of music that would support our well-being at that moment. As we become more attuned, angel numbers serve as direct guidance on balancing our own energy, working with specific chakras, or engaging with subtle healing practices. Classic works on chakra energy, such as *Wheels of Life: A User's Guide to the Chakra System* by *Anodea Judith (1987)*, offer insights into the significance of each chakra and can deepen our understanding of these messages. Judith's exploration of the chakra system provides valuable techniques for harmonising our energy centres, enabling us to align more fully with the guidance we receive.

In this way, single or duo digits move beyond general messages, offering an intimate and personal dialogue with our guides about our spiritual path. This transformation in how we receive angelic guidance is a testament to our growing connection with the spiritual realm, marking a significant phase in our journey where we're able to interpret simpler sequences while remaining fully present and connected to their meaning. It's often during the later phases of our spiritual evolution that we notice these simpler sequences, as our mind becomes more naturally attuned to receiving them and understanding their nuanced meanings.

I can recall a few times when the single unit "1" appeared vividly in my life—like a TikTok post with exactly 111 likes, 1 comment, and 1 share. The timing felt like a gentle reminder to ground myself, calling me to balance my root chakra after a stressful period where I felt on the verge of disconnecting from the Earth's elements.

21.1 Angel Numbers and Chakras Associations

Number 1 - Red - Root Chakra (Muladhara)

Number 1 symbolizes leadership, initiative, and new beginnings.

Color Association

Connected with the vibrant and energizing color red

111

Root Chakra Association

The Root Chakra, located at the base of the spine, is our foundational energy center. It governs our feelings of safety, stability, and basic needs.

The frequency of red, in the lower spectrum of visible light, resonates with the Root Chakra's low, grounding energy. This synchronicity strengthens our sense of security and physical presence in the world.

Crystals

Primary Crystals: Red Jasper and Garnet are known for their stabilizing properties.

Additional Crystals: Bloodstone and Black Tourmaline, also resonating with red frequencies, aid in grounding and protective qualities.

Carrying or meditating with these crystals can amplify the grounding energy of the Root Chakra, enhancing courage and physical vitality.

Aura Color Significance

Individuals with a red aura often exhibit strong physical energy, practicality, and a grounded approach to life.

Practices like grounding meditation, engaging in physical activity, or surrounding oneself with red objects can strengthen this aura. Wearing or meditating with red crystals can also enhance the aura's vibrancy and protect it from negative energies.

Interconnected Frequencies

The frequency of number 1, associated with beginnings and leadership, aligns with the vibrational frequency of red. This alignment amplifies the Root Chakra's energy, reinforcing our physical and emotional foundation.

When angel number 1 or sequences like 11 appear, it could be a message to focus on your foundational needs or to initiate new beginnings. This message might relate to strengthening your Root Chakra, enhancing your physical energy, or developing a more pragmatic approach to life.

Incorporating red into your environment, wearing red clothing, or meditating with red crystals can help align your personal energy with the empowering frequency of number 1.

Listening to music tuned to *396 Hz*, the frequency associated with liberating guilt and fear, can also resonate with the Root Chakra, promoting a sense of safety and grounding.

Balance in the Root Chakra, influenced by the number 1, can be achieved by consciously engaging with the color red and its associated crystals. This might involve practices like visualizing red light during meditation or placing red crystals on the body during energy work.

Recognizing the appearance of angel number 1 in your life, especially in relation to your aura and chakra health, can guide you towards areas needing attention or development. It invites you to explore your potential for leadership, new projects, and establishing a solid foundation for your endeavors.

Number 2 - Orange - Sacral Chakra (Svadhisthana)

Number 2 embodies balance, duality, and harmony.

Color Association

Linked with the vibrant and stimulating color orange.

Sacral Chakra Connection

The Sacral Chakra, situated in the lower abdomen, is pivotal in our emotional depth, sexuality, and creative expression.

Orange's frequency, situated in the visible light spectrum, vibrates with the Sacral Chakra's energy, fostering creativity, pleasure, and emotional fluidity.

Crystals

Primary Crystals: Carnelian and Orange Calcite are renowned for stimulating and balancing the Sacral Chakra.

Additional Crystals: Tiger's Eye and Sunstone, aligning with orange frequencies, can also be used to enhance creativity and emotional strength.

Utilizing these crystals through carrying, wearing, or meditating can significantly amplify the Sacral Chakra's energy, promoting emotional balance and creative inspiration.

Aura Color Significance

An orange aura signifies a creative, passionate, and adventurous spirit.

Engaging in creative activities, expressing emotions healthily, and meditating with orange crystals can deepen and protect this aura color. Surrounding oneself with orange colors in daily life can also enhance its vibrancy.

The frequency of number 2, denoting balance and harmony, synchronizes with the vibrational frequency of orange, enhancing emotional intelligence and creativity.

Interconnected Frequencies

Seeing angel number 2 or sequences like 22 suggests a call to focus on emotional balance, embrace creativity, or nurture relationships. This message might relate to activating your Sacral Chakra and embracing its qualities.

Incorporating orange into your environment, wearing orange clothing, or engaging with orange crystals like Carnelian can help align your energy with number 2's frequency. Listening to music tuned to *417 Hz*, associated with facilitating change and undoing situations, can resonate with the Sacral Chakra, promoting creativity and emotional release.

Achieving balance in the Sacral Chakra, influenced by the number 2, can involve consciously engaging with the color orange and its related crystals. Practices such as visualizing orange light during meditation or placing orange crystals on the body can be beneficial.

Recognizing the presence of angel number 2 in your life, especially in the context of your aura and chakra health, can guide you toward nurturing your emotional and creative aspects. It invites exploration into the realms of relationships, artistic pursuits, and understanding your emotional depths.

Number 3 - Yellow - Solar Plexus Chakra (Manipura)

Number 3 embodies self-expression, creativity, and enthusiasm.

Color Association

Bright and uplifting yellow, a color that stimulates and energizes.

Solar Plexus Chakra Association

The Solar Plexus Chakra, situated in the upper abdomen, is the core of our identity, self-esteem, and personal power.

Yellow's frequency in the visible spectrum aligns with the energy of the Solar Plexus Chakra, enhancing personal empowerment and self-confidence.

Crystals

Primary Crystals: Yellow Citrine and Tiger's Eye are powerful in activating and balancing the Solar Plexus Chakra.

Additional Crystals: Pyrite and Yellow Jasper can also be utilized to augment personal power and clarity.

Integrating these crystals in daily life through jewelry, meditation, or placing them in your living space can boost the Solar Plexus Chakra's vibrancy, aiding in self-confidence and personal growth.

Aura Color Significance

A yellow aura represents a joyful, intellectual, and confident personality.

Engaging in confidence-boosting activities, positive thinking, and using yellow crystals can enrich the yellow aura. Surrounding yourself with yellow hues and sunlight can also amplify its strength.

Interconnected Frequencies

Number 3's vibrancy resonates with the energizing frequency of yellow, fostering self-expression, confidence, and intellectual pursuits.

Encountering angel number 3 or sequences like 33 can be an indication to focus on personal growth, express your creativity, or step into your power. It's a nudge towards embracing and empowering your Solar Plexus Chakra.

Incorporating yellow into your surroundings, wearing yellow clothing, or engaging with yellow crystals like Citrine can align your energy with the vibrancy of number 3. Listening to music tuned to *528 Hz*, associated with transformation and miracles, can resonate with the Solar Plexus Chakra, facilitating personal empowerment and clarity.

Cultivating a strong Solar Plexus Chakra, influenced by the number 3, involves actively working with the color yellow and its corresponding crystals. Visualizing a bright yellow light during meditation or placing yellow crystals on your body can be effective.

Recognizing the presence of angel number 3 in your life, especially in relation to your aura and chakra health, can guide you toward strengthening your self-esteem, assertiveness, and personal identity. It encourages a journey of self-discovery, intellectual growth, and a confident approach to life's challenges.

This detailed analysis of angel number 3, the color yellow, and the Solar Plexus Chakra reveals their combined influence on our sense of self, confidence, and intellectual vibrancy. By embracing these connections, you can pave a path towards personal empowerment and a brighter, more self-assured life.

Number 4 - Green - Heart Chakra (Anahata)

Number 4 represents stability, reliability, and grounding.

Color Association

Calming and nurturing green, symbolizing growth and renewal.

Heart Chakra Relation

The Heart Chakra, centered in our chest, governs our ability to love, empathize, and connect with others.

Green's soothing frequency aligns with the Heart Chakra's energy, enhancing emotional balance and the capacity to love.

Crystals

Primary Crystals: Green Aventurine and Rose Quartz are potent for nurturing the Heart Chakra, promoting love, compassion, and emotional healing.

Additional Crystals: Malachite and Emerald can also be beneficial in supporting heart-centered emotions and healing.

Carrying, wearing, or meditating with these crystals can amplify the Heart Chakra's energies, facilitating deeper emotional connections and fostering unconditional love.

Aura Color Significance

A green aura suggests a compassionate, caring, and empathetic nature, often found in healing professions.

Activities that promote love, compassion, and connection with nature can enrich a green aura. Using green crystals and surrounding oneself with greenery can fortify this aura color.

Interconnected Frequencies

Number 4's energy resonates with the nurturing frequency of green, fostering stability in relationships and emotional well-being.

Encountering angel number 4, such as in sequences like 44, can be a message to focus on emotional stability, nurture relationships, or foster inner peace and empathy. It's an encouragement to balance and heal the Heart Chakra.

Integrating green into your environment, wearing green clothing, or engaging with heart-healing crystals like Green Aventurine can align your energy with the healing qualities of number 4. Listening to music tuned to *639 Hz,* associated with harmonizing relationships, can resonate with the Heart Chakra, enhancing love and empathy.

Fostering a healthy Heart Chakra, influenced by the number 4, involves actively working with the color green and its corresponding crystals. Visualizing a vibrant green light during meditation or placing heart-healing crystals on your chest can be effective in promoting emotional stability and love.

Recognizing the presence of angel number 4 in your life, in relation to your aura and chakra health, guides you toward nurturing your emotional bonds, developing empathy, and finding balance in giving and receiving love. It encourages a journey of heart-centered growth and deep, meaningful connections with others.

This comprehensive analysis of angel number 4, the color green, and the Heart Chakra highlights their combined influence on our emotional stability, capacity for love, and empathetic connections. By embracing these connections, you can cultivate a nurturing, compassionate approach to your relationships and emotional well-being.

Number 5 - Blue - Throat Chakra (Vishuddha)

Number 5 represents transformation, adaptability, and freedom.

Color Association
Expressive and serene blue, symbolizing clarity and communication.

The Throat Chakra, positioned at the throat, is the center of communication, self-expression, and truth.

Blue's soothing and clear frequency aligns with the Throat Chakra, facilitating open and authentic communication.

Crystals

Primary Crystals: Blue Lace Agate and Turquoise enhance the Throat Chakra, promoting clear expression and truthfulness.

Additional Crystals: Lapis Lazuli and Aquamarine can also support effective communication and self-expression.

Using these crystals during meditation or wearing them as jewelry can help in expressing your true self and enhancing verbal communication.

Aura Color Significance

A blue aura indicates calmness, clarity, and a gift for articulation and communication. To enrich a blue aura, engage in activities that foster peaceful communication and self-expression. Blue crystals can be used for meditation, and surrounding yourself with tranquil blue environments can be beneficial.

Interconnected Frequencies

Number 5's dynamic energy harmonizes with the clear and calm frequency of blue, enhancing adaptability in communication and self-expression.

Encountering angel number 5, such as in sequences like 55, is a sign to focus on clear communication, embrace changes, and express your true self. It's a nudge to balance and energize the Throat Chakra.

Integrating blue into your daily life, through attire or decor, and engaging with communication-enhancing crystals like Turquoise can align your energy with the expressive qualities of number 5. Listening to music tuned to *741 Hz*, associated with awakening intuition, can resonate with the Throat Chakra, boosting self-expression.

Color, Aura, and Chakra Synergy

Working with the Throat Chakra, influenced by number 5, involves actively using the color blue and its corresponding crystals. Visualizing a bright blue light during meditation or placing communication-enhancing crystals on your throat can be effective in promoting honest and clear communication.

Recognizing the presence of angel number 5 in your life, in relation to your aura and chakra health, guides you toward improving your communication skills, expressing your thoughts clearly, and embracing your authentic voice. It encourages a journey of expressive growth and meaningful interpersonal connections.

This comprehensive look at angel number 5, the color blue, and the Throat Chakra reveals their combined influence on our communication abilities, self-expression, and the pursuit of truth. By embracing these connections, you can cultivate a calm, clear approach to expressing yourself and communicating with others.

Number 6 - Indigo - Third Eye Chakra (Ajna)

Number 6 symbolizes responsibility, nurturing, and intuition.

Color Association

Deep and mystical indigo, representing insight and intuition.

Third Eye Chakra Connection

The Third Eye Chakra, situated on the forehead, is the center of intuition and foresight. Indigo's deep and introspective frequency aligns with the Third Eye Chakra, fostering intuition and inner wisdom.

Crystals

Primary Crystals: Lapis Lazuli and Amethyst are powerful for enhancing the Third Eye Chakra, boosting intuition and spiritual clarity.

Additional Crystals: Sodalite and Azurite can also be used to support insight and intuition.

Using these crystals in meditation or carrying them can help unlock deeper intuitive abilities and enhance spiritual understanding.

Aura Color Significance

An indigo aura suggests profound intuitive abilities and a deep connection to the subconscious mind. To nurture an indigo aura, engage in activities that foster intuition and self-reflection. Meditation with indigo crystals and visualization of an indigo light can be beneficial.

666

Interconnected Frequencies

Number 6's nurturing energy harmonizes with the mystical frequency of indigo, enhancing intuition and inner knowing. Encountering angel number 6, such as in sequences like 66, is a call to trust your intuition and nurture your spiritual insights. It's an invitation to activate and balance the Third Eye Chakra.

Incorporating indigo in your environment and working with intuition-boosting crystals like Amethyst can align your energy with the insightful qualities of number 6. Listening to music tuned to *852 Hz*, associated with awakening intuition, can resonate with the Third Eye Chakra, enhancing your intuitive abilities.

Color, Aura, and Chakra Synergy

Engaging with the Third Eye Chakra, influenced by number 6, involves utilizing the color indigo and its corresponding crystals. Meditating while visualizing an indigo light or placing crystals like Lapis Lazuli on your forehead can enhance spiritual insight.

Recognizing the presence of angel number 6 in your life, in relation to your aura and chakra health, guides you toward trusting your intuition, exploring your spiritual path, and understanding life's deeper meanings. It encourages a journey of intuitive growth and self-discovery.

Number 7 - Violet - Crown Chakra (Sahasrara)

Number 7 symbolizes mysticism, spiritual awakening, and enlightenment.

777

Color Association
The color violet, representing spiritual awareness and higher consciousness.

Crown Chakra Association
The Crown Chakra, located at the top of the head, is our spiritual connection point.

Frequency Resonance
Violet's high frequency resonates with the Crown Chakra, enhancing spiritual connection and universal awareness.

Crystals
Primary Crystals: Selenite and Clear Quartz, known for their high vibrational frequencies, are ideal for stimulating the Crown Chakra.

Additional Crystals: Amethyst and White Topaz can also be beneficial in enhancing spiritual connection.

Placing these crystals on or near the top of the head during meditation can deepen spiritual experiences and heighten awareness.

Aura Color Significance

A violet aura suggests a deep spiritual understanding and a connection to the divine.

To nurture a violet aura, engage in spiritual practices like meditation and mindfulness. Using violet crystals and visualizing a violet light around the crown can amplify spiritual awareness.

Interconnected Frequencies

The mystical energy of number 7 harmonizes with the spiritual frequency of violet, fostering enlightenment and universal connection. Encountering angel number 7 is an invitation to explore your spiritual path and seek deeper universal truths. It's a call to embrace higher wisdom and connect with the divine. Integrating violet into your environment and working with crystals like Selenite can align your energy with the enlightening qualities of number 7. Listening to music tuned to *963 Hz*, associated with higher consciousness, can resonate with the Crown Chakra, enhancing spiritual connection.

Color, Aura, and Chakra Synergy

Focusing on the Crown Chakra, influenced by number 7, involves utilizing the color violet and its corresponding crystals. Meditating with Selenite or Clear Quartz at the crown can facilitate a deeper spiritual connection.

Recognizing the presence of angel number 7 in your life, in harmony with your aura and chakra health, encourages a journey towards spiritual enlightenment. It invites you to explore the mysteries of the universe and understand your place within it.

This comprehensive exploration of angel number 7, the color violet, and the Crown Chakra highlights the profound spiritual connection and enlightenment they foster together. By embracing these elements, you can deepen your spiritual journey and connect more profoundly with the universe and your higher self.

Number 8 - Pink or Light Red - Lower Heart Chakra

Number 8 represents abundance, material success, and inner strength.

Color Association

Aligns with pink or light red, symbolizing love, compassion, and nurturing.

Lower Heart Chakra Connection

The Lower Heart Chakra, not traditionally recognized in the seven-chakra system, is seen as a bridge between earthly and spiritual love.

Frequency Resonance

The soothing frequencies of pink and light red resonate with this chakra, promoting compassionate and nurturing energies.

Crystals

Primary Crystals: Pink Quartz and Rhodonite are ideal for enhancing the energies of the Lower Heart Chakra.

Additional Crystals: Kunzite and Pink Opal can also be beneficial in promoting love and compassion.

Wearing these crystals or placing them near the heart during meditation can foster a sense of nurturing love and emotional healing.

Aura Color Significance

A pink aura indicates a caring, nurturing nature, often found in individuals who are deeply compassionate and loving.

Engaging in loving-kindness meditation and surrounding oneself with pink hues can nurture a pink aura. Wearing pink crystals can also support and protect this aura color.

Interconnected Energies

Number 8's association with abundance and inner strength harmonizes with the nurturing qualities of pink and light red, enhancing earthly connections and compassion.

Seeing angel number 8 invites you to focus on material success and personal strength, while maintaining a compassionate and nurturing heart.

Integrating pink and light red in your daily life, along with crystals like Rose Quartz, can align your energy with the nurturing qualities of number 8. Listening to soothing music or sounds tuned to frequencies that resonate with love and compassion can further enhance this alignment.

Color, Aura, and Chakra Synergy

Embracing the Lower Heart Chakra's energies, influenced by number 8, involves utilizing pink and light red hues and their corresponding crystals. Focusing on earthly compassion and nurturing relationships is key.

The presence of angel number 8 in your life, along with a healthy aura and chakra system, encourages the cultivation of nurturing and compassionate relationships. It's a reminder to balance material success with emotional fulfillment and to spread love and kindness in your daily interactions.

Exploring angel number 8, along with the colors pink and light red, and the Lower Heart Chakra, highlights the importance of balancing abundance and strength with compassion and nurturing. By embracing these elements, you can deepen your connections on Earth and cultivate a life rich in love and emotional fulfillment.

Number 9 - Gold or White - Soul Star Chakra (Vyapini)

Number 9 symbolizes completion, enlightenment, and the culmination of a spiritual journey.

Color Association

Connected with gold and white, representing purity, higher consciousness, and spiritual illumination.

Soul Star Chakra Association

The Soul Star Chakra, located above the head, is our gateway to the divine, higher self, and universal knowledge.

Frequency Resonance

Gold and white frequencies resonate with this chakra, facilitating a connection to higher realms and divine consciousness.

999

Crystals

Primary Crystals: Gold Sheen Obsidian and White Howlite are potent for the Soul Star Chakra, enhancing spiritual connection and cosmic awareness.

Additional Crystals: Selenite and Clear Quartz are also excellent for fostering divine connection and clarity.

Placing these crystals above the head during meditation can elevate spiritual awareness and deepen the connection to the cosmos.

Aura Color Significance

These aura colors signify a deep spiritual connection and access to higher wisdom.

Meditation with Gold Sheen Obsidian or White Howlite can strengthen these aura colors. Engaging in spiritual practices and maintaining a high vibrational lifestyle supports and protects these aura colors.

Interconnected Energies

Number 9's association with completion and spiritual enlightenment aligns beautifully with the purity and illumination of gold and white.

Encountering angel number 9 is a call to embrace your spiritual journey, seeking deeper understanding and connection with the divine.

Integrating gold and white in your surroundings, along with crystals like Gold Sheen Obsidian, can foster a deeper spiritual connection. Listening to high-frequency music or sounds can also resonate with these colors, enhancing your spiritual experience:

963 Hz: This frequency is often referred to as the "Frequency of the Gods." It's linked to the activation of the higher chakras, especially the Soul Star Chakra. It aids in connecting with the divine and universal consciousness.

852 Hz: This frequency helps in awakening intuition and a higher purpose. It's beneficial for those seeking deeper spiritual connections and resonates with the insights offered by angel number 9.

Golden Frequency (528 Hz): Known as the "Miracle Tone," it resonates with love, transformation, and miracles. It aligns well with the golden aspect of angel number 9, fostering spiritual growth and enlightenment.

White Light Meditation Music: Often found in various frequency ranges, this music embodies the purity and spiritual illumination associated with white color. It's perfect for meditation sessions focusing on cosmic connections and divine guidance.

Color, Aura, and Chakra Synergy

The Soul Star Chakra, influenced by number 9, encourages a profound spiritual awakening, enhanced by the purity and illumination of gold and white.

The appearance of angel number 9, combined with a vibrant gold or white aura and an active Soul Star Chakra, signifies a strong connection to spiritual realms. It's an invitation to explore the depths of your soul and embrace your higher purpose.

I want to introduce to you one more way that you can use the angel numbers with chakra association. You can use them to identify your Lightworker category.

To identify your Lightworker category (see ch. 11.2) through angel numbers, simply engage in meditation and ask your Spirit Guides to reveal which Lightworker role you are meant to embrace in this lifetime. Use your inner voice during this meditative state to pose the question clearly and with intent. The first angel number that appears to you following this inquiry will serve as a direct answer from your guides, indicating your designated Lightwo1rker category. This technique taps into the profound connection between your consciousness and the spiritual realm, allowing for guidance to be communicated through the universal language of numbers.

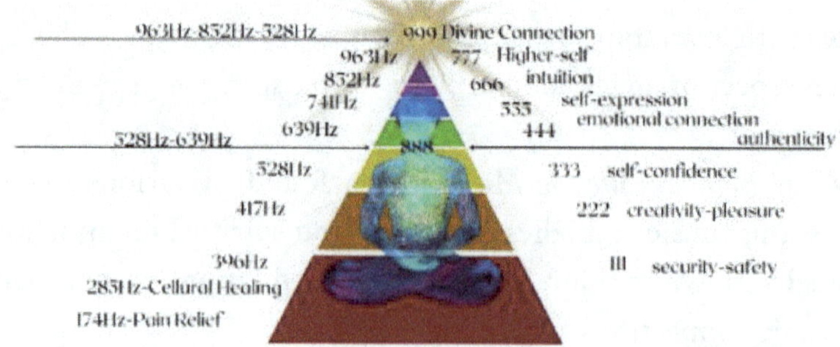

I want to introduce to you one more way that you can use the angel numbers with chakra association. You can use them to identify your Lightworker category.

To identify your Lightworker category (see ch. 11.2) through angel numbers, simply engage in meditation and ask your Spirit Guides to reveal which Lightworker role you are meant to embrace in this life-time. Use your inner voice during this meditative state to pose the question clearly and with intent. The first angel number that appears to you following this inquiry will serve as a direct answer from your guides, indicating your designated Lightwo1rker category. This technique taps into the profound connection between your consciousness and the spiritual realm, allowing for guidance to be communicated through the universal language of numbers.

22

Spiritual Awakening Journey-Phase 4

2.1 Integration

2 In the profound journey of spiritual awakening, the pinnacle is often described not merely as an arrival at a new state of being but as a process of integration. This integration is multifaceted, encompassing the harmonious unification of the physical, energetic, and consciousness levels of our existence with the collective consciousness of all awakened beings and, ultimately, with the Source itself. Understanding this stage requires delving into the nuances of what integration truly means in the context of spiritual awakening.

At the heart of this integration is the seamless alignment between the physical body and the energetic. This is not merely a state of physical health or vitality but a profound synchronization where our most tangible aspects are in perfect harmony with our energy or subtle body. This energetic body, understood in many traditions as consisting of chakras, meridians, or auras, becomes fully activated and aligned, facilitating a constant flow of universal energy through us. This harmonization eradicates the boundaries between the physical and energetic, leading to a heightened state of health, vitality, and a deep sense of well-being.

The journey further deepens as our individual consciousness integrates into the collective consciousness of all awakened beings. This is a realization that we are not isolated entities navigating a spiritual path in solitude. Instead, our awakening contributes to and is supported by the collective field of awakened consciousness. This integration signifies a shift from the personal to the universal, where our personal awakenings ripple outwards, contributing to the collective enlightenment and being enriched by it. It's a realization that our individual insights, growth, and enlightenment are part of a larger tapestry of collective consciousness, moving together towards greater awakening.

The ultimate aspect of integration is the merging with the Source, the origin of all that is. This is often described as the dissolution of the ego or the sense of a separate self, leading to an experiential understanding and felt sense of oneness with the Source. This union transcends intellectual understanding, becoming a direct experience where distinctions between self and Source blur and eventually disappear. It's a state of being where the illusion of separation is dissolved, and the reality of oneness is lived and experienced. This integration with the Source is the final dissolution of any sense of duality, marking the culmination of the spiritual journey.

Living from this place of integration brings profound transformations. It manifests as living in the present moment, engaging with the world with compassion, and an effortless flow of actions aligned with higher wisdom. This integrated state is characterized by a life lived in harmony with the universe, where actions are an expression of the divine, and existence is a constant dance with the cosmos.

The last stage of the spiritual awakening journey, is characterized by a profound sense of unity, peace, and enlightenment. While the journey itself can be highly individual, many describe this final stage with similar attributes. Here are key elements often associated with the last stage of spiritual awakening:

Unity with All That Is

At this stage, individuals often experience a deep sense of connection with the universe, feeling a oneness with all living beings, nature, and the cosmos. This unity transcends the illusion of separation, leading to a profound understanding that everything is interconnected.

Inner Peace and Serenity

A hallmark of reaching the final stage is the enduring presence of peace within. This peace isn't contingent on external circumstances but stems from an inner wellspring of serenity, understanding, and acceptance of what is.

Enlightenment or Self-Realization

Enlightenment, or the full realization of one's true nature, is often described as the pinnacle of the spiritual journey. It involves the direct experience or insight into the essence of being, beyond the ego or individual self. This realization brings clarity, joy, and a profound sense of liberation.

Unconditional Love and Compassion

There's an overwhelming sense of love and compassion for oneself and others. This love is unconditional, not based on personal gain or relationships but emanates from the recognition of the unity and shared essence among all beings.

Detachment and Non-Attachment

Individuals in this stage often exhibit a healthy detachment from material possessions, outcomes, and even personal identities. This doesn't mean apathy or disengagement from the world but a freedom from being controlled by desires, aversions, and the ego.

Continuous Presence and Mindfulness

Living in the present moment becomes the natural state. The mind is free from the habitual patterns of dwelling on the past or worrying about the future, leading to a full engagement with the now.

Service and Contribution

With the realization of oneness and love, there often comes a natural desire to serve and contribute to the well-being of others and the planet. This service is not driven by a sense of duty but flows naturally from the understanding of interconnectedness.

It's important to note that these descriptions are broad and can vary significantly among different spiritual traditions and individual experiences. The journey to this stage is deeply personal, and the manifestation of these attributes can differ widely among those who reach it.

In summary, integration in the final stage of spiritual awakening is a deep and profound unification of our entire being with the energetic fabric of the universe and the Source. It's a stage where the journey inward culminates in a realization that we are, in essence, never separate from the whole. This realization is not the end but a new beginning of living in a state of constant awakening, where every moment is an expression of this integrated truth.

This final stage of spiritual awakening is not a destination guaranteed to everyone in this lifetime. It's essential to recognize that this journey may span across lifetimes, and reaching this ultimate phase is not a prerequisite for a meaningful or spiritually fulfilled life. Embracing the journey at any stage, whether you find yourself at the beginning or potentially nearing this profound stage of integration, is crucial. Understanding that each step, each moment, is part of your unique earthly experience, chosen by you for a specific purpose, brings a deeper acceptance and appreciation for your path.

My reflections on this journey, especially considering the events of the past months and how they've shaped my path, have led me to a profound realization: everything indeed happens for a reason. This perspective is key to understanding the intricate tapestry of choices, experiences, joys, and challenges that compose our lives. Accepting this, embracing the flow of life with all its fluctuations, can usher in a profound sense of inner peace.

Harmony emerges from acknowledging our free will, recognizing that love is an unconditional unity with all of existence. Reaching this stage of spiritual awakening can also bring about a feeling of completeness, where the urge to manifest specific desires dissipates. You come to understand that there is no need for more, for everything you've ever wanted or needed is already with you and within you. This realization doesn't negate the beauty of exploration, travel, or creation, but it highlights that true happiness comes from within, not from external achievements or acquisitions.

At this pinnacle of spiritual awakening, you experience a gentle surrender to the present, free from sadness over the past or anxiety about the future. This surrender is devoid of any sense of loss for the paths not taken or the people no longer by your side. It's a state where past traumas no longer define your energy because you recognize your essence is not tethered to past events.

This clarity, this profound understanding of your own power and the essence of your being, is what many seek throughout their spiritual journey. So, wherever you are in your journey, remember the importance of embracing the present moment. Seize the day, find joy in the simplicity of life, and cherish your experience on this Earth. This mindset isn't just about finding peace; it's about recognizing the incredible journey of growth and realization that life is, in all its complexity and beauty.

In the context of angel numbers and wisdom, you'll find yourself approaching the final stage of your spiritual awakening journey. Here, a sense of ongoing, effortless communication emerges, akin to the natural interactions you have with those around you. While this communication may not be verbal and might appear to be a one-sided form of guidance, it is actually a reciprocal dialogue. This realization serves as a comforting reminder that we are never truly isolated. This remarkable connection with the Source manifests in various ways, continually reassuring us of its presence.

you'll also discover that decoding the messages behind angel numbers becomes an intuitive and effortless process. You'll possess an innate understanding, allowing your intuition to immediately unravel the meanings these numbers convey.

22.2 The Other Dimensions

At this point, I want to explain to you my perspective of what the other dimensions are. A simple way to understand dimensions is like this: Imagine yourself standing outside a building. This building is entirely made of one-way glass. You can see the building and its glass surface but cannot see inside. If you decide to enter the building, you realize that everyone inside could see you, but you couldn't see them. Now inside, you can see both the people outside the building and the interior as you are in it. This building has many floors and rooms. The rooms are again made of one-way glass. Whoever is in another room can see you and the other rooms, but you can only really see the room if you step inside. And with every room you enter, you gain the ability to see the other rooms. These represent the densities in the 3rd dimension.

From the 1st floor, which is the 4th dimension, the floor is again made of glass, and the entities living there can look down at you, but you cannot see them. The floors above work the same way. On each floor (each dimension), the entities can communicate with those below them, see them, but the entities from the lower floors can only see the ones above on very specific occasions. These occasions occur when these floors and the rooms within them start to merge. So, now you have the 1st floor merging and becoming one with the ground floor. Your body allows you to see whatever is on the 1st floor but only in specific rooms (densities). This can also happen if you leave your body on the ground floor and your energetic body, your astral body, decides to fly and go through the floor to see and communicate with the entities there.

However, there is a restriction. To achieve this merging, the frequency must match. Every floor and the rooms within it operate at a specific frequency. The higher the room, the higher the frequency. For your astral body to reach these floors (dimensions), your frequency must be raised enough. Of course, the highest floors will only be achievable if, at the same time with your intention of entering, they allow the merging; otherwise, it is impossible to reach the top floor where the main source is. Conversely, whenever there is a need for the higher dimensions to be seen, then the entities have the power to move down and merge.

Now, back on the ground floor, the other rooms, the other densities, have entities living there that are closer to us and more easily approachable. Also, on the 1st floor, which is the 4th dimension, there are rooms with entities that remain there and are slightly higher in the hierarchy than those on the ground floor. All these entities operate at low frequencies hence they cannot move further above but can easily move in the 3rd dimension. Lastly, there is a basement and many floors beneath, with their own rooms (densities). These operate at a frequency even lower than us and the entities on the ground and 4th dimension. They again can look up and approach us, but we cannot see them unless we decide to lower our frequency. Now, all these lower frequency entities cannot raise their frequency enough to enter the higher floors, but they can reach ours.

Conclusion

Exploring psychic abilities offers a unique pathway into these multidimensional realms. By tuning into and raising our vibrational frequency, individuals can align with the energies of higher dimensions. Spirit guides, residing in the 5th dimension, provide guidance and support from a place of elevated consciousness. Past souls, remaining in the 4th dimension, offer insights from their experiences. Elemental spirits, Spirit Orbs, and lower frequency entities inhabit the ground floor in different densities, accessible to those who seek to understand the fabric of our existence more deeply. The dark entities and lower vibrational beings reside in the basements, where the hierarchy is inversely related to frequency— the lower the frequency, the higher their standing. However, in the higher dimensions, it is the elevation of frequency that determines one's ascension. Through intentional practice and spiritual development, people can navigate these dimensions, encountering a spectrum of entities and energies, thereby enriching their understanding of the universe and their place within it.

The concept of dimensions in the realm of metaphysics can be likened to different levels of frequency. Essentially, the universe operates on the principle that the higher the frequency, the higher the dimension, and vice versa. This understanding opens up a profound pathway for personal development and spiritual exploration, particularly in how we can navigate ourselves into higher dimensions by raising our frequency.

The frequency referred to here is not just a measure of physical vibrations but pertains to the frequency of our energetic body, which is intrinsically connected to our physical form. Since everything in the universe is interconnected, maintaining a clean physical body becomes crucial. This cleanliness is not only about hygiene but also about the purity from substances such as alcohol, tobacco, drugs, and toxins that can lower our vibrational state. Beyond the physical, it extends to how we operate on emotional and spiritual levels—practicing love, understanding, respect, releasing grudges, eschewing jealousy, and adhering to a universal ethical code that respects the energy of others.

By balancing the physical with the ethereal body, we create a harmonious vibration that facilitates our ability to 'jump' into other dimensions. This leap is often achieved through meditation, a practice through which our consciousness can separate from our physical body and traverse different realms. Within the constraints of our 3D world, our frequency typically allows us to ascend only as high as the 4th dimension, and more rarely, into the 5th. However, this limitation does not preclude connections with entities of the highest hierarchies or even with the source itself, God. Such profound connections occur when these higher-dimensional beings choose to come down to our level as we simultaneously strive to elevate our vibrational frequency.

This dynamic interplay highlights a critical aspect of spiritual ascension: the journey is both inward and outward. It requires a conscientious effort to purify and uplift every aspect of our being to resonate with the higher frequencies of existence. The higher dimensions are not just spaces of elevated frequency but realms of profound wisdom, understanding, and connectivity to the universal consciousness.

Thus, the process of ascending through dimensions is deeply transformative, offering insights into the nature of reality and our place within it. It's a journey of expanding consciousness, where the vibrational alignment between the physical and the ethereal unlocks the doors to realms beyond our current comprehension. In embracing this journey, we acknowledge the boundless potential within us to connect with the vast expanse of the cosmos, guided by love, respect, and a deep commitment to spiritual growth.

22.3 Ascension

In the landscape of New Age spiritual awakening, there exists a misconception that reaching the final stage of one's spiritual journey inherently leads to a spiritual Ascension in the after life. This belief posits that upon passing, an individual's soul transforms into an angelic being, embarking on a new journey through the celestial hierarchy. However, my understanding diverges from this theory, suggesting that true Ascension occurs during our earthly existence. It unfolds as we achieve harmony between our physical and ethereal bodies, maintaining a seamless connection with both the physical and spiritual realms. This state of being transcends the fear of judgment or the dread of encounters with lower frequency entities, embracing a respectful and profound comprehension of energy, and utilizing it for the greater good.

True Ascension is the realization of our authentic selves and mastering the art of navigating our time here as complete beings, free from the shackles of both physical and spiritual attachments. It involves making the most of our earthly sojourn, operating within the realm of Christ consciousness—this consciousness transcends the limitations imposed by religions and man-made control mechanisms.

It's about fostering a community where individuals can coexist in pure harmony, integrating their psychic abilities to enhance communal living, resonating closely with the ideal society envisioned by Plato. In this utopia, every individual understands and applies the Universal Law of Love, an ethical guideline that promotes living in alignment with love's true essence.

Ascension, therefore, is not an event awaiting us at life's end but a continuous process that unfolds as we live. It is about evolving within our current existence, learning to balance and bridge our physical experiences with our spiritual insights. This balance allows us to live more fully, more aware, and in deeper harmony with the universe and its myriad expressions of life. By aspiring to this level of consciousness, we aim to create a society where harmony with nature, both in the physical and spiritual realms, is not just an ideal but a lived reality. Here, psychic abilities aren't just personal gifts but tools for communal upliftment, facilitating a harmonious existence that benefits all.

In essence, the journey of Ascension is about realizing our potential as whole beings, unbound and free to explore the depths of our existence while contributing to the collective good. It's a call to live beyond the confines of the material and spiritual dichotomy, embracing a holistic approach that nourishes our journey on Earth and beyond. This vision of Ascension invites us to embody the highest expressions of love, understanding, and unity, paving the way for a world where the physical and spiritual are inextricably linked in the dance of existence.

Bridging the insights from our exploration of dimensions with the concept of true Ascension reveals a profound interconnectedness in our spiritual journey. As we've learned, the universe's fabric is woven with varying frequencies, each corresponding to different dimensions of existence. This mosaic of vibrational states offers us a pathway to navigate through these dimensions by elevating our own frequency—essentially, by harmonizing our physical and ethereal bodies. Similarly, the essence of true Ascension, as elucidated above, is not merely a post-mortem transformation but an active, lived experience of rising through these vibrational states during our earthly existence.

The journey of Ascension, then, can be seen as a conscious endeavor to align with these higher dimensions while we are still bound to the physical plane. It involves cultivating a state of being that transcends the limitations of our immediate physical reality, embodying principles that resonate with higher vibrational frequencies—love, understanding, and a profound connection to the universal energy that binds all of existence. By operating in balance and harmony, and fostering a community that lives by the Universal Law of Love, we not only elevate our own vibrational frequency but contribute to the upliftment of the collective consciousness.

This connection between understanding dimensions and pursuing true Ascension underscores a fundamental truth: our spiritual evolution and the expansion of our consciousness are deeply entwined with the vibrational nature of the universe. Each step we take towards balancing our physical and ethereal selves, towards living in harmony and without fear, is a step towards navigating these higher dimensions. It is through this journey that we realize our full potential as beings of light, capable of transcending the boundaries between dimensions and living in the fullest expression of our true selves. Herein lies the quintessence of our spiritual odyssey—melding the wisdom of the dimensions with the heart of Ascension to manifest a reality where the physical and spiritual coalesce, guiding us towards a higher existence marked by unity, love, and an enlightened consciousness.

23

Personal Decoding

Before we dive into the list of common angel numbers and their combinations, I want to stress how deeply personal and unique the journey of spiritual awakening and communication with Spirit Guides truly is. The meanings of angel numbers, while they often follow familiar patterns, evolve as you progress on your path and strengthen your connection with your Guides. As your intuition grows, so does your ability to interpret these numbers in more profound, personalized ways.

Let me share a recent experience that demonstrates this evolution. In the beginning, whenever I saw the angel number 333, I interpreted it as a sign to break free from my limitations and expand my network. It was a number that pushed me out of my comfort zone, encouraging creativity and new perspectives.

However, recently, I noticed a significant shift in its meaning. One night, I suddenly woke up and glanced at the clock—it was 3:33 a.m. The following morning, I saw the number 333 twice more: first on the last digits of a taxi's license plate and then again on a Facebook post with 333 likes. Later that same day, I found myself in the hospital with severe chest pains, worried I was having a heart attack. Fortunately, it turned out to be an esophageal spasm, which, while painful, wasn't life-threatening.

A month later, when I began seeing 333 again, I immediately felt a need for caution. This time, I knew it was connected to my health.

Sure enough, shortly after, I contracted a virus that left me bedridden for a week. These events showed me how the meaning of angel numbers can evolve and take on new layers as our relationship with our Spirit Guides deepens.

As you move further along this journey, you'll notice the messages from your Guides become more specific and clear, tailored to your individual experiences. This communication becomes increasingly two-way—you can ask questions and receive guidance in return. Stay open to these insights as they unfold, and trust that your Guides are leading you along the path you are meant to follow.

24

List with the Basic Angel Numbers

Angel Number sequence of 1, 11, 111, 111:

Basic Meanings: Manifestation, awakening, inspirational insights.

Category: Supportive

Specifically, the number 1 – a number that stands as a symbol of beginnings, leadership, and the very essence of existence. In this exploration, I'll share with you the profound meanings behind this fundamental digit.

The Essence of Beginnings

The number 1 in numerology is often seen as the starting point, the very first step in a sequence that shapes the universe. It represents new beginnings, a chance to start afresh. Think about the number 1 as the dawn of day – the first light that pierces through the dark night, offering hope and new opportunities.

In many cultures and spiritual beliefs, 1 is seen as the number of creation, the very foundation of existence. In monotheistic religions, it symbolizes the unity and supremacy of the divine force. It reminds us that at the core of everything, there's a singular energy that connects us all.

A Symbol of Leadership and Individuality

The number 1 also stands for leadership, individuality, and assertiveness. It's about being the one who leads the way, the pioneer forging new paths. When you encounter the number 1, especially in the form of angel numbers like 111 or 1111, it's often a call to embrace your leadership qualities, to stand tall and be confident in your individuality. It encourages you to trust your instincts and take the lead in your life journey.

In my own experiences, whenever I've encountered the number 1, especially in sequences, it has been a reminder to stay true to myself. It's about understanding and embracing your uniqueness, realizing that being different isn't just okay – it's powerful.

The Link to Ambition and Motivation

Number 1 is also intrinsically linked to ambition and motivation. It's a number that energizes, pushes you forward, and ignites the fires of willpower and determination. In the realm of numerology, encountering the number 1 can be a sign to harness your inner strength, to aim high and chase your dreams with relentless passion.

The Spiritual Dimensions

In the spiritual domain, the number 1 resonates with self-reliance and tenacity. It's about self-discovery and understanding your place in the universe. This number beckons you to embark on a spiritual journey of self-awareness, where you realize the power of your thoughts and intentions in shaping your reality.

The Number 1 in Your Life

As you journey through life, pay attention to how the number 1 appears to you. It might pop up in significant moments, nudging you to take action or to ponder your life's direction. It could be a sign to start a new project, to change paths, or simply to remember your worth.

Remember, the number 1 isn't just a digit; it's a symbol of the potential that lies within you – the potential to start anew, to lead, and to carve out your path in this world.

Intuitive meaning

1. Love:

When you see 1111 while seeking guidance for love, it signals a fresh start or new chapter in your love life. If you're single, it could mean a new romantic relationship is on the horizon, encouraging you to remain open and positive about meeting someone new. If you're in a relationship, 1111 suggests that it's time to take your relationship to the next level, be it through deeper commitment or more open communication. Trust your instincts, as 1111 is a sign of alignment in your love life.

2. Finance/Employment:

In the context of finance or employment, seeing 1111 is a sign that new opportunities are coming your way. It urges you to take initiative and lead in your career, perhaps through a promotion or starting a new business. This number encourages innovation, so if you've been contemplating a new venture, now is the time to act. Financially, it indicates a prosperous period if you remain focused and assertive in your goals.

3. Health:

For health-related questions, 1111 is a reminder to focus on self-care and new wellness practices. It suggests that taking a proactive approach to your health—whether it's starting a new fitness routine, adopting better eating habits, or exploring holistic health practices—will lead to positive changes. Trust your body's signals and start fresh in areas that need attention.

The number 111 is also linked to the Root Chakra, which governs the lower body—specifically the legs, feet, lower back, and spine. Seeing 111 may suggest that it's time to address issues related to your physical stability, such as posture, balance, or any discomfort in these areas. Grounding activities like walking in nature, yoga, or strengthening your lower body can help restore balance and promote overall well-being.

In Conclusion

The number 1, with its multifaceted meanings, is truly a fascinating aspect of numerology and spirituality. It teaches us about the power of beginnings, the importance of individuality, and the strength that lies in taking that first step. As you encounter this number, let it be a reminder of your own potential and the endless possibilities that await.

Angel Number sequence of 2, 22, 222, 2222:

Basic Meanings: Balance, harmony, partnership,

faith.

Category: Confirming

let's explore the number 2 – a symbol of balance, relationships, and duality. It's a number that speaks to the heart of cooperation and harmony.

The Dance of Duality

At its core, the number 2 represents duality – the yin and yang, light and shadow, masculine and feminine. It reminds us that life is about balance and that opposing forces can exist in harmony. Think of it as a gentle nudge towards understanding and accepting the different aspects of our world and ourselves.

In many spiritual beliefs, 2 signifies the necessity of opposites in the natural order. It's about the interconnectedness of all things, where one part complements the other, creating a whole that is greater than the sum of its parts.

A Symbol of Partnership and Cooperation

If the number 1 was about individuality and leadership, the number 2 is all about partnership and cooperation. It's the number that seeks connection, understanding, and diplomacy. When you come across the number 2, especially in patterns like 222 or 2222, consider it a sign to foster relationships, to collaborate, and to seek peace.

In my life, whenever the number 2 has made its presence felt, it's been a reminder to listen, to empathize, and to connect deeply with others. It's about building bridges, not walls, and recognizing the strength that lies in unity. It was also a confirmation that love is on the way. Love not only for others, but self-love, acceptance and balance.

Harmony and Balance

The Spiritual Significance In spiritual terms, the number 2 often signals a need for patience, faith, and trust in the journey. It's about understanding the timing of the universe and knowing that everything happens for a reason. The appearance of 2 can be a reminder that you're not alone, that your life is in a state of balance, and that harmony is being cultivated in the background, even if it's not immediately apparent.

The Number 2 in Your Life

As you journey through life, observe how the number 2 appears and influences your path. It may show up during times when cooperation is needed, when you're seeking balance, or when you're called to be patient and trust the flow of life.

The number 2 isn't just a figure; it embodies the essence of togetherness and harmony. It teaches us the importance of relationships, the power of patience, and the beauty of balance and connection.

Intuitive meaning

1. Love:

When 2222 appears in matters of love, it's all about balance, harmony, and cooperation in relationships. If you're in a partnership, it signifies that maintaining balance and patience is key to nurturing a healthy relationship. If you're single, it's a message to focus on self-love and patience, as the right relationship will come at the right time. It encourages you to trust that love is aligning for you.

2. Finance/Employment:

Seeing 2222 in relation to work or finances indicates that collaboration is essential to success. It may suggest a new business partnership or teamwork that will enhance your career prospects. Financially, it's a reminder to balance your spending and saving habits, maintaining harmony between your desires and practical needs.

3. Health:

For health inquiries, 2222 is a message to maintain balance in your physical, emotional, and spiritual well-being. It reminds you to avoid extremes—whether in diet, exercise, or stress levels—and find peace in taking a balanced approach to your health. It could also indicate healing through nurturing relationships, as emotional support plays a key role in your overall wellness.

This number is connected to the Sacral Chakra, which governs the reproductive organs, lower abdomen, and kidneys. You may need to focus on maintaining emotional harmony and ensuring that your reproductive and digestive systems are in good health. Activities like gentle stretching, creative expression, or improving your hydration levels could help in balancing this chakra and fostering both emotional and physical wellness.

In Conclusion

The number 2, with its gentle energy, brings the message of peace, partnership, and balance. It invites us to embrace cooperation, to understand the dual nature of our existence, and to find harmony in our lives. As you encounter this number, let it remind you of the strength found in unity and the importance of walking life's path with others.

Angel Number sequence of 3, 33, 333, 3333:
Basic Meanings: Creative expression, social interaction, optimism.
Category: Confirming

Now we'll dive into the number 3 – a symbol of creativity, self-expression, and growth. It's a number that radiates joy, inspiration, and an expansive view of life.

The Essence of Creativity

At its essence, the number 3 is the embodiment of creativity. It represents the birth of something new, the fusion of two entities to create a third. This can be seen in various aspects of life and the universe – the blending of mind and body to create spirit, for instance.

In many spiritual and cultural traditions, the number 3 is considered sacred. It's seen in the Christian Holy Trinity, the three jewels of Buddhism, and the triple aspects of the Goddess in neopaganism. This trinity aspect underscores the idea of wholeness and completion.

A Symbol of Self-Expression and Communication

While the number 1 symbolizes leadership and independence, and 2 denotes partnership and cooperation, the number 3 brings forth the energy of communication and self-expression. It encourages us to express our ideas, emotions, and creativity. When patterns like 333 or 3333 appear in your life, consider it a sign to embrace your creative soul, to express yourself boldly, and to inspire others through your words and actions. You can be the leader of the group, stand out and innovate!

In my life, the number 3 has often been a prompt to let my creative juices flow, to engage in artistic pursuits, and to communicate more openly with the world around me.

Growth and Expansion

The number 3 is also about growth, expansion, and moving beyond your current boundaries. It's a reminder that life is an ever-unfolding journey of learning and evolving. The appearance of 3 can be a nudge to expand your horizons, to learn new skills, and to embrace the joy of living.

The Spiritual Significance

Spiritually, the number 3 often signifies the presence of guides and ascended masters. It suggests that you're supported in your creative and expressive endeavors, and that the universe is conspiring to help you grow and expand. The number 3 is a beacon of positive energy, optimism, and joy.

The Number 3 in Your Life

As you navigate through life, take note of how the number 3 manifests in your experiences. It may appear during phases when you're called to express yourself more fully, when creativity is knocking at your door, or when you're ready for personal growth and expansion.

The number 3 isn't just a digit; it's a symbol of life's joyous, creative, and expressive nature. It teaches us the importance of articulation, the value of expanding our minds and spirits, and the beauty of living life vibrantly.

Intuitive Meaning

1. Love:

When you see 3333 and you're asking about love, it signals a period of growth and open communication in relationships. If you're single, this number encourages you to express your true self in social situations, which may lead to new romantic connections. If you're in a relationship, 3333 invites you to nurture your bond through creativity and joy, promoting deeper emotional intimacy.

2. Finance/Employment:

In terms of career and finances, 3333 represents creativity and the manifestation of new ideas. It suggests that now is the time to put your creative talents to use in your work, possibly through a new project, role, or career path. Financially, it indicates that positive results will come from thinking outside the box and taking a creative approach to challenges.

3. Health:

For health-related questions, 3333 encourages you to explore creative ways to improve your well-being. This could involve trying alternative therapies, engaging in artistic activities for stress relief, or finding joy in movement and exercise. It's a sign to prioritize fun and joy as part of your health journey, as a positive mindset can greatly impact physical health.

This number is linked to the Solar Plexus Chakra, which governs the digestive system, liver, and pancreas. It may be urging you to take care of your gut health, addressing digestive issues, or working on boosting your confidence and personal power. Incorporating digestive-supporting foods, practicing mindful breathing, or engaging in activities that help build your self-esteem can help balance this chakra and improve your overall health.

In Conclusion

The number 3, with its dynamic energy, brings the message of creativity, self-expression, and growth. It invites us to embrace our expressive selves, to find joy in creation, and to recognize the importance of communication and expansion in our lives. As you encounter this number, let it inspire you to live life to the fullest, to express your innermost thoughts and feelings, and to embrace the growth that comes from every experience.

Angel Number sequence of 4, 44, 444, 4444:
Basic Meanings: Protection, stability, practicality.
Category: Supportive
we're now focusing on the number 4 – a symbol of stability, practicality, and strong foundations. It's a number that brings a sense of order and structure to our lives.

The Essence of Stability

The number 4 is all about creating stability and building solid foundations for the future. It represents the practical aspects of life – the need to plan, to work diligently, and to establish a sense of order and routine. In the universe, the number 4 is reflected in the four seasons, the four cardinal directions, and the four elements (earth, air, fire, water), each contributing to the balance and stability of nature.

In various traditions, the number 4 is seen as grounding and solid. For instance, in Buddhism, there are the Four Noble Truths, a core aspect of the Buddha's teachings. In many cultures, the number 4 is associated with the earth, embodying strength, endurance, and steadfastness.

Symbol of Practicality and Organization

While the number 3 is about creativity and growth, the number 4 brings us back to reality, grounding us in the practicalities of life. It urges us to be organized, disciplined, and to build our dreams on a solid foundation. When you encounter patterns like 444 or 4444, it's a message to focus on building a stable and secure future, to pay attention to the details, and to plan carefully.

In my journey, I've learned that the appearance of 4 is a reminder to get back to basics, to organize my life, and to focus on creating a stable and secure environment.

Growth Through Stability

The number 4 also signifies growth through stability. It's about laying down roots so that you can grow and flourish. It's a reminder that sometimes the most exciting growth comes from the most mundane activities – organizing your life, planning for the future, and working steadily towards your

Image by Olga Gerogianni
The Spiritual Significance

In a spiritual sense, the number 4 often represents the need to return to your roots and to find stability in your spiritual practice. It suggests that grounding and centering yourself will enable you to pursue your spiritual path more effectively. The number 4 is a call to fortify your spiritual foundation and to find harmony in the physical realm. Connected with your heart chakra it serves as a reminder to balance your emotions before moving on. Heal and love.

The Number 4 in Your Life

As you encounter the number 4 in your daily life, consider it a prompt to examine the stability and structure of your life. It might appear during times when you need to focus more on practical matters, when establishing a routine is necessary, or when it's time to work diligently towards your goals.

The number 4 teaches us about the importance of stability, organization, and practicality. It's a reminder that sometimes the most extraordinary achievements are built on the most ordinary foundations.

Intuitive meaning

1. Love:

In matters of love, seeing 4444 is a sign that stability and security are key in your relationship. If you're single, it may indicate that you're laying the groundwork for a long-term relationship, and now is the time to focus on build-

goals. It's a gentle reminder to not rush but take time and organize.

ing a solid emotional foundation. In a relationship, 4444 encourages you to work on strengthening trust, commitment, and stability in your partnership.

2. Finance/Employment:

When 4444 shows up regarding work or finances, it's a message that hard work and discipline will lead to success. This is a sign that you're on the right path and that your dedication will pay off. Financially, 4444 suggests being practical and focused on creating a stable financial foundation. It's a time for saving, investing, and planning for long-term success.

3. Health:

For health questions, 4444 is a reassuring message of stability and progress. It indicates that consistent efforts towards maintaining your health—whether through diet, exercise, or routine check-ups—are laying the foundation for long-term wellness. It also encourages you to stick to routines and disciplined practices that promote a stable and healthy lifestyle.

This number is connected to the Heart Chakra, which governs the heart, lungs, chest, and circulatory system. It may suggest the need

to address any heart health issues or to focus on emotional healing, particularly with feelings of love and forgiveness. Practices such as cardiovascular exercise, deep breathing, or working on healing past emotional wounds can help strengthen the heart chakra and bring both emotional and physical balance.

In Conclusion

The number 4, with its down-to-earth energy, is a powerful symbol of stability, practicality, and structure. It encourages us to build our lives on a solid foundation, to focus on the practical aspects of our goals, and to understand the value of hard work and discipline. Let the number 4 be a guide to creating a balanced, stable, and structured life that can support your dreams and ambitions.

Angel Number sequence of 5, 55, 555, 5555:

Basic Meanings: Major life changes, freedom, adaptability

Category: Advisory

the number 5 emerges as a symbol of change, freedom, and adaptability. It's a number that represents the spirit of adventure and the pursuit of personal freedom.

Embracing Change

The essence of the number 5 is all about embracing change. It signifies the need for growth through new experiences. When you see patterns like 555 or 5555, it's often a sign that significant changes are on the horizon. These changes bring opportunities for personal growth and greater understanding of yourself and the world around you.

In my experience, encountering the number 5 has been a clear indicator that it's time to break free from routines and explore new horizons. It's about stepping out of the comfort zone and experiencing life more fully.

The Spirit of Adventure

Number 5 is closely linked to the idea of adventure and trying new things. It encourages curiosity and exploration, urging you to see life as an exciting journey with endless possibilities. This number inspires you to be brave, to take risks, and to live life more spontaneously. It's also time to cut attachments and break free. Break your life's patterns and explore.

Adaptability and Versatility

One of the key strengths of the number 5 is adaptability. It's about being versatile and flexible, able to adjust to new situations with ease. The energy of 5 is dynamic and resourceful, always finding innovative ways to solve problems and navigate through life's uncertainties.

A Call for Personal Freedom

At its core, the number 5 is a call for personal freedom. It urges you to live life on your own terms, to seek your own path, and to value your independence. It's a reminder that true freedom comes from being true to yourself and from having the courage to follow your heart. Connected with the throat chakra it leads your expression, to speak out, transform with no fear and be the butterfly after the cocoon phase.

Spiritual Exploration

Spiritually, the number 5 can indicate a time of transformation and spiritual awakening. It's a phase where you may feel a strong desire to seek deeper truths, to explore different spiritual paths, and to expand your consciousness. Activate and develop new psychic abilities, expand your knowledge and change existing habits.

The Number 5 in Your Life

When you encounter the number 5, consider it an invitation to welcome change, to embrace new opportunities, and to enjoy the freedom it brings. It's a time to be adventurous, to be open to new experiences, and to trust that these changes will bring positive growth.

The number 5 reminds us of the joy of living freely and the importance of adapting to the ever-changing nature of life. It encourages us to be flexible, to embrace the unknown, and to trust in the journey.

Intuitive meaning

1. Love:

Seeing 5555 in love indicates that change is on the horizon. If you're single, this could mean a new and exciting relationship is coming your way, one that will challenge and inspire you. If you're in a relationship, 5555 suggests a period of transformation—this could be a move, a change in the dynamic of the relationship, or a new chapter. Embrace the change, as it will lead to growth.

2. Finance/Employment:

When it comes to career or finances, 5555 signals major changes that could lead to new opportunities. It may indicate a job change, a career shift, or a financial breakthrough. Be open to taking risks and embracing new paths. Although change can be unsettling, 5555 suggests that these changes will lead to positive growth and freedom.

3. Health:

For health inquiries, 5555 indicates a time of transformation. It suggests that embracing change—whether through adopting new habits, letting go of old routines, or trying new treatments—will bring improvement to your overall health. Be open to exploring new ways to nurture your well-being and release what no longer serves you.

This number is associated with the Throat Chakra, which governs the throat, neck, thyroid, and vocal cords. It could be urging you to express yourself more clearly or to address any physical issues in these areas. Ensuring you are speaking your truth, practicing vocal exercises, and paying attention to your neck and throat health—possibly through stretching and hydration—could bring balance and vitality to this chakra.

In Conclusion

The number 5, with its vibrant and adventurous energy, symbolizes change, freedom, and adaptability. It inspires us to embrace life's changes, to explore new horizons, and to enjoy the journey of personal and spiritual growth. Let the number 5 be your guide to a more adventurous and fulfilling life.

Angel Number sequence of 6, 66, 666, 6666:

Basic Meanings: Balance, nurturing, self-care.

Category: Advisory

In the realm of numbers, the number 6 stands as a symbol of harmony, refocus responsibility, and nurturing. It's a number that embodies the essence of care, compassion, and familial love.

Balance and Harmony

The number 6 is often associated with balance and harmony. It represents the need to create a stable, peaceful environment, both at home and in the wider community. When you see patterns like 666 or 6666, it's a gentle reminder to focus on creating balance in your life, paying attention to your well-being and the well-being of those around you.

In my journey, the number 6 has often appeared as a sign to take a step back and assess where I'm putting my energy, ensuring that I'm not neglecting important areas of my life, especially personal relationships. It also appears as a reminder that you need to re-evaluate your choices, and obtain a holistic view to see clearly.

The Call of Responsibility

Number 6 carries with it a sense of duty and responsibility. It's about being reliable and taking care of your obligations, particularly towards family and close friends. This number encourages you to be someone others can depend on, offering support and guidance when needed. Remember though that to help others you must first heal and love yourself.

The Heart of Nurturing

At its core, the number 6 is deeply nurturing. It's about caring for others, showing compassion, and being kind-hearted. It reminds us of the importance of love and empathy in our lives, urging us to offer a helping hand and a listening ear to those in need.

Seeking Peace and Harmony

The energy of the number 6 is all about seeking peace and harmony. It's about striving for a life that is not only balanced but also peaceful. This number encourages you to resolve conflicts, to promote understanding and to create an atmosphere of tranquillity in your surroundings.

Personal and Spiritual Growth

On a spiritual level, the number 6 can signify a period of growth and inner development. It's a time to nurture your own soul, to engage in self-reflection, and to cultivate inner peace. This growth often radiates outward, positively impacting those around you. Connected with the 3rd eye chakra, it appears when your spiritual practices are not harmonised with your Life's purpose (or mission). Trust your intuition but always remember to follow the Universal Ethical Laws.

The Number 6 in Your Life

When the number 6 appears in your life, see it as an invitation to embrace your responsibilities, to nurture your relationships, and to strive for harmony. It's a time to focus on your home life, to strengthen your connections, and to create a loving, supportive environment.

The number 6 reminds us that true strength lies in our ability to care for and support others. It encourages us to be compassionate, understanding, and to create a balanced, harmonious life.

Intuitive meaning

1. Love:

When 6666 appears in relation to love, it suggests a strong focus on nurturing and balance in your relationships. If you're single, it may signal that now is the time to heal any emotional wounds and practice self-love before entering a new relationship. For those in a partnership, 6666 encourages you to bring more care, compassion, and attention to your relationship. It's a reminder to balance giving and receiving love, creating a harmonious and nurturing environment with your partner.

2. Finance/Employment:

In the context of work or finances, 6666 is a message to find balance between your career ambitions and personal life. It suggests that you may have been overly focused on material concerns or work at the expense of your emotional and spiritual well-being. Now is the time to reassess your priorities, make time for self-care, and ensure that your financial pursuits align with your deeper values. It's also a sign that financial stability will come when you focus on creating balance in all areas of your life.

3. Health:

For health-related matters, 6666 encourages you to refocus on self-care and nurturing your body, mind, and spirit. It's a reminder that neglecting any aspect of your well-being—whether emotional, physical, or spiritual—can lead to imbalance. This number suggests that it's time to adopt a more holistic approach to health, paying attention to nurturing your body with proper nutrition, exercise, and emotional self-care. Harmony in your life will lead to better overall health.

This number is connected to the Third Eye Chakra, which governs the eyes, forehead, and brain. It may suggest the need for mental clarity, addressing vision issues, or focusing on stress and anxiety management. Practices such as meditation, reducing screen time, or engaging in activities that stimulate mental clarity, such as journaling or visualization exercises, can help balance this chakra and improve your mental and physical well-being.

In Conclusion

The number 6, with its nurturing and harmonious energy, symbolizes balance, responsibility, and care. It inspires us to create harmony in our lives, to nurture our relationships, and to grow both personally and spiritually. Let the number 6 guide you to a more balanced and fulfilling life.

Angel Number sequence of 7, 77, 777, 7777:

Basic Meanings: Spiritual awakening, divine guidance, inner wisdom.

Category: Guiding

the number 7 is often seen as the most mystical and introspective. It's a number that speaks to the deeper understanding of the self and the universe.

A Symbol of Spiritual Awakening

The number 7 is widely regarded as a symbol of spiritual awakening and enlightenment. It calls on us to delve deeper into the realms of the spiritual and the metaphysical. When encountering patterns like 777 or 7777, it's an invitation to explore your spirituality, to seek answers to life's deeper questions, and to connect more profoundly with the spiritual realm.

In my own life, the appearance of the number 7 has often coincided with phases of introspection and spiritual exploration. It's been a prompt to look beyond the surface, to seek a deeper truth. It was guiding me to fulfil my Life's Mission.

The Quest for Knowledge

Number 7 is also associated with a thirst for knowledge. It's about seeking wisdom, not just information, but understanding the mysteries of life. This number inspires a learning journey, not just through books and study, but through life experiences and self-reflection. It's also a reminder that the knowledge is already inside you, it's time to visit your Akashic records and reconnect with the collective memory. To remember!

Introspection and Self-Analysis

At its essence, the number 7 is about introspection. It invites you to look inward, to understand your inner world, and to contemplate your life's purpose. This introspective journey is key to personal growth and self-awareness.

Connection to the Mystical

The energy of the number 7 is closely connected to the mystical and the esoteric. It's a number that resonates with the mysterious aspects of life and the unseen forces that shape our existence. It's an energetically strong number that reminds you the connection with the Source. God's essence that is inside of you.

Personal Growth and Development

On a spiritual and personal level, the number 7 signifies growth and development. It's a time to deepen your understanding of yourself and the world around you, to grow spiritually, and to develop a more profound sense of wisdom. You are now ready to fulfil your spiritual journey. You are supported.

The Number 7 in Your Life

When the number 7 appears in your life, view it as a signal to embrace your spiritual journey, to seek deeper understanding, and to engage in introspection. It's an opportunity to explore the mysteries of life and to grow in wisdom and spiritual understanding.

The number 7 encourages you to look within, to seek answers, and to cultivate a deeper sense of knowing and wisdom. It's a reminder that the path to enlightenment starts with understanding oneself.

Intuitive meaning

1. Love:

Seeing 7777 in love is a sign of deep spiritual connection and alignment. If you're single, it indicates that a relationship rooted in spiritual growth and understanding is on its way. This person may be someone with whom you share a soul connection. If you're in a relationship, 7777 suggests that your partnership is moving to a deeper, more spiritual level. It's a time to nurture the emotional and spiritual aspects of your bond.

2. Finance/Employment:

In terms of career and finances, 7777 is a powerful indicator of divine guidance and luck. This number suggests that you're on the right path and that you should trust the process, even if results aren't immediately visible. Opportunities related to spiritual or creative endeavors may arise, and financial gains will come through trusting your intuition and aligning your work with your higher purpose.

3. Health:

For health inquiries, 7777 encourages you to focus on spiritual well-being as part of your health journey. Meditation, mindfulness, and inner work are key to achieving balance and harmony in your physical health. It's a reminder that true healing comes from within and that spiritual growth can positively impact your physical and mental well-being.

This number is linked to the Crown Chakra, which governs the top of the head, brain, and nervous system. It could be prompting you to focus on your spiritual connection and mental well-being. Engaging in meditation, practicing mindfulness, or working on connecting to a higher purpose can help balance this chakra and foster a sense of overall peace and alignment.

In Conclusion

The number 7, with its deep connection to mysticism and introspection, symbolizes spiritual awakening, the pursuit of wisdom, and personal growth. It invites us to embark on a journey of self-discovery and spiritual enlightenment. Let the number 7 inspire you to explore the depths of your soul and uncover the mysteries of the universe.

Angel Number sequence of 8, 88, 888, 8888:
Basic Meanings: Abundance, financial stability, cosmic balance.
Category: Guiding

The number 8 is a powerful symbol of abundance, authority, and the never-ending cycle of infinity. It's a number that represents balance and achievement, often associated with material and financial success.

Symbol of Abundance and Prosperity

The number 8 is often seen as a beacon of abundance and prosperity. It's a reminder that the universe is abundant and that there's enough for everyone. When you encounter patterns like 888 or 8888, consider it a sign to focus on abundance, whether it's in wealth, happiness, or love. Open up your heart and mind and ask, because your time to receive has come.

In my own life, I've found that the appearance of the number 8 is a positive omen, indicating that prosperity and success are within reach, reminding me to stay focused and to persevere.

Authority and Power

The number 8 also resonates with authority and power. It speaks of confidence, capability, and achieving success through determination and leadership. It's about taking charge of your life and realizing your ambitions.

The Infinity Symbol

Interestingly, the number 8, when laid on its side, becomes the symbol of infinity. This represents the infinite flow of energy, the eternal cycle of life and death, and the continuous journey of the soul.

Balance and Harmony

The energy of the number 8 is also about balance. It's a reminder that for every action, there is an equal and opposite reaction, and maintaining balance in all aspects of life is key.

Material and Spiritual Harmony

The number 8 encourages a harmony between material and spiritual worlds. It's a reminder that financial and material success should not come at the expense of your spiritual growth and inner peace.

The Number 8 in Your Life

When you encounter the number 8, see it as a signal to focus on achieving your goals, particularly those related to financial and material success. It's a reminder to harness your inner power and authority, to strive for balance, and to remember the infinite nature of the universe and your own spirit.

Intuitive meaning

1. Love:

In the context of love, 8888 is a sign of abundance and emotional fulfillment. If you're single, it suggests that you're entering a phase where love flows naturally, and abundance in relationships is forthcoming. If you're in a relationship, 8888 indicates a time of growth, harmony, and deep emotional connection. It suggests that your relationship will reach a new level of stability and abundance in mutual support.

2. Finance/Employment:

When it comes to finances and work, 8888 is a powerful message of material success and financial abundance. It's a sign that all your hard work is about to pay off, and you'll be rewarded with financial security and success. This number encourages you to keep moving forward with confidence, as you're on the path to achieving your material goals.

3. Health:

For health-related questions, 8888 suggests focusing on balance and well-being in all areas of your life. This number indicates that health improvements are coming, especially if you've been working hard to maintain balance in your physical and emotional life. It's a reminder that abundance in health is just as important as material success, so focus on holistic well-being.

This number is connected to the Root Chakra, which governs the spine, legs, and feet. It suggests grounding yourself by addressing any issues related to physical security or stress related to finances, which can manifest in the lower body. Grounding exercises like walking barefoot on natural surfaces, strengthening your legs, or engaging in balancing exercises like yoga can help restore your physical and energetic balance.

In Conclusion

The number 8, with its connections to abundance, authority, and the infinite, is a powerful symbol in the journey of life. It encourages you to embrace your personal power, to seek material and spiritual harmony, and to remember the endless cycle of energy in the universe. Let the number 8 inspire you to achieve balance and success in every aspect of your life.

Angel Number sequence of 9, 99, 999, 9999:
Basic Meanings: Completion, release, higher purpose
Category: Advisory
The number 9 holds a special place as it symbolizes completion, the culmination of all the numbers before it. It is a number that beckons us towards humanitarianism and spiritual enlightenment. It's connected with the collective consciousness.
Symbol of Completion and Fulfillment

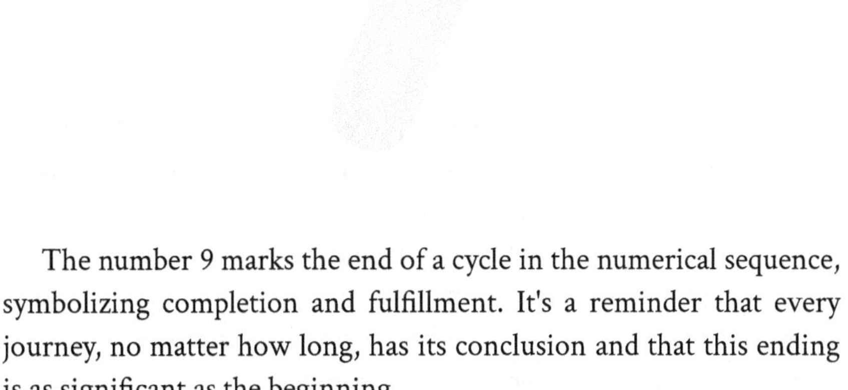

The number 9 marks the end of a cycle in the numerical sequence, symbolizing completion and fulfillment. It's a reminder that every journey, no matter how long, has its conclusion and that this ending is as significant as the beginning.

In my own experiences, whenever I've encountered the number 9, particularly in patterns like 999 or 9999, it has often heralded a phase of completion or the end of a significant chapter in my life. It reminds me that endings are natural and necessary for growth and evolution.

Humanitarianism and Compassion

The number 9 resonates strongly with humanitarian ideals. It speaks of empathy, compassion, and serving humanity. This number urges us to look beyond our individual needs and to consider the greater good.

Spiritual Enlightenment

The number 9 also has deep spiritual connotations. It is associated with enlightenment, awakening, and the pursuit of higher knowledge. This number often appears when we are being called to trust our intuition and to delve deeper into our spiritual practice.

Universal Love and Perspective

Embodying universal love and a broad perspective, the number 9 encourages us to embrace a more holistic view of the world. It challenges us to think globally and act selflessly.

The Number 9 in Your Life

When the number 9 repeatedly appears in your life, it might be a signal to focus on completing ongoing projects or to prepare for a significant closure. It's also a call to elevate your view and to engage in acts of kindness and philanthropy.

Intuitive meaning

1. Love:

In love, seeing 9999 signals the completion of a significant chapter in your love life. If you're single, it could indicate the end of a cycle of emotional healing, making space for new and deeper relationships. If you're in a relationship, 9999 may suggest that you and your partner are moving towards a resolution of past issues, or it could signal that a relationship is reaching its natural conclusion, making way for personal growth and new opportunities for love.

2. Finance/Employment:

In relation to work and finances, 9999 suggests the completion of a major project or phase in your career. You may be wrapping up a long-term effort, and this completion will open doors to new opportunities. Financially, it could indicate the end of a cycle of debt or financial struggle, bringing a time of closure and new beginnings in your financial life.

3. Health:

For health inquiries, 9999 is a powerful symbol of healing and release. It encourages you to let go of old habits, patterns, or health conditions that no longer serve you. This number signals the completion of a phase in your health journey, marking the end of a difficult period and the start of a more balanced, healthier phase. It's a call to focus on healing and transformation.

This number is linked to the Crown Chakra, which governs the brain and nervous system. It might indicate that you need to let go of stress or patterns that no longer serve you, focusing on peace and spiritual release. Meditation, rest, and practices that encourage mental clarity and calm can help bring this chakra into balance, promoting overall health and well-being.

In Conclusion

The number 9, with its vibrations of completion, humanitarianism, and spiritual awakening, is a powerful guide in the numerological journey. It encourages us to bring things to a close with grace, to open our hearts to the needs of others, and to seek a deeper understanding of the spiritual aspects of our lives.

Let the energy of the number 9 inspire you to embrace endings as new beginnings, to engage in acts of kindness and compassion, and to pursue a path of spiritual enlightenment. Remember, in every ending, there is the seed of a new beginning.

25

List with the Basic Paired Angel Numbers

1

212-9898

Angel Number 1212

Primary Number: 1 (New beginnings, independence)

Secondary Number: 2 (Harmony, relationships)

Analysis: Angel number 1212 is a blend of the energies of 1 and 2. The primary number 1 suggests a time of new beginnings and taking initiative, while the secondary number 2 adds an element of harmony and balance, particularly in relationships. This combination indicates a period where starting new projects or relationships will be beneficial, as long as there's a focus on cooperation and harmony.

1. Love:

Seeing 1212 in the context of love suggests that new beginnings and harmony are on the horizon. If you're single, this number encourages you to open your heart and mind to new relationships, focusing on balance and mutual understanding. If you're in a relationship, 1212 indicates that cooperation and harmony are key. It may be time to address any imbalances and work together to create a more fulfilling partnership.

2. Finance/Employment:

In matters of finance or employment, 1212 indicates a fresh start with balanced and harmonious outcomes. It's a sign that you should take initiative in your career while ensuring that teamwork and cooperation are prioritized. A new job or business venture that requires collaboration could be on the way, and maintaining balance between work and personal life will be essential for success.

3. Health:

For health matters, 1212 is a reminder to bring balance into your physical and emotional well-being. It suggests that you may need to make changes to create a more harmonious lifestyle, whether it's through diet, exercise, or stress management. New approaches to wellness could help you restore balance, leading to greater overall health.

Angel Number 1313

Primary Number: 1 (Leadership, assertiveness)

Secondary Number: 3 (Creativity, communication)

Analysis: In 1313, the primary number 1 emphasizes leadership and assertiveness, suggesting you should take the lead in your endeavors. The secondary number 3 brings a creative and communicative energy, indicating that expressing your ideas and engaging in creative pursuits will lead to success. This combination encourages you to confidently express your creativity and innovative ideas.

1. Love:

When 1313 appears, it signals a time to take the lead in your love life and express yourself more creatively. If you're single, it suggests being more assertive in seeking love, while for those in relationships, it's a reminder to keep communication open and creative. This number encourages you to explore new ways of connecting with your partner to keep the relationship fresh and engaging.

2. Finance/Employment:

In a professional setting, 1313 suggests that leadership and creative solutions will bring success. You are encouraged to take initiative and assert your ideas confidently. This is also a good time to communicate your innovative thoughts at work. Your creativity will be appreciated, and this can lead to positive changes in your job or business.

3. Health:

For health, 1313 emphasizes the importance of being proactive. Take control of your wellness journey and be open to creative solutions. Whether it's trying a new workout routine or exploring holistic therapies, this number urges you to lead with positivity and innovation to improve your health.

Angel Number 1414

Primary Number: 1 (Independence, motivation)

Secondary Number: 4 (Stability, practicality)

Analysis: Angel number 1414 combines the pioneering spirit of 1 with the solid foundation of 4. The primary number 1 is about taking action and moving forward, while the secondary number 4 suggests building a stable and practical foundation for these actions. This number sequence encourages a balanced approach to achieving your goals, combining ambition with pragmatism.

1. Love:

Seeing 1414 in love matters suggests stability and practicality are key. If you're single, it encourages you to take a grounded approach in your search for love, focusing on long-term stability. For those in relationships, 1414 signals that it's time to work together to build a solid foundation for your future, whether through communication, shared goals, or practical planning.

2. Finance/Employment:

In finances or employment, 1414 is a reminder that hard work and practicality are the foundation of success. It's a time to stay disciplined and focused on long-term goals, ensuring that you are building a stable career or financial situation. This is a sign that your efforts will be rewarded if you maintain a structured and diligent approach.

3. Health:

For health, 1414 encourages a structured approach. Focus on building healthy habits that will create a solid foundation for your well-being. This might involve creating a routine for exercise or managing stress in a practical way. Stability and consistency are key to maintaining good health at this time.

Angel Number 1515

Primary Number: 1 (Innovation, new beginnings)

Secondary Number: 5 (Change, adventure)

Analysis: In 1515, the primary number 1's influence of new beginnings and innovation is strong, indicating a time to embrace new ideas and directions. The secondary number 5 adds an element of change and excitement, suggesting that these new beginnings will bring adventure and significant changes to your life. This combination is a powerful sign of transformation and embracing new opportunities.

1. Love:

Angel number 1515 signals significant changes in your love life. If you're single, it's time to embrace new opportunities in love, while those in relationships may experience transformations that bring excitement and growth. The number 1515 encourages adaptability and openness to change, which will lead to greater harmony in your romantic connections.

2. Finance/Employment:

In a professional or financial context, 1515 is a strong indicator that changes are coming. Whether it's a new job, promotion, or career shift, this number encourages you to embrace the changes with optimism. It's also a sign that new opportunities could bring financial freedom or exciting ventures that align with your goals.

3. Health:

For health, 1515 suggests that changes are needed to improve your well-being. This could be a time to break old habits and embrace new, healthier routines. It encourages flexibility and openness to trying new methods of self-care or treatment to achieve better health outcomes.

Angel Number 1616
Primary Number: 1 (Self-leadership, assertiveness)
Secondary Number: 6 (Balance, nurturing)
Analysis: Angel number 1616 suggests taking the lead (1) in creating balance and harmony (6) in your life. The primary number 1 focuses on self-leadership and assertiveness, while the secondary number 6 brings in the energy of care, nurturing, and responsibility. This combination encourages you to take charge of creating a harmonious and nurturing environment for yourself and others.

1. Love:
When 1616 appears, it's time to focus on creating balance and nurturing relationships. If you're single, this number encourages you to take the lead in finding love while ensuring emotional balance. For those in a relationship, 1616 suggests nurturing your connection with care and responsibility, ensuring that both partners feel valued and supported.

2. Finance/Employment:
In financial or employment matters, 1616 is a sign to take initiative in creating a more stable and balanced work environment. It may indicate a need to nurture your career growth while being practical about your financial goals. Balancing ambition with responsibility will lead to greater success in the long run.

3. Health:
For health, 1616 suggests focusing on self-care and nurturing your body, mind, and spirit. It's a reminder to take the lead in maintaining a healthy lifestyle and balancing your responsibilities so that your well-being is not neglected. Prioritize both physical and emotional health for holistic well-being.

Angel Number 1717
Primary Number: 1 (New opportunities, ambition)
Secondary Number: 7 (Spiritual awakening, inner wisdom)

Analysis: In 1717, the primary number 1 indicates new opportunities and an ambitious spirit. The secondary number 7 adds a layer of spiritual depth, suggesting that these new opportunities will also bring spiritual growth and a deeper understanding of your inner wisdom. This combination is a reminder to pursue your ambitions while staying aligned with your spiritual path.

1. Love:

Seeing 1717 in love indicates new opportunities for spiritual growth within relationships. If you're single, this number encourages you to seek a partner who aligns with your spiritual journey. For those in a relationship, 1717 suggests deepening your connection by exploring spiritual or personal growth together, fostering a stronger bond.

2. Finance/Employment:

In the context of work or finances, 1717 signals a time for new beginnings that are aligned with your spiritual purpose. It suggests that pursuing opportunities that resonate with your inner wisdom will lead to professional and financial success. Be ambitious, but also ensure that your work aligns with your higher values.

3. Health:

For health matters, 1717 encourages you to focus on spiritual growth and inner healing. It may be time to address your emotional or spiritual health as part of your overall well-being. Meditation, mindfulness, and spiritual practices will help restore balance and vitality.

Angel Number 1818
Primary Number: 1 (Initiative, leadership)
Secondary Number: 8 (Abundance, power)
Analysis: Angel number 1818 combines the forward-moving energy of 1 with the abundance and success represented by 8. The primary number 1 suggests taking initiative and leading your path towards success, while the secondary number 8 indicates that this path will be accompanied by financial or material abundance. This sequence is a positive sign of prosperity through initiative.

1. Love:

When 1818 appears in love, it signals the potential for abundance and leadership in your relationships. If you're single, it suggests that love is on the way, especially if you take the lead in seeking it. In relationships, 1818 encourages you to take initiative in creating a prosperous and fulfilling partnership, where both partners thrive.

2. Finance/Employment:

In professional and financial matters, 1818 is a sign of abundance and success. It encourages you to take the initiative in your career, as your efforts will lead to material rewards. This is a time for stepping into leadership roles and embracing the prosperity that follows hard work.

3. Health:

For health, 1818 is a positive sign that good health and vitality are on the horizon. It suggests that taking control of your health—whether through diet, exercise, or positive thinking—will lead to long-term wellness and abundance in your life. Leadership in self-care is key.

Angel Number 1919

Primary Number: 1 (New phase, self-reliance)

Secondary Number: 9 (Completion, humanitarianism)

Analysis: In 1919, the primary number 1 signifies the start of a new phase or chapter in life, characterized by self-reliance and independence. The secondary number 9 suggests that this new phase involves completing a significant cycle and possibly engaging in humanitarian or altruistic activities. This combination indicates a time of personal growth and contributing to the greater good.

1. Love:

Seeing 1919 in the context of love suggests that a phase of your love life is coming to completion, making way for new beginnings. If you're single, it may indicate that you're ready to move on from past relationships and start fresh. For those in relationships, it suggests the completion of an important cycle, such as moving to the next stage in the relationship or resolving long-standing issues.

2. Finance/Employment:

In work or finances, 1919 signals the completion of one phase and the beginning of a new one. You may be finishing a project, leaving a job, or completing a financial goal, and this number encourages you to look forward to the new opportunities that are coming. Trust in the process of closing one chapter to open another.

3. Health:

For health, 1919 indicates the end of a cycle and the start of a new health journey. If you've been struggling with health issues, this number suggests that healing and renewal are on the way. It's time to let go of old habits and embrace new, healthier routines that will lead to greater well-being.

Angel Number 2121

Primary Number: 2 (Harmony, relationships)

Secondary Number: 1 (New beginnings, independence)

Analysis: Angel number 2121 brings together the harmonious energy of 2 with the fresh start energy of 1. The primary number 2 emphasizes balance, partnership, and cooperation, while the secondary number 1 adds an element of new beginnings and individualism. This combination suggests a phase where forming or nurturing partnerships will be beneficial, especially when they encourage personal growth.

1. Love:

Angel number 2121 in love indicates a harmonious balance between independence and partnership. If you're single, this number suggests that a new relationship may be on the horizon, one that allows you to maintain your individuality while building a strong partnership. For those in relationships, it's a reminder to nurture harmony and balance within the relationship, ensuring that both partners feel supported and independent.

2. Finance/Employment:

In financial or employment matters, 2121 suggests that maintaining balance and cooperation in the workplace will lead to success. It may indicate the start of a new project or career opportunity that requires teamwork, while also allowing you to assert your individuality. Balance between collaboration and self-leadership is key.

3. Health:

For health, 2121 encourages balance in your approach to well-being. It's a reminder to take care of both your physical and mental health while ensuring that you maintain a harmonious lifestyle. Incorporating both independence in your self-care routine and cooperation with healthcare providers or loved ones will support your health journey.

Angel Number 2323

Primary Number: 2 (Diplomacy, balance)

Secondary Number: 3 (Creativity, expression)

Analysis: In 2323, the primary number 2 focuses on diplomacy and balance, encouraging harmonious relationships. The secondary number 3 enhances this with creative expression and communication. This combination indicates a time to communicate effectively and creatively in relationships, promoting understanding and harmony.

1. Love:

When 2323 appears in love, it suggests a time of joyful communication and harmony in your relationships. If you're single, this number encourages you to express your feelings openly, as creative expression can lead to new romantic connections. For those in relationships, 2323 emphasizes the importance of communication and creativity to maintain harmony and mutual understanding.

2. Finance/Employment:

In finances or work, 2323 is a sign that creative collaboration will bring success. It encourages you to express your ideas and embrace teamwork. This is a good time for partnerships that involve innovative thinking and problem-solving, as your creative efforts will lead to professional growth and financial stability.

3. Health:

For health, 2323 suggests that positive communication and self-expression are key to your well-being. It encourages you to release any stress or emotional blockages by speaking your truth or engaging in creative activities. Maintaining a balance between mind, body, and spirit will improve your health.

Angel Number 2424

Primary Number: 2 (Partnerships, harmony)

Secondary Number: 4 (Stability, structure)

Analysis: Angel number 2424 combines the cooperative nature of 2 with the stabilizing influence of 4. The primary number 2 is about finding harmony in relationships, while the secondary number 4 suggests building a solid, stable foundation. This number sequence encourages a balanced and pragmatic approach in your partnerships, ensuring long-term stability.

1. Love:

Seeing 2424 in love signifies a time for creating stability in your relationships. If you're single, it's a sign to focus on building a solid foundation before entering a new relationship. For those in relationships, this number encourages you to strengthen your connection by creating a secure and stable environment for your partnership to thrive.

2. Finance/Employment:

In work or finance, 2424 suggests that now is the time to focus on structure and stability. It's a good time to lay down solid foundations for future success, whether through careful planning, saving, or seeking job security. Stability in your professional life will lead to long-term financial rewards.

3. Health:

For health, 2424 is a reminder to focus on creating a balanced and stable routine. Whether it's setting a regular exercise schedule or maintaining a healthy diet, building structure into your daily life will bring long-term health benefits. Stability and consistency are essential for your well-being.

Angel Number 2525
Primary Number: 2 (Balance, adaptability)
Secondary Number: 5 (Change, adventure)
Analysis: In 2525, the primary number 2's influence of balance and adaptability is combined with the dynamic energy of 5. This suggests an important period of change and growth in your life, where maintaining balance and adapting to new situations will be key. Expect significant changes that require a flexible yet balanced approach.

1. Love:

Angel number 2525 indicates that changes in your love life are on the horizon. If you're single, it's a sign that new and exciting relationships may be approaching, so be open to new possibilities. For those in relationships, this number suggests that adaptability and flexibility will be key as you navigate changes together. Embrace the changes, as they will lead to growth and harmony.

2. Finance/Employment:

In a professional or financial context, 2525 suggests that significant changes are coming. These changes may involve new opportunities or shifts in your career, and adaptability will be essential. Stay flexible, as these changes are likely to bring positive growth, but you may need to adjust your plans accordingly.

3. Health:

For health, 2525 encourages you to be open to change and adaptability in your wellness routine. You may need to adjust your habits or try new approaches to improve your health. Flexibility and a willingness to embrace new methods will bring positive changes to your well-being.

Angel Number 2626
Primary Number: 2 (Cooperation, harmony)

Secondary Number: 6 (Nurturing, responsibility)

Analysis: Angel number 2626 suggests a focus on nurturing and caring relationships (6), supported by a foundation of harmony and cooperation (2). The primary number 2 emphasizes the need for balance in relationships, while the secondary number 6 brings an element of care and responsibility. This combination encourages you to nurture your relationships while maintaining a harmonious balance.

1. Love:

Seeing 2626 in the context of love indicates a time to focus on nurturing and caring relationships. If you're single, it suggests that someone nurturing and supportive may enter your life. For those in relationships, this number encourages you to focus on building a harmonious and nurturing environment, emphasizing mutual care and emotional balance.

2. Finance/Employment:

In financial or work matters, 2626 suggests that cooperation and responsibility will bring success. It's a good time to nurture professional relationships and focus on teamwork, as working together with others will lead to long-term stability and success. Careful management of resources will also be beneficial.

3. Health:

For health, 2626 is a reminder to nurture your body and mind. Focus on self-care and create a balanced lifestyle that supports your well-being. This number encourages you to take responsibility for your health by adopting practices that bring harmony and care to your routine.

Angel Number 2727

Primary Number: 2 (Duality, relationships)

Secondary Number: 7 (Spiritual awakening, introspection)

Analysis: In 2727, the primary number 2 indicates a focus on relationships and partnerships, while the secondary number 7 brings a deeper, spiritual dimension. This combination suggests that your relationships may be entering a phase of spiritual growth or that you should seek deeper spiritual connections within your relationships.

1. Love:

Angel number 2727 in love suggests that spiritual growth within relationships is important at this time. If you're single, it encourages you to seek a partner who aligns with your spiritual values. For those in relationships, this number suggests deepening your connection through spiritual exploration and mutual introspection.

2. Finance/Employment:

In financial or employment matters, 2727 indicates that your inner wisdom will guide you towards the right decisions. Trust your intuition when making career or financial choices, and look for opportunities that align with your higher purpose. Spiritual growth and material success can go hand in hand during this time.

3. Health:

For health, 2727 suggests focusing on spiritual healing and introspection as part of your overall wellness. Meditation, mindfulness, and inner reflection will help you maintain balance and harmony in your health. Trust your inner guidance when it comes to making health-related decisions.

Angel Number 2828

Primary Number: 2 (Harmony, cooperation)

Secondary Number: 8 (Abundance, power)

Analysis: Angel number 2828 blends the harmonizing energy of 2 with the abundance and success of 8. The primary number 2 suggests that maintaining harmony and balance will lead to success, while the secondary number 8 indicates that this success will likely be in the form of material or financial gain. This sequence is a positive sign of prosperity through cooperation.

1. Love:

Seeing 2828 in love signifies that harmony and abundance are on the way. If you're single, this number encourages you to focus on creating a balanced emotional environment to attract a prosperous relationship. For those in relationships, 2828 suggests that maintaining harmony and cooperation will lead to abundance and joy within your partnership.

2. Finance/Employment:

In finance or employment, 2828 is a powerful sign of financial success and abundance through cooperation. It indicates that partnerships or collaborations will lead to prosperity. Now is the time to focus on teamwork and harmony in the workplace, as these efforts will bring material rewards.

3. Health:

For health, 2828 encourages you to maintain balance in your physical and emotional well-being. Harmonizing your lifestyle and taking a cooperative approach to health—such as working with a professional or adopting holistic methods—will lead to greater vitality and abundance in your health.

Angel Number 2929

Primary Number: 2 (Partnership, balance)

Secondary Number: 9 (Completion, humanitarianism)

Analysis: In 2929, the primary number 2 signifies the importance of partnerships and maintaining balance in relationships. The secondary number 9 suggests a phase of completion or culmination, possibly involving humanitarian or altruistic endeavors. This combination indicates a time to bring balance to relationships while working towards fulfilling higher goals or completing significant life chapters.

1. Love:

Angel number 2929 in love indicates that a cycle is coming to an end, making way for new beginnings. If you're single, it suggests that it's time to release past relationships and embrace a fresh start. For those in relationships, 2929 encourages you to bring balance to your relationship as you move toward a new phase of growth or completion.

2. Finance/Employment:

In financial or employment matters, 2929 suggests that you are nearing the completion of an important project or phase. This is a time to prepare for the next steps and bring balance to your career or finances. New opportunities will arise once you complete this cycle, and it's important to be ready to embrace them.

3. Health:

For health, 2929 indicates the need to bring closure to any lingering health issues. It's time to focus on healing and balance, ensuring that you're ready to embrace a new chapter of well-being. This number encourages you to complete any ongoing treatments or lifestyle changes to pave the way for better health.

Angel Number 3131

Primary Number: 3 (Creativity, communication)

Secondary Number: 1 (New beginnings, independence)

Analysis: Angel number 3131 emphasizes the expressive and creative energies of 3, supported by the pioneering spirit of 1. This combination suggests a phase of creative self-expression and effective communication, leading to new beginnings. It encourages you to embrace your unique talents and express your individuality.

1. Love:

Seeing 3131 in love indicates that self-expression and creativity will play a significant role in your relationships. If you're single, it encourages you to express your feelings openly, which could attract new romantic opportunities. For those in relationships, 3131 suggests that bringing creativity and communication into your partnership will strengthen your bond.

2. Finance/Employment:

In finance or work, 3131 signals a time to embrace your creative talents and take the lead in new projects. Your ability to communicate effectively and think outside the box will bring success. This is a time for innovation and leadership, so don't be afraid to step into a new role or start a new venture.

3. Health:

For health, 3131 encourages you to be proactive in expressing your needs and trying creative approaches to improve your well-being. It may be time to explore alternative therapies or creative activities that promote healing and balance in your life.

Angel Number 3232

Primary Number: 3 (Expression, joy)

Secondary Number: 2 (Harmony, relationships)

Analysis: In 3232, the primary number 3 focuses on creativity and joy, while the secondary number 2 adds elements of harmony and cooperation. This sequence suggests a harmonious blend of self-expression and collaboration, indicating a period where your creative output can enhance your relationships and bring joy.

1. Love:

Angel number 3232 in love suggests a time of joy, creativity, and balance in your relationships. If you're single, it encourages you to embrace social opportunities and express your true self. For those in relationships, 3232 emphasizes the importance of maintaining harmony and joy by communicating openly and creatively with your partner.

2. Finance/Employment:

In work or financial matters, 3232 suggests that creativity and harmonious collaboration will bring success. It's a time to focus on partnerships and teamwork, allowing your creative ideas to flourish in a balanced environment. Your joy and enthusiasm will attract positive results in your career.

3. Health:

For health, 3232 encourages you to maintain a joyful and balanced approach to your well-being. Incorporate creative activities and social interactions into your health routine to bring emotional and physical vitality. Harmony and self-expression will lead to a healthier, more balanced life.

Angel Number 3434

Primary Number: 3 (Creativity, social)

Secondary Number: 4 (Stability, structure)

Analysis: Angel number 3434 combines the social, communicative energy of 3 with the organizational and foundational aspects of 4. This indicates a time to express your ideas and creativity in a structured and disciplined manner. It's an encouragement to bring your creative visions into reality with careful planning.

1. Love:

Seeing 3434 in love indicates that it's time to bring stability and structure to your romantic life. If you're single, this number encourages you to seek a relationship that offers long-term stability. For those in relationships, 3434 suggests that creating a strong foundation through communication and practical efforts will strengthen your bond.

2. Finance/Employment:

In finance or employment, 3434 is a reminder to combine creativity with practicality. It's a good time to organize your ideas and bring them into reality through structured planning. Discipline and hard work, combined with creative thinking, will lead to success.

3. Health:

For health, 3434 encourages you to focus on creating a structured and disciplined routine that supports your well-being. Whether it's establishing a regular exercise schedule or maintaining a balanced diet, creating stability in your health habits will bring long-term benefits.

Angel Number 3535

Primary Number: 3 (Communication, enthusiasm)

Secondary Number: 5 (Change, freedom)

Analysis: In 3535, the primary number 3's influence of communication and enthusiasm is combined with the transformative energy of

5. This suggests significant changes are coming, fueled by your ability to adapt and communicate effectively. Embrace these changes with optimism and flexibility.

1. Love:

Angel number 3535 in love indicates that exciting changes are on the horizon. If you're single, it suggests that new, adventurous relationships may be approaching. For those in relationships, 3535 encourages you to embrace change and keep the excitement alive through communication and spontaneity.

2. Finance/Employment:

In finance or work, 3535 suggests that you're entering a period of transformation and growth. Stay flexible and open to new opportunities, as changes in your career or financial situation will bring positive results. Communication and adaptability are key to navigating these changes successfully.

3. Health:

For health, 3535 encourages you to be open to new approaches and changes in your wellness routine. Trying different methods, such as new fitness programs or alternative therapies, will bring positive results. Embrace change with optimism and stay adaptable.

Angel Number 3636

Primary Number: 3 (Creativity, sociability)

Secondary Number: 6 (Care, family)

Analysis: Angel number 3636 suggests focusing on creative expression (3) in a nurturing and caring environment (6). The primary number 3 encourages you to share your talents and social skills, while the secondary number 6 emphasizes the importance of responsibility and care, particularly in family or domestic matters.

1. Love:

In love, 3636 suggests a nurturing and compassionate approach. If you're single, it indicates that you may soon meet someone who values family and home life. For those in relationships, this number encourages you to create a harmonious and caring environment, focusing on mutual support and understanding.

2. Finance/Employment:

In work or finances, 3636 signals that you should use your creativity to build stability. This number encourages finding balance between your professional and personal life. It's also a reminder to manage your responsibilities at work carefully while ensuring you nurture your personal goals.

3. Health:

For health, 3636 highlights the importance of balancing your physical and emotional well-being. Focus on nurturing yourself through a healthy lifestyle and caring for your emotional needs. Creative outlets and spending time with family can improve your overall health and bring emotional balance.

Angel Number 3737

Primary Number: 3 (Expression, joy)

Secondary Number: 7 (Spirituality, introspection)

Analysis: In 3737, the primary number 3 indicates a period of joyful expression and social interaction, while the secondary number 7 adds a layer of spiritual depth and introspection. This combination encourages you to explore your spiritual path through creative endeavors and social connections.

1. Love:

In love, 3737 suggests a time of spiritual growth within your relationships. If you're single, it encourages you to seek a partner who shares your spiritual values. For those in relationships, this number highlights the importance of spiritual connection and mutual growth on your journey together.

2. Finance/Employment:

In financial or work matters, 3737 indicates that your intuition and spiritual wisdom will guide you to success. Focus on aligning your career or financial goals with your inner purpose. Creative solutions inspired by your spiritual insights can bring new opportunities for growth.

3. Health:

For health, 3737 encourages a holistic approach, integrating your spiritual practices into your well-being routine. Meditation, spiritual healing, and mindfulness will enhance your physical health and bring emotional balance. Trust your intuition when making health-related decisions.

Angel Number 3838

Primary Number: 3 (Creativity, optimism)

Secondary Number: 8 (Abundance, success)

Analysis: Angel number 3838 blends the optimistic and creative vibrations of 3 with the material and financial abundance of 8. This sequence suggests that your creative endeavors and positive outlook will lead to material success and abundance. It's a reminder to stay positive and creative in your pursuits.

1. Love:

Angel number 3838 in love indicates that creativity and optimism will strengthen your relationships. If you're single, this number encourages you to remain positive and express yourself openly to attract a fulfilling relationship. For those in relationships, 3838 suggests that creativity and positive communication will bring abundance and joy to your partnership.

2. Finance/Employment:

In finance or employment, 3838 is a sign of material success and financial abundance. Your creative efforts and positive outlook will lead to prosperous outcomes in your work. Stay focused on your goals, and your innovative ideas will bring financial rewards.

3. Health:

For health, 3838 suggests that a positive mindset and creative outlets will lead to improved well-being. Engage in activities that bring you joy and optimism, as these will support both your mental and physical health. Positive energy is key to maintaining vitality.

Angel Number 3939

Primary Number: 3 (Creativity, social)

Secondary Number: 9 (Completion, humanitarianism)

Analysis: In 3939, the primary number 3 focuses on creativity and social connections, while the secondary number 9 suggests a phase of completion or humanitarian efforts. This combination indicates that your creative and social skills may play a significant role in concluding important life chapters or contributing to humanitarian causes.

1. Love:

In love, 3939 suggests that it's time to complete a chapter in your romantic life and move forward. If you're single, it may indicate that you are ready to let go of past relationships and open yourself to new possibilities. For those in relationships, this number encourages closure on old issues and the beginning of a new phase of growth and creativity.

2. Finance/Employment:

In finance or employment, 3939 signifies that a creative project or job cycle may be coming to an end, making room for new opportunities. Use your creativity and communication skills to complete your current tasks and prepare for the next phase of growth.

3. Health:

For health, 3939 suggests that it's time to conclude any health issues you've been addressing and focus on a fresh start. Completing a wellness plan or treatment will lead to renewed vitality. Use creative methods to maintain your health and bring closure to lingering concerns.

Angel Number 4141

Primary Number: 4 (Stability, practicality)

Secondary Number: 1 (New beginnings, leadership)

Analysis: Angel number 4141 emphasizes the stable and practical aspects of 4, supported by the innovative energy of 1. This combination suggests a period of building solid foundations for new projects or phases in life. It encourages you to combine practicality with a pioneering spirit to achieve your goals.

1. Love:

In love, 4141 suggests that stability and leadership will strengthen your relationship. If you're single, this number encourages you to take charge of your romantic life and seek a relationship built on a strong foundation. For those in relationships, 4141 emphasizes the importance of creating a stable environment that supports mutual growth.

2. Finance/Employment:

In financial or work matters, 4141 is a sign that building a solid foundation is key to your success. Use your leadership skills to organize your work and focus on long-term goals. This number encourages you to combine practicality with ambition to achieve lasting financial stability.

3. Health:

For health, 4141 suggests that a structured approach to wellness will bring lasting benefits. Creating a consistent routine, such as regular exercise or a balanced diet, will improve your health. Stability and discipline in your health habits are essential to achieving long-term vitality.

Angel Number 4242

Primary Number: 4 (Foundation, order)

Secondary Number: 2 (Duality, cooperation)

Analysis: In 4242, the primary number 4 focuses on building a strong, organized foundation, while the secondary number 2 adds elements of balance and partnership. This sequence suggests a time for creating stability in your life, with the support of harmonious relationships and cooperation.

1. Love:

Angel number 4242 in love suggests that balance and cooperation are essential for maintaining harmony in your relationships. If you're single, it's a reminder to seek a partner who values stability and cooperation. For those in relationships, 4242 encourages you to work together with your partner to create a balanced and supportive relationship.

2. Finance/Employment:

In finance or work, 4242 signals that cooperation and teamwork are crucial for achieving long-term stability. Focus on building strong relationships with colleagues and partners, as these will help create a solid foundation for future success. Organization and cooperation will lead to financial rewards.

3. Health:

For health, 4242 encourages you to create balance in your daily life. Focus on maintaining harmony between your work, personal life, and wellness. Cooperation with others, such as seeking guidance from health professionals or support from loved ones, will enhance your overall well-being.

Angel Number 4343

Primary Number: 4 (Structure, discipline)

Secondary Number: 3 (Creativity, communication)

Analysis: Angel number 4343 combines the structured and disciplined nature of 4 with the creative and expressive energies of 3. This indicates a need to bring creative ideas into a more organized form. It's a call to use disciplined efforts to realize your creative visions.

1. Love:

In love, 4343 suggests that structured communication and discipline will help strengthen your relationships. If you're single, it encourages you to be disciplined in your search for love, focusing on building a relationship with clear communication and mutual respect. For those in relationships, 4343 emphasizes the need to establish boundaries and create a stable, organized environment for love to thrive.

2. Finance/Employment:

In finance or work, 4343 is a reminder to combine creativity with discipline. It's a time to focus on organizing your creative ideas and turning them into practical, structured plans. Your ability to balance creativity with responsibility will lead to professional success and financial stability.

3. Health:

For health, 4343 encourages you to bring structure and discipline to your wellness routine. Focus on creating a balanced lifestyle that supports both your physical and emotional health. A structured approach, such as following a specific health plan or regimen, will lead to long-term vitality.

Angel Number 4545

Primary Number: 4 (Organization, determination)

Secondary Number: 5 (Adventure, change)

Analysis: In 4545, the primary number 4's influence of organization and determination is combined with the transformative and adventurous energy of 5. This suggests significant changes that require a structured approach. Embrace these changes with an organized mindset and a sense of adventure.

1. Love:

Angel number 4545 in love suggests that exciting changes are coming, but they require a structured approach. If you're single, it indicates that new romantic opportunities will arise, but you'll need to stay grounded and organized in your approach. For those in relationships, 4545 encourages embracing changes while maintaining stability in your partnership.

2. Finance/Employment:

In finance or employment, 4545 signals that significant changes are on the horizon. However, these changes will be successful if approached with organization and determination. Embrace new opportunities, but stay focused on maintaining structure and discipline in your work to achieve financial growth.

3. Health:

For health, 4545 encourages you to embrace changes in your wellness routine while staying disciplined and organized. Whether it's trying a new exercise program or adopting healthier habits, a balanced approach will ensure that these changes lead to improved well-being.

Angel Number 4646

Primary Number: 4 (Solidity, reliability)

Secondary Number: 6 (Family, nurturing)

Analysis: Angel number 4646 suggests a focus on creating a stable and secure environment (4) in your family and personal life (6). The primary number 4 encourages you to build and maintain a strong foundation, while the secondary number 6 emphasizes the importance of nurturing and caring for loved ones.

1. Love:

In love, 4646 suggests that creating a stable and nurturing environment will enhance your relationships. If you're single, it encourages you to seek a partner who values family and security. For those in relationships, 4646 emphasizes the importance of building a solid foundation through care, responsibility, and mutual support.

2. Finance/Employment:

In finance or employment, 4646 signals that focusing on stability and practicality will bring success. It's a time to manage your resources carefully and create a strong financial foundation for the future. Hard work and responsible management will lead to long-term financial security.

3. Health:

For health, 4646 encourages you to create a stable and nurturing routine that supports your well-being. Focus on self-care and maintaining a healthy environment for yourself and your loved ones. Consistency and care in your health habits will lead to long-term vitality.

Angel Number 4747

Primary Number: 4 (Discipline, hard work, stability)

Secondary Number: 7 (Spirituality, wisdom)

Analysis: In 4747, the primary number 4 indicates a period of disciplined effort and hard work, while the secondary number 7 adds a layer of spiritual understanding and wisdom. This combination encourages you to ground your spiritual insights in practical reality, applying your wisdom in tangible ways.

1. Love:

Angel number 4747 in love suggests that spiritual growth and stability are essential for building strong relationships. If you're single, this number encourages you to seek a partner who shares your spiritual values and is grounded in their approach to life. For those in relationships, 4747 highlights the importance of building a stable foundation for spiritual growth together.

2. Finance/Employment:

In finance or employment, 4747 indicates that a combination of discipline and spiritual wisdom will lead to success. Stay grounded and organized in your work while trusting your intuition to guide you toward the right decisions. This balance between practicality and spiritual insight will lead to professional growth and financial rewards.

3. Health:

For health, 4747 encourages you to integrate spiritual practices into your wellness routine. Meditation, mindfulness, or spiritual reflection can help create balance and harmony in your health. A disciplined approach to both physical and spiritual well-being will lead to long-term health benefits.

Angel Number 4848

Primary Number: 4 (Practicality, endurance)

Secondary Number: 8 (Abundance, power)

Analysis: Angel number 4848 blends the practical and enduring vibrations of 4 with the material success and empowerment of 8. This sequence suggests that your hard work and practical efforts will lead to material success and abundance. It's a reminder to stay persistent and grounded in your endeavors.

1. Love:

In love, 4848 suggests that creating stability and focusing on long-term goals will enhance your relationships. If you're single, this number encourages you to seek a partner who shares your values of stability and commitment. For those in relationships, 4848 emphasizes the importance of building a solid foundation for future growth.

2. Finance/Employment:

In finance or employment, 4848 is a sign of material success and financial abundance. Your practical efforts and hard work will lead to financial rewards and long-term security. Stay focused on your goals, and your persistence will pay off with material success.

3. Health:

For health, 4848 encourages you to stay committed to your wellness routine and maintain a balanced approach to your physical health. Consistency and determination in your health habits will lead to long-lasting benefits and improved vitality.

Angel Number 4949

Primary Number: 4 (Organization, responsibility)

Secondary Number: 9 (Completion, universal love)

Analysis: In 4949, the primary number 4 focuses on organization and responsibility, while the secondary number 9 suggests a phase of completion or involvement in humanitarian causes. This combination indicates that your organized and responsible nature may play a key role in concluding significant life projects or contributing to the greater good.

1. Love:

In love, 4949 suggests that a phase of your romantic life may be coming to an end. If you're single, it's a sign to let go of old emotional baggage and open yourself to new possibilities. For those in relationships, 4949 encourages both partners to work through their responsibilities and move forward with clarity and love, perhaps completing an important phase in the relationship.

2. Finance/Employment:

In financial or employment matters, 4949 signifies that you may be wrapping up a significant project or position. This number encourages you to stay organized and responsible as you prepare to complete one chapter and move on to new opportunities. Focus on closure and finishing your tasks with integrity.

3. Health:

For health, 4949 advises you to bring closure to ongoing health issues. It's time to organize your routine and take responsibility for your well-being. This number suggests that completing a wellness plan or treatment cycle will bring a sense of fulfillment and health improvement.

Angel Number 5151

Primary Number: 5 (Change, freedom)

Secondary Number: 1 (New beginnings, leadership)

Analysis: Angel number 5151 brings together the energies of change and new beginnings. It suggests that significant life changes are on the horizon, which will require your initiative and leadership. Embrace the changes, as they are likely to lead you to fresh opportunities and personal growth.

1. Love:

In love, 5151 suggests that significant changes are coming, leading to new beginnings. If you're single, this number encourages you to embrace new romantic opportunities with confidence. For those in relationships, 5151 signifies a time of transformation within the partnership, urging both partners to adapt to changes and grow together.

2. Finance/Employment:

In finance or employment, 5151 indicates that new opportunities are on the horizon. It's a time for embracing change and taking the lead in new projects or ventures. This number encourages you to trust in your ability to navigate through transitions with confidence and create new pathways to financial success.

3. Health:

For health, 5151 signals that changes are needed to improve your well-being. It's time to take charge of your health by adopting new habits or trying different approaches. Embrace the changes with a positive attitude, knowing that they will lead to greater health and vitality.

Angel Number 5252

Primary Number: 5 (Adaptability, adventure)

Secondary Number: 2 (Harmony, partnership)

Analysis: In 5252, the adventurous and adaptable nature of 5 is combined with the harmonious and cooperative energy of 2. This suggests a time for embracing changes and new experiences, while also seeking balance and harmony in relationships and partnerships.

1. Love:

In love, 5252 emphasizes the importance of maintaining balance during times of change. If you're single, this number suggests that adaptability will help you find a harmonious relationship. For those in relationships, 5252 encourages cooperation and flexibility as you and your partner navigate through changes together.

2. Finance/Employment:

In finance or employment, 5252 suggests that change is inevitable, but balance and adaptability will lead to success. Be open to new opportunities or shifts in your career, and focus on maintaining harmony in your work environment. Flexibility will help you thrive during periods of transition.

3. Health:

For health, 5252 indicates that changes in your health routine may be necessary to restore balance. Focus on adaptability and seek a harmonious approach to wellness. Whether it's adjusting your diet, exercise, or mental health practices, maintaining balance will support your overall well-being.

Angel Number 5353

Primary Number: 5 (Versatility, exploration)

Secondary Number: 3 (Creativity, expression)

Analysis: Angel number 5353 suggests a period of exploration and creativity. The number 5's energy of versatility and change is amplified by 3's focus on self-expression and communication. It's a time to explore new avenues of creativity and to express yourself more freely.

1. Love:

In love, 5353 suggests that exploring new creative ways of expressing love and communication will bring excitement to your relationships. If you're single, it encourages you to be open and creative in how you connect with others. For those in relationships, this number suggests that communicating openly and creatively will strengthen the bond.

2. Finance/Employment:

In finance or employment, 5353 signifies that your creative approach to challenges will lead to new opportunities and success. Embrace change and use your versatility to explore new ways of generating income or improving your career. Creativity and communication will be key to navigating this period.

3. Health:

For health, 5353 encourages you to explore new methods of maintaining well-being. Engage in creative activities that support both your mental and physical health, such as artistic expression or innovative fitness routines. Being adaptable and versatile in your approach to health will lead to positive outcomes.

Angel Number 5454

Primary Number: 5 (Freedom, curiosity)

Secondary Number: 4 (Stability, structure)

Analysis: In 5454, the freedom-loving and curious nature of 5 is grounded by the stable and structured energy of 4. This combination indicates a time to explore new horizons while maintaining a sense of stability and order in your life. It's about finding balance between adventure and responsibility.

1. Love:

In love, 5454 encourages you to explore new horizons while maintaining a sense of stability. If you're single, it's a time to be adventurous in your love life but ensure that you remain grounded in your values. For those in relationships, this number suggests that while it's important to embrace change, it's equally vital to provide stability and security within the partnership.

2. Finance/Employment:

In finance or employment, 5454 signals that you should pursue new opportunities while maintaining a structured and organized approach. It's a time for balancing adventure with responsibility in your career or financial ventures. By keeping a steady foundation, you can embrace change without jeopardizing your long-term goals.

3. Health:

For health, 5454 indicates that while it's important to try new health practices or routines, you should also focus on maintaining a stable foundation. Balance adventurous activities with a structured approach to your well-being, ensuring you stay grounded while exploring new methods for health improvement.

Angel Number 5656

Primary Number: 5 (Adventurous, transformative)

Secondary Number: 6 (Nurturing, family)

Analysis: Angel number 5656 suggests a dynamic period of transformation (5) that also focuses on the nurturing and caring aspects of your life (6). Embrace changes that enhance your family life or personal relationships. It's a time for growth both in personal freedom and in your close connections.

1. Love:

In love, 5656 indicates that changes are coming that will positively affect your relationships. If you're single, this number encourages you to embrace new romantic experiences that align with your values of family and harmony. For those in relationships, 5656 suggests that personal and relationship growth will come through changes that promote nurturing and care.

2. Finance/Employment:

In finance or employment, 5656 suggests that changes in your career or financial situation will bring opportunities for personal growth and stability. Embrace new challenges with a nurturing attitude, focusing on how these changes can support both your material goals and your personal values.

3. Health:

For health, 5656 signals that positive changes are needed to nurture your well-being. Focus on transforming your health habits in a way that supports both physical and emotional harmony. Embrace new routines that bring balance to your personal and family life, enhancing your overall well-being.

Angel Number 5757

Primary Number: 5 (Change, progress)

Secondary Number: 7 (Spirituality, inner-wisdom)

Analysis: In 5757, the transformative energy of 5 is blended with the spiritual and introspective qualities of 7. This sequence encourages you to embrace changes that are not only external but also deeply spiritual. It's a call to progress in life while staying aligned with your inner wisdom.

1. Love:

In love, 5757 suggests that spiritual growth and change will play a significant role in your relationships. If you're single, this number encourages you to seek a partner who aligns with your spiritual values. For those in relationships, 5757 highlights the importance of embracing change as a path to deeper spiritual connection and mutual growth.

2. Finance/Employment:

In finance or employment, 5757 signals that you should embrace change as part of your spiritual and professional growth. Trust in your inner wisdom to guide you through transitions, and use your spiritual insights to navigate challenges and make decisions that align with your higher purpose.

3. Health:

For health, 5757 encourages you to focus on spiritual practices that support your physical and mental well-being. Meditation, mindfulness, or other spiritual activities will enhance your health, helping you adapt to changes in your body and mind with a deeper sense of wisdom and peace.

Angel Number 5858

Primary Number: 5 (Flexibility, resourcefulness)

Secondary Number: 8 (Abundance, power)

Analysis: Angel number 5858 is about the flexibility and adaptability of 5, coupled with the material and financial focus of 8. This combination suggests that changes you're currently undergoing or considering could lead to material abundance and empowerment. Stay open and adaptable to these possibilities.

1. Love:

In love, 5858 suggests that changes in your romantic life will bring abundance and growth. If you're single, this number encourages you to embrace new romantic opportunities with an open heart, knowing that they will lead to positive outcomes. For those in relationships, 5858 indicates that changes will lead to a deeper, more prosperous connection.

2. Finance/Employment:

In finance or employment, 5858 signals that changes in your career or financial situation will lead to material abundance and personal freedom. Embrace new opportunities with confidence, and trust that your adaptability and resourcefulness will bring financial success.

3. Health:

For health, 5858 indicates that changes in your health routine will lead to greater freedom and vitality. Focus on adopting practices that support both your physical and emotional well-being. Embrace the flexibility to try new methods that will enhance your overall health and empower you to feel your best.

Angel Number 5959

Primary Number: 5 (Adventure, experiential learning)

Secondary Number: 9 (Completion, humanitarianism)

Analysis: In 5959, the adventurous spirit of 5 is combined with the concluding and universal energy of 9. This sequence indicates a phase of life where you're not only exploring new horizons but also wrapping up important life lessons. It might also hint at a shift towards more humanitarian pursuits.

1. Love:

In love, 5959 suggests that you are nearing the completion of an important phase in your romantic life. If you're single, it may indicate that you're wrapping up emotional lessons and preparing for a new beginning. For those in relationships, 5959 signals that a significant cycle is ending, allowing for personal growth and humanitarian love to emerge.

2. Finance/Employment:

In finance or employment, 5959 indicates that you're completing an important chapter in your career or financial journey. It's a time to reflect on what you've learned and prepare for a new phase. This number encourages you to pursue new adventures or projects that align with your higher calling.

3. Health:

For health, 5959 signals the completion of a health challenge or phase, allowing you to embrace a new approach to your well-being. Focus on bringing closure to old habits or health issues and prepare to embrace new practices that support your long-term health and growth.

Angel Number 6161

Primary Number: 6 (Balance, family, refocus)

Secondary Number: 1 (New beginnings, leadership)

Analysis: Angel number 6161 signifies a blend of refocusing on family harmony and embracing new beginnings. It calls for leadership in redefining personal or family life, paving the way for balance and a fresh start.

1. Love:

In love, 6161 suggests that you should focus on nurturing your relationships while embracing new beginnings. If you're single, it encourages you to take the lead in finding a partner who values harmony and balance. For those in relationships, 6161 emphasizes the importance of creating a stable, nurturing environment for love to grow.

2. Finance/Employment:

In finance or employment, 6161 signals that new beginnings are on the horizon, and they will be built on the foundation of harmony and balance. Focus on nurturing your financial goals and creating a balanced work-life dynamic to ensure long-term success.

3. Health:

For health, 6161 encourages you to refocus on nurturing both your physical and emotional well-being. Embrace new health practices that bring balance and stability to your life, and focus on creating a supportive environment that enhances your overall vitality.

Angel Number 6262

Primary Number: 6 (Nurturing, responsibility, refocus)

Secondary Number: 2 (Partnership, diplomacy)

Analysis: In 6262, the nurturing and responsible nature of 6 is combined with a need to refocus on partnerships, calling for diplomacy and mutual understanding in relationships.

1. Love:

In love, 6262 emphasizes cooperation and balance within relationships. If you're single, this number suggests that a harmonious partnership is on the horizon. For those in relationships, 6262 encourages both partners to nurture their relationship through cooperation and mutual support.

2. Finance/Employment:

In finance or employment, 6262 indicates that balance and cooperation will lead to success. Focus on building strong partnerships in your professional life, and work collaboratively to achieve your financial goals.

3. Health:

For health, 6262 encourages you to create balance in your wellness routine. Focus on nurturing yourself through both physical and emotional care, and seek support from loved ones or professionals when needed. Balance and harmony are key to improving your health.

Angel Number 6363

Primary Number: 6 (Home, compassion, refocus)

Secondary Number: 3 (Creativity, communication)

Analysis: Angel number 6363 suggests a harmonious blend of refocusing on home and compassionate aspects (6) with creativity and expression (3). It's time to channel your nurturing nature into creative communication within your family.

1. Love:

In love, 6363 emphasizes the importance of creativity and compassionate communication within relationships. If you're single, this number encourages you to approach romantic connections with an open heart and a creative mindset. For those in relationships, 6363 suggests nurturing your partnership through empathy and thoughtful expression, fostering deeper emotional bonds.

2. Finance/Employment:

In finance or employment, 6363 signals that your creativity and communication skills will lead to success. This is a time to bring innovative ideas into your work or financial ventures, while also ensuring you are compassionate and considerate in your professional relationships.

3. Health:

For health, 6363 encourages you to focus on nurturing yourself with care and compassion. Explore creative ways to improve your well-being, whether it's through art, meditation, or engaging in activities that bring you joy and emotional balance. Compassionate self-care will be key to maintaining your overall health.

Angel Number 6464

Primary Number: 6 (Caregiving, domesticity, refocus)

Secondary Number: 4 (Structure, determination)

Analysis: 6464 emphasizes refocusing on providing care and stability in your domestic life, grounded by the structured energy of 4. It's a call for harmonious and structured family environments.

1. Love:

In love, 6464 suggests a focus on building stability and structure in your relationships. If you're single, it's a sign to seek partners who value commitment and reliability. For those in relationships, 6464 emphasizes the need for both partners to create a strong, stable foundation in their relationship, ensuring long-term harmony and growth.

2. Finance/Employment:

In finance or employment, 6464 signals that hard work, organization, and a stable approach will lead to success. Focus on creating a solid plan for your financial goals, and be disciplined in executing your work. A stable and structured approach will help you achieve your ambitions.

3. Health:

For health, 6464 encourages you to take a structured and disciplined approach to your well-being. This is a time to focus on creating a strong foundation for long-term health, through consistency in your routines and a balanced lifestyle. Stay committed to practices that enhance your physical and emotional stability.

Angel Number 6565

Primary Number: 6 (Harmony, service, refocus)

Secondary Number: 5 (Change, freedom)

Analysis: 6565 combines the harmonious and service-oriented 6 with the dynamic energy of 5. This sequence encourages embracing changes that bring balance and refocus your relationships and service to others.

1. Love:

In love, 6565 signals that changes are coming, but these changes will ultimately lead to greater harmony. If you're single, embrace new romantic opportunities that bring balance and growth into your life. For those in relationships, 6565 encourages both partners to adapt to changes while maintaining a harmonious and nurturing connection.

2. Finance/Employment:

In finance or employment, 6565 suggests that changes in your career or financial situation will bring new opportunities for balance and growth. Embrace these changes with an adaptable and flexible mindset, knowing that they will lead to long-term financial harmony.

3. Health:

For health, 6565 indicates that embracing changes in your health routine will lead to greater balance and well-being. Be open to trying new methods that promote harmony in both your physical and emotional health, and adapt to changes with a positive attitude.

Angel Number 6767

Primary Number: 6 (Family, empathy, refocus)

Secondary Number: 7 (Spiritual growth, introspection)

Analysis: 6767 brings together family-oriented and empathetic qualities (6) with spiritual growth (7), encouraging a refocus on family relationships while engaging in personal spiritual development.

1. Love:

In love, 6767 suggests that spiritual growth will play a significant role in your relationships. If you're single, seek partners who align with your spiritual values. For those in relationships, 6767 encourages both partners to explore spiritual growth together, fostering deeper emotional and spiritual connections.

2. Finance/Employment:

In finance or employment, 6767 signals that spiritual insights and inner wisdom will guide you through professional changes. Trust your intuition when making decisions about your career or financial ventures, and stay aligned with your higher purpose to achieve success.

3. Health:

For health, 6767 encourages you to focus on spiritual practices that support your well-being. Engaging in mindfulness, meditation, or other spiritual activities will enhance your health and bring inner peace. Spiritual growth will be key to maintaining balance in your physical and emotional health.

Angel Number 6868

Primary Number: 6 (Nurturing, stability, refocus)

Secondary Number: 8 (Abundance, power)

Analysis: 6868 blends nurturing and stability-focused aspects of 6 with the material abundance of 8. This sequence suggests that refocusing nurturing actions could lead to material and empowering benefits.

1. Love:

In love, 6868 emphasizes the importance of nurturing relationships while also focusing on material stability. If you're single, this number suggests that building a strong, secure foundation in your personal life will attract the right partner. For those in relationships, 6868 encourages both partners to balance emotional nurturing with creating a stable, supportive environment.

2. Finance/Employment:

In finance or employment, 6868 signals that your efforts to nurture and support your financial goals will lead to material abundance. Focus on creating a stable foundation for success, and trust that your hard work will result in financial rewards and empowerment.

3. Health:

For health, 6868 encourages you to nurture your well-being by focusing on both emotional and material stability. Create a balanced lifestyle that supports your physical and emotional health, ensuring you have the resources and support needed for long-term vitality.

Angel Number 6969

Primary Number: 6 (Caring, family-focused, refocus)

Secondary Number: 9 (Humanitarian, completion)

Analysis: In 6969, the family and community-focused 6 meets the humanitarian energy of 9. This sequence encourages refocusing your nurturing qualities on broader humanitarian efforts or completing significant family or community projects.

1. Love:

In love, 6969 suggests a time of completion and transformation in your relationships. If you're single, this number may indicate that you are finishing an emotional healing process and preparing for new romantic opportunities. For those in relationships, 6969 encourages both partners to focus on nurturing their connection while contributing to a higher purpose, such as humanitarian efforts.

2. Finance/Employment:

In finance or employment, 6969 signals that you are completing a significant phase in your career or financial journey. It's a time to reflect on what you've achieved and prepare for a new chapter that aligns with your values of service and compassion.

3. Health:

For health, 6969 indicates that you are completing an important phase in your well-being and preparing for transformation. Focus on nurturing yourself and completing any necessary healing processes, while also considering how your health practices align with your higher purpose.

Angel Number 7171

Primary Number: 7 (Spirituality, introspection)

Secondary Number: 1 (New beginnings, independence)

Analysis: Angel number 7171 emphasizes a deep spiritual journey and introspection (7) combined with the energy of new beginnings and independence (1). This sequence suggests a phase of personal spiritual growth and the start of a new chapter in your spiritual path.

1. Love:

In love, 7171 emphasizes the importance of spiritual connection and new beginnings. If you're single, this number encourages you to seek partners who align with your spiritual values. For those in relationships, 7171 suggests that spiritual growth will strengthen the bond between partners, leading to new opportunities for deeper emotional connection.

2. Finance/Employment:

In finance or employment, 7171 signals that new beginnings in your career will be guided by spiritual insights and inner wisdom. Trust in your intuition and stay aligned with your higher purpose to achieve success in your professional life.

3. Health:

For health, 7171 encourages you to focus on spiritual practices that support your well-being. This is a time for personal growth and introspection, where spiritual activities such as meditation or mindfulness will enhance your health and lead to new beginnings in your physical and emotional well-being.

Angel Number 7272

Primary Number: 7 (Inner wisdom, contemplation)

Secondary Number: 2 (Harmony, relationships)

Analysis: 7272 blends the pursuit of inner wisdom and contemplation (7) with the need for harmony in relationships (2). This number suggests a time for deep reflection on your connections with others, fostering balance and understanding.

1. Love:

In love, 7272 suggests that maintaining harmony in your relationships will lead to spiritual growth. If you're single, this number encourages you to seek partnerships that promote both emotional and spiritual balance. For those in relationships, 7272 emphasizes the importance of introspection and spiritual connection in maintaining a harmonious relationship.

2. Finance/Employment:

In finance or employment, 7272 signals that balancing harmony in your professional relationships will lead to success. Focus on maintaining peaceful and cooperative partnerships, and use your inner wisdom to navigate any challenges in your career.

3. Health:

For health, 7272 encourages you to find balance between your physical and spiritual well-being. Engage in practices that promote both inner peace and physical health, such as meditation, yoga, or other holistic activities. Harmony in both aspects of your life will lead to improved overall health.

Angel Number 7373

Primary Number: 7 (Mysticism, inner-knowing)

Secondary Number: 3 (Creativity, communication)

Analysis: With 7373, the mystical and introspective qualities of 7 are united with the expressive and creative energies of 3. It encourages communicating your spiritual insights and creative expression, possibly through artistic or spiritual endeavors.

1. Love:

In love, 7373 emphasizes the importance of spiritual connection and creative self-expression. If you're single, this number encourages you to explore romantic connections that inspire your creativity and align with your spiritual values. For those in relationships, 7373 suggests that open communication and spiritual growth will strengthen the bond between partners.

2. Finance/Employment:

In finance or employment, 7373 signals that your creative and spiritual insights will lead to success. This is a time to explore new ideas and express your unique talents in your career or financial ventures, while staying aligned with your spiritual path.

3. Health:

For health, 7373 encourages you to focus on creative self-expression and spiritual practices that support your well-being. Engage in activities that nurture both your body and soul, such as artistic expression or spiritual exploration, to enhance your overall health and vitality.

Angel Number 7474

Primary Number: 7 (Spiritual awakening, enlightenment)

Secondary Number: 4 (Stability, structure)

Analysis: Angel number 7474 signifies a spiritual awakening or enlightenment (7) that requires a solid foundation and structure (4) in your life. It's a call to build a stable environment that supports your spiritual growth.

1. Love:

In love, 7474 suggests that spiritual growth and stability are essential for building a strong relationship. If you're single, this number encourages you to seek partners who value both spiritual and emotional growth. For those in relationships, 7474 emphasizes the importance of creating a stable foundation for the relationship while exploring spiritual growth together.

2. Finance/Employment:

In finance or employment, 7474 signals that spiritual insights and a structured approach will lead to success. This is a time to build a stable foundation for your career while staying aligned with your spiritual goals. Discipline and organization will help you achieve long-term success.

3. Health:

For health, 7474 encourages you to focus on creating a stable and structured approach to your well-being. Engage in spiritual practices that support your physical health, and establish consistent routines that promote long-term vitality and balance in your life.

Angel Number 7575

Primary Number: 7 (Inner growth, spiritual development)

Secondary Number: 5 (Adventure, change)

Analysis: In 7575, the quest for inner growth and spiritual development (7) is combined with a craving for adventure and change (5). This sequence encourages embracing new experiences as part of your spiritual journey.

1. Love:

In love, 7575 indicates that changes in your romantic life will lead to spiritual growth. If you're single, this number encourages you to seek partners who inspire both personal and spiritual development. For those in relationships, 7575 suggests that embracing change will bring deeper spiritual connection and growth within the partnership.

2. Finance/Employment:

In finance or employment, 7575 signals that embracing changes in your career will lead to both personal and spiritual growth. Be open to new opportunities and trust that these changes will guide you toward success while aligning with your higher purpose.

3. Health:

For health, 7575 encourages you to embrace changes that promote both physical and spiritual well-being. Engage in practices that support personal growth, such as meditation or exercise, and stay open to new methods of improving your health.

Angel Number 7676

Primary Number: 7 (Intuition, soul-searching)

Secondary Number: 6 (Harmony, family)

Analysis: 7676 suggests a deep dive into intuition and soul-searching (7) while maintaining harmony and balance in family and relationships (6). It's about finding inner peace while nurturing your close bonds.

1. Love:

In love, 7676 highlights the importance of nurturing family and emotional bonds while seeking spiritual growth. If you're single, this number encourages you to find someone who values both emotional depth and spiritual connection. For those in relationships, 7676 suggests focusing on maintaining harmony in family relationships while also engaging in personal spiritual exploration.

2. Finance/Employment:

In finance or employment, 7676 signals that your spiritual development and intuitive insights will lead to balanced professional growth. Trust your instincts and focus on nurturing professional relationships, as they will play a key role in achieving success.

3. Health:

For health, 7676 encourages you to maintain a balance between emotional well-being and spiritual development. Nurturing your close relationships and seeking inner peace through spiritual practices will positively impact your physical and emotional health.

Angel Number 7878

Primary Number: 7 (Spiritual exploration, self-reflection)

Secondary Number: 8 (Abundance, success)

Analysis: 7878 brings together spiritual exploration and self-reflection (7) with the manifestation of abundance and success (8). This sequence indicates that your spiritual journey will lead to material and spiritual prosperity.

1. Love:

In love, 7878 emphasizes the importance of spiritual exploration and material success within relationships. If you're single, this number suggests finding a partner who shares your spiritual aspirations while also being grounded in practical life. For those in relationships, 7878 encourages spiritual growth together while focusing on building a stable and prosperous future.

2. Finance/Employment:

In finance or employment, 7878 signals that spiritual self-reflection and personal development will lead to material success and abundance. Trust in your spiritual journey and stay committed to achieving your financial goals through balanced efforts.

3. Health:

For health, 7878 encourages a focus on spiritual exploration and inner reflection to enhance your overall well-being. Engaging in mindfulness and meditation practices will bring clarity, which can lead to positive physical and emotional changes.

Angel Number 7979

Primary Number: 7 (Soul mission, higher learning)

Secondary Number: 9 (Universal love, completion)

Analysis: In 7979, the focus is on pursuing your soul mission and higher learning (7), which aligns with the energies of universal love and the completion of a significant phase (9). This number sequence suggests reaching a pivotal point in your spiritual journey, culminating in a deeper understanding of universal love and interconnectedness.

1. Love:

In love, 7979 suggests a deep focus on your soul mission and spiritual learning. If you're single, this number indicates that a relationship aligned with your spiritual growth is on the horizon. For those in relationships, 7979 encourages both partners to explore their spiritual paths together, strengthening the bond through shared wisdom.

2. Finance/Employment:

In finance or employment, 7979 signals that your focus on spiritual understanding and karmic lessons will lead to fulfilling your soul mission. Trust that your financial or career success will align with the deeper spiritual truths you uncover.

3. Health:

For health, 7979 encourages you to focus on deep spiritual practices that lead to inner wisdom and healing. By aligning your life with spiritual laws, you will experience improvements in both physical and emotional health.

Angel Number 8181

Primary Number: 8 (Abundance, authority)

Secondary Number: 1 (Leadership, new beginnings)

Analysis: Angel number 8181 signals a powerful blend of abundance and personal authority (8) with the drive for leadership and new beginnings (1). This sequence suggests a time to take charge and manifest prosperity in your life, embracing new opportunities with confidence.

1. Love:

In love, 8181 signifies the potential for new beginnings through personal empowerment and leadership. If you're single, this number encourages you to take charge of your romantic life, leading the way to new and exciting opportunities. For those in relationships, 8181 suggests taking the initiative to strengthen the partnership and bring a sense of renewal.

2. Finance/Employment:

In finance or employment, 8181 signals a time for leadership and personal authority in achieving material success. This number encourages you to take the lead in your financial endeavors and trust in your ability to manifest abundance.

3. Health:

For health, 8181 encourages you to take responsibility for your well-being and embrace a proactive approach. Focus on maintaining balance and strength in your health routines, as personal empowerment will lead to improvements in your physical and emotional health.

Angel Number 8282

Primary Number: 8 (Financial success, confidence)

Secondary Number: 2 (Diplomacy, cooperation)

Analysis: 8282 combines the energies of material and financial success (8) with the qualities of diplomacy and cooperation (2). This number encourages finding balance between achieving material goals and maintaining harmonious relationships.

1. Love:

In love, 8282 emphasizes the importance of balance and cooperation in relationships. If you're single, this number suggests that finding harmony within yourself will attract a balanced and fulfilling partnership. For those in relationships, 8282 encourages both partners to maintain a cooperative and diplomatic approach to nurture the relationship.

2. Finance/Employment:

In finance or employment, 8282 signals that finding balance between material success and collaboration will lead to financial growth. Focus on cooperative efforts in your career or financial ventures, as partnerships will enhance your ability to achieve success.

3. Health:

For health, 8282 encourages balance in all aspects of your well-being. Pay attention to both physical health and emotional harmony, as maintaining a cooperative approach in relationships and self-care will lead to overall well-being.

Angel Number 8383

Primary Number: 8 (Karma, material wealth)

Secondary Number: 3 (Creativity, self-expression)

Analysis: With 8383, the karmic lessons and focus on material wealth (8) are interwoven with creativity and self-expression (3). It suggests that your material and spiritual pursuits should be creatively aligned, expressing your true self in your quest for abundance.

1. Love:

In love, 8383 highlights the importance of creativity and self-expression in relationships. If you're single, this number encourages you to embrace your unique qualities and express them confidently in romantic pursuits. For those in relationships, 8383 suggests that creative self-expression will deepen the bond between partners and bring joy to the relationship.

2. Finance/Employment:

In finance or employment, 8383 signals that your creative ideas and self-expression will lead to material abundance. Focus on using your talents to manifest financial success, and trust that your innovative approach will bring positive outcomes.

3. Health:

For health, 8383 encourages you to use creative outlets and self-expression as a means to enhance your well-being. Engaging in artistic activities or other forms of creativity will support your emotional and mental health, leading to overall vitality.

Angel Number 8484

Primary Number: 8 (Achievement, efficiency)

Secondary Number: 4 (Stability, practicality)

Analysis: Angel number 8484 signifies a period of achievement and efficiency (8) that requires a solid and practical approach (4). This sequence calls for building a stable foundation to support your ambitious goals.

1. Love:

In love, 8484 suggests the need for stability and structure within relationships. If you're single, this number encourages you to seek a partner who values commitment and long-term stability. For those in relationships, 8484 emphasizes the importance of creating a solid foundation for the relationship, ensuring its long-term success.

2. Finance/Employment:

In finance or employment, 8484 signals that hard work, discipline, and a structured approach will lead to material success. Focus on building a stable foundation for your financial goals, and stay persistent in your efforts to achieve long-term prosperity.

3. Health:

For health, 8484 encourages you to establish a disciplined and structured approach to maintaining your well-being. Creating consistent health routines and focusing on stability will lead to lasting improvements in your physical and emotional health.

Angel Number 8585

Primary Number: 8 (Wealth, material freedom)

Secondary Number: 5 (Change, freedom)

Analysis: In 8585, the pursuit of wealth and material freedom (8) is coupled with a desire for change and personal freedom (5). This number encourages embracing transformative experiences to achieve financial and personal independence.

1. Love:

In love, 8585 emphasizes the importance of personal freedom and embracing change in relationships. If you're single, this number suggests that new romantic opportunities will arise when you embrace your independence and seek adventure. For those in relationships, 8585 encourages both partners to embrace changes that promote growth and personal freedom.

2. Finance/Employment:

In finance or employment, 8585 signals that embracing change and adapting to new opportunities will lead to financial freedom and material success. Stay flexible in your approach to career and financial goals, as this will lead to prosperous outcomes.

3. Health:

For health, 8585 encourages you to embrace changes in your health routines that promote personal freedom and well-being. Be open to new methods of self-care that align with your evolving lifestyle, and trust that these changes will lead to improved health.

Angel Number 8686

Primary Number: 8 (Prosperity, empowerment)

Secondary Number: 6 (Family, responsibility)

Analysis: 8686 suggests a focus on prosperity and empowerment (8) while also attending to family responsibilities and domestic harmony (6). It's a reminder to balance your drive for success with your duties and relationships at home.

1. Love:

In love, 8686 emphasizes the importance of balancing emotional nurturing with material stability. If you're single, this number encourages you to seek a partner who is both emotionally supportive and grounded in practical life. For those in relationships, 8686 suggests focusing on creating a secure and stable environment while nurturing emotional bonds.

2. Finance/Employment:

In finance or employment, 8686 signals that your efforts to balance nurturing relationships and material success will lead to financial abundance. Focus on creating a stable foundation for your financial goals while also maintaining strong relationships in your professional life.

3. Health:

For health, 8686 encourages you to nurture your well-being by balancing emotional and material stability. Ensure that your physical health routines are supported by emotional care, creating a balanced approach to long-term health and vitality.

Angel Number 8787

Primary Number: 8 (Authority, personal power) *Secondary Number: 7* (Spiritual development, introspection) *Analysis:* 8787 brings together personal power and authority (8) with spiritual development and introspection (7). This sequence indicates a phase where achieving material goals is aligned with spiritual growth and self-discovery.

Analysis: Angel number 8787 merges personal authority and empowerment (8) with spiritual growth and introspection (7). It signifies a phase where material success is intricately tied to your spiritual journey and self-discovery.

1. Love:

In love, 8787 suggests that spiritual development and personal empowerment will enhance your relationships. If you're single, this number encourages you to focus on your spiritual growth before seeking romantic connections. For those in relationships, 8787 emphasizes the importance of personal growth and spiritual development within the partnership.

2. Finance/Employment:

In finance or employment, 8787 signals that aligning your personal power and spiritual development will lead to financial success. Trust in your spiritual path and use your personal authority to make decisions that lead to material abundance.

3. Health:

For health, 8787 encourages you to focus on spiritual practices that support your physical and emotional well-being. Aligning your spiritual growth with personal empowerment will lead to improvements in your overall health.

Angel Number 8989

Primary Number: 8 (Abundance, self-reliance)

Secondary Number: 9 (Humanitarianism, endings)

Analysis: In 8989, the themes of abundance and self-reliance (8) meet the energies of humanitarianism and the completion of cycles (9). This number sequence suggests that your material success will play a significant role in broader humanitarian efforts or mark the end of a major life phase, leading to a new beginning.

1. Love:

In love, 8989 highlights the completion of significant life phases and the start of new beginnings. If you're single, this number suggests that you are finishing an emotional healing process and preparing for a new, fulfilling relationship. For those in relationships, 8989 encourages both partners to focus on humanitarian efforts and to embrace new chapters in their shared journey.

2. Finance/Employment:

In finance or employment, 8989 signals the completion of a major project or financial goal, followed by the start of new opportunities. This number encourages you to use your material success to contribute to humanitarian causes, as this will lead to even greater fulfillment.

3. Health:

For health, 8989 suggests that you are completing a significant healing process and preparing for transformation. Focus on maintaining balance in your physical and emotional health, while also considering how your well-being contributes to the greater good.

Angel Number 9191

Primary Number: 9 (Completion, humanitarianism)

Secondary Number: 1 (New beginnings, leadership)

Analysis: Angel number 9191 signifies the culmination of a significant phase or project (9), coupled with the excitement of new beginnings (1). This sequence suggests you're closing one important chapter and embarking on a new journey with leadership and initiative.

1. Love:

In love, 9191 signals the end of an important chapter and the beginning of new opportunities. If you're single, this number suggests that you are ready to start a new relationship after completing a phase of personal growth. For those in relationships, 9191 encourages both partners to embrace new beginnings while celebrating the completion of shared goals.

2. Finance/Employment:

In finance or employment, 9191 signals that you are finishing a significant phase in your career and preparing for new beginnings. This number encourages you to take leadership in your new ventures while reflecting on your accomplishments.

3. Health:

For health, 9191 encourages you to complete any ongoing health projects or routines and embrace new approaches to your well-being. Focus on releasing old patterns and starting fresh in your health journey.

Angel Number 9292

Primary Number: 9 (Universal love, spiritual awakening)

Secondary Number: 2 (Harmony, partnerships)

Analysis: 9292 blends the energies of universal love and spiritual enlightenment (9) with harmony and partnerships (2). It encourages you to embrace spiritual growth while fostering cooperative and harmonious relationships.

1. Love:

In love, 9292 emphasizes the importance of spiritual growth and harmonious partnerships. If you're single, this number encourages you to seek a partner who supports your spiritual awakening. For those in relationships, 9292 suggests focusing on deepening your spiritual connection within the partnership.

2. Finance/Employment:

In finance or employment, 9292 signals that spiritual growth and harmonious cooperation will lead to success. Focus on creating balanced partnerships in your career while staying aligned with your spiritual values.

3. Health:

For health, 9292 encourages you to seek balance between your physical health and spiritual well-being. Engaging in practices that nurture both aspects will lead to overall health improvements.

Angel Number 9393

Primary Number: 9 (Philanthropy, endings)

Secondary Number: 3 (Creativity, communication)

Analysis: Angel number 9393 combines the energy of philanthropy and the closure of life cycles (9) with creativity and effective communication (3). This number calls for using your creative talents in service of others, especially as one phase of your life comes to a close.

1. Love:

In love, 9393 emphasizes the importance of creativity and compassionate communication in relationships. If you're single, this number encourages you to express your true self creatively in your romantic pursuits. For those in relationships, 9393 suggests that open communication and compassion will strengthen the bond between partners.

2. Finance/Employment:

In finance or employment, 9393 signals that using your creative talents and effective communication will lead to success. This number encourages you to focus on completing important projects that align with your humanitarian values.

3. Health:

For health, 9393 encourages you to express your emotions creatively and communicate openly with others. Focusing on creative outlets and compassionate connections will enhance your overall well-being.

Angel Number 9494

Primary Number: 9 (Spiritual enlightenment, altruism)

Secondary Number: 4 (Stability, pragmatism)

Analysis: In 9494, the pursuit of spiritual enlightenment and altruism (9) is grounded by the need for stability and practicality (4). This sequence suggests a balance between high spiritual ideals and the practical aspects of life.

1. Love:

In love, 9494 suggests that spiritual enlightenment and practical stability are key to fulfilling relationships. If you're single, this number encourages you to seek a partner who values both spiritual growth and stability. For those in relationships, 9494 emphasizes the importance of balancing spiritual ideals with practical actions to build a strong foundation.

2. Finance/Employment:

In finance or employment, 9494 signals that balancing spiritual enlightenment with practical efforts will lead to success. This number encourages you to focus on creating a stable foundation for your financial and career goals.

3. Health:

For health, 9494 encourages you to integrate spiritual practices with practical health routines. Focusing on both aspects will lead to long-term stability in your physical and emotional health.

Angel Number 9595

Primary Number: 9 (Service to humanity, completion)

Secondary Number: 5 (Adventure, change)

Analysis: 9595 signifies a period of service to humanity and the completion of significant life chapters (9), combined with a longing for adventure and change (5). It encourages embracing transformative experiences that benefit others.

1. Love:

In love, 9595 suggests that embracing change and focusing on humanitarian efforts will bring fulfillment in relationships. If you're single, this number encourages you to focus on personal growth and humanitarian pursuits before seeking romantic connections. For those in relationships, 9595 emphasizes the importance of change and service to others in strengthening the bond.

2. Finance/Employment:

In finance or employment, 9595 signals that significant changes and humanitarian efforts will lead to career success. This number encourages you to embrace new opportunities that align with your higher purpose and contribute to the greater good.

3. Health:

For health, 9595 encourages you to embrace changes that promote both physical well-being and service to others. Focusing on humanitarian efforts and personal transformation will enhance your overall health.

Angel Number 9696

Primary Number: 9 (Global consciousness, wisdom)

Secondary Number: 6 (Family, responsibility)

Analysis: Angel number 9696 brings together the wisdom of global consciousness (9) with the nurturing energy of family and domestic responsibilities (6). It's a reminder to balance your global and spiritual aspirations with your personal and familial duties.

1. Love:

In love, 9696 emphasizes the importance of balancing global consciousness with family responsibilities. If you're single, this number encourages you to seek a partner who shares your humanitarian values and commitment to family. For those in relationships, 9696 suggests focusing on nurturing both family bonds and global service.

2. Finance/Employment:

In finance or employment, 9696 signals that balancing your global aspirations with family responsibilities will lead to success. This number encourages you to focus on both your professional and personal responsibilities, ensuring that neither is neglected.

3. Health:

For health, 9696 encourages you to focus on both personal well-being and family harmony. Balancing your health routines with family responsibilities will lead to overall well-being.

Angel Number 9797

Primary Number: 9 (Spiritual laws, karmic conclusions)

Secondary Number: 7 (Inner wisdom, introspection)

Analysis: 9797 indicates a phase of understanding spiritual laws and reaching karmic conclusions (9), enhanced by inner wisdom and introspection (7). This sequence suggests deep self-reflection and spiritual understanding are key to navigating this phase.

1. Love:

In love, 9797 suggests that spiritual laws and karmic conclusions are influencing your relationships. If you're single, this number encourages you to focus on inner wisdom and karmic lessons before entering new relationships. For those in relationships, 9797 emphasizes the importance of spiritual growth and karmic balance in maintaining a healthy relationship.

2. Finance/Employment:

In finance or employment, 9797 signals that understanding spiritual laws and karmic lessons will lead to success. This number encourages you to reflect on past experiences and use them to guide your career or financial decisions.

3. Health:

For health, 9797 encourages you to focus on spiritual practices that enhance your inner wisdom and overall well-being. Engaging in self-reflection and understanding karmic lessons will lead to improvements in your health.

Angel Number 9898

Primary Number: 9 (Spiritual fulfillment, humanitarian goals)

Secondary Number: 8 (Material abundance, leadership)

Analysis: In 9898, the themes of spiritual fulfillment and humanitarian goals (9) are paired with material abundance and leadership skills (8). This number sequence suggests using your material success and leadership abilities to achieve spiritual and humanitarian objectives.

1. Love:

In love, 9898 suggests that your material success will contribute to your humanitarian goals and relationship fulfillment. If you're single, this number encourages you to focus on building a strong foundation for personal growth and humanitarian efforts before seeking a relationship. For those in relationships, 9898 emphasizes the importance of using material abundance to contribute to the greater good.

2. Finance/Employment:

In finance or employment, 9898 signals that your material success and leadership skills will play a significant role in achieving humanitarian goals. This number encourages you to focus on using your financial and professional success to contribute to global causes.

3. Health:

For health, 9898 encourages you to focus on both material well-being and spiritual fulfillment. Balancing physical health routines with humanitarian efforts will lead to overall well-being and fulfillment.

26

List with the Basic Mirrored Angel Numbers

1 221-9119

Angel Number 1221

Primary Number: 2 (Harmony, relationships)

Secondary Number: 1 (New beginnings, independence)

Category: Confirming

Analysis: Angel number 1221 brings a message of harmony (2) in relationships, supported by new beginnings (1). This sequence encourages focusing on maintaining balance in relationships while embracing personal independence.

1. Love:

   In love, 1221 suggests that balance and harmony are key to successful relationships. If you're single, this number encourages you to focus on self-love and personal growth, which will prepare you for a new romantic chapter. For those in relationships, it emphasizes the importance of maintaining balance and respecting each other's independence.

2. Finance/Employment:

   In finance or employment, 1221 indicates that cooperation with colleagues and taking initiative will lead to success. It's a time to balance your independent projects with teamwork, as this will create a productive and harmonious work environment.

3. Health:

For health, 1221 encourages creating harmony in your daily routines. Balance self-care with new health habits, ensuring you're nurturing both your physical and mental well-being. Focus on maintaining your sacral chakra (linked to the number 2), which governs emotional balance and relationships.

Angel Number 1331

Primary Number: 3 (Creativity, expression)

Secondary Number: 1 (New beginnings, independence)

Category: Confirming

Analysis: Angel number 1331 emphasizes creative self-expression (3) and new beginnings (1). This sequence encourages embracing your creativity while stepping into new opportunities with confidence.

1. Love:

In love, 1331 suggests that expressing yourself openly will lead to new and exciting romantic opportunities. If you're single, this number encourages you to show your true self to attract the right partner. For those in relationships, it emphasizes the importance of creativity and communication in maintaining a fresh and fulfilling connection.

2. Finance/Employment:

In finance or employment, 1331 highlights the need for creative problem-solving and innovation. It's a time to use your unique talents and ideas to create new career opportunities or projects that can lead to success.

3. Health:

For health, 1331 encourages adopting creative approaches to your well-being, such as trying new fitness routines or engaging in artistic activities for mental health. Focus on nurturing your solar plexus chakra (linked to the number 3), which governs self-confidence and personal power.

Angel Number 1441

Primary Number: 4 (Stability, structure)

Secondary Number: 1 (New beginnings, independence)

Category: Supportive

Analysis: Angel number 1441 emphasizes the importance of building a solid foundation (4) while embracing new beginnings (1). This sequence encourages you to take practical steps toward creating stability in your life while pursuing new ventures.

1. Love:

   In love, 1441 suggests that stability is key to fostering a strong relationship. If you're single, this number indicates that focusing on creating a secure emotional foundation will help attract a lasting partnership. For those in relationships, it emphasizes the importance of maintaining stability while exploring new experiences together.

2. Finance/Employment:

   In finance or employment, 1441 encourages focusing on building a stable career path or financial foundation. It's a time to take practical steps toward your goals while being open to new professional opportunities.

3. Health:

   For health, 1441 advises creating a structured and consistent routine to promote well-being. Establish healthy habits and focus on maintaining balance. This number connects with your root chakra (linked to the number 4), which governs physical stability and grounding.

Angel Number 1551

Primary Number: 5 (Change, freedom)
Secondary Number: 1 (New beginnings, independence)
Category: Advisory
Analysis: Angel number 1551 brings a message of major change (5) and new beginnings (1). This sequence encourages embracing transformation and stepping into new opportunities with confidence.

1. Love:
   In love, 1551 suggests that changes are on the horizon. If you're single, this number signals the potential for a new and exciting relationship. For those in relationships, it encourages embracing change and growth together to strengthen your bond.
2. Finance/Employment:
   In finance or employment, 1551 indicates that significant changes may be approaching. It's time to take risks and embrace new career paths or financial strategies that will lead to personal growth and success.
3. Health:
   For health, 1551 encourages adopting new habits and routines that promote positive change. Focus on physical and mental well-being by breaking free from old patterns. This number resonates with the throat chakra (linked to the number 5), which governs communication and self-expression.

Angel Number 1661
Primary Number: 6 (Nurturing, responsibility)
Secondary Number: 1 (New beginnings, independence)
Category: Advisory
Analysis: Angel number 1661 emphasizes the need for nurturing and responsibility (6) while embracing new beginnings (1). This sequence encourages you to take care of your personal relationships and responsibilities while stepping into new opportunities.

1. Love:

   In love, 1661 suggests that nurturing and care are essential for building a strong relationship. If you're single, this number indicates that focusing on self-love and care will prepare you for a new relationship. For those in relationships, it emphasizes the importance of nurturing your bond while embracing new experiences together.

2. Finance/Employment:

   In finance or employment, 1661 encourages taking responsibility for your career or financial situation while being open to new opportunities. It's a time to balance nurturing existing projects with pursuing new goals.

3. Health:

   For health, 1661 advises taking responsibility for your well-being by focusing on self-care and nurturing routines. Establish healthy habits that support your physical and mental health. This number connects with the heart chakra (linked to the number 6), which governs love, compassion, and healing.

Angel Number 1771

Primary Number: 7 (Spirituality, inner wisdom)

Secondary Number: 1 (New beginnings, independence)

Category: Guiding

Analysis: Angel number 1771 encourages spiritual growth (7) alongside new beginnings (1). This sequence suggests a time of personal development and spiritual awakening as you embrace new opportunities in your life.

1. Love:

   In love, 1771 suggests that spiritual connection is vital for a strong relationship. If you're single, this number encourages you to seek partners who share your spiritual values. For those in relationships, it emphasizes deepening your spiritual bond and growing together on a spiritual level.

2. Finance/Employment:

In finance or employment, 1771 signals that spiritual insights and intuition will guide you toward success. It's a time to trust your inner wisdom as you embark on new projects or career paths.

3. Health:

For health, 1771 encourages incorporating spiritual practices such as meditation or mindfulness into your daily routine. Focus on maintaining your crown chakra (linked to the number 7), which governs spiritual connection and enlightenment.

Angel Number 1881

Primary Number: 8 (Abundance, power)

Secondary Number: 1 (New beginnings, independence)

Category: Guiding

Analysis: Angel number 1881 combines the energy of abundance and personal power (8) with new beginnings (1). This sequence encourages you to take charge of your life and manifest success through new opportunities.

1. Love:

In love, 1881 suggests that personal empowerment will lead to new and fulfilling relationships. If you're single, this number encourages you to focus on self-confidence and attracting a partner who values your strength. For those in relationships, it emphasizes building a partnership based on mutual respect and personal growth.

2. Finance/Employment:

In finance or employment, 1881 indicates that abundance and success are within reach. It's time to take the initiative and pursue new career opportunities that align with your personal goals and ambitions.

3. Health:

For health, 1881 encourages focusing on personal empowerment and taking control of your well-being. Establish routines that promote physical strength and mental resilience. This number connects with the solar plexus chakra (linked to the number 8), which governs personal power and confidence.

Angel Number 1991

Primary Number: 9 (Completion, humanitarianism)

Secondary Number: 1 (New beginnings, independence)

Category: Advisory

Analysis: Angel number 1991 signifies the completion of a significant life phase (9) and the beginning of a new chapter (1). This sequence encourages you to embrace new beginnings while contributing to the greater good.

1. Love:

In love, 1991 suggests that one chapter of your romantic life is ending, making way for new beginnings. If you're single, this number indicates that healing from past relationships will prepare you for new love. For those in relationships, it encourages moving forward with a renewed sense of purpose and connection.

2. Finance/Employment:

In finance or employment, 1991 signals that you are wrapping up a significant project or phase in your career, allowing you to start fresh. It's a time to focus on new opportunities that align with your values and long-term goals.

3. Health:

For health, 1991 encourages completing old health routines that no longer serve you and embracing new practices that promote well-being. Focus on nurturing your crown chakra (linked to the number 9), which governs spiritual connection and universal love.

Angel Number 2112

Primary Number: 1 (New beginnings, independence)
Secondary Number: 2 (Harmony, relationships)
Category: Confirming
Analysis: Angel number 2112 highlights the importance of creating balance (2) while pursuing new beginnings (1). This sequence encourages you to focus on building harmonious relationships while asserting your independence in new endeavors.

1. Love:
   In love, 2112 suggests that a fresh start may be on the horizon, either by improving an existing relationship or attracting a new one. It emphasizes maintaining harmony while expressing your individual needs.
2. Finance/Employment:
   In finance or employment, 2112 encourages teamwork and collaboration while taking the lead in your projects. Balancing cooperative efforts with independent initiatives will lead to success.
3. Health:
   For health, 2112 advises creating balance in your daily routines while introducing new practices for personal well-being. Focus on your sacral chakra (linked to the number 2), which governs emotional health and relationships, alongside the root chakra (linked to the number 1), which ensures grounding and vitality.

Angel Number 2332

Primary Number: 3 (Creativity, expression)
Secondary Number: 2 (Harmony, relationships)

Category: Confirming

Analysis: Angel number 2332 emphasizes creative expression (3) within harmonious relationships (2). This sequence encourages you to use your creativity to foster joy and balance in your connections with others.

1. **Love:**

   In love, 2332 suggests that open communication and creative expression will strengthen your relationships. If you're single, it encourages you to express your true self to attract a partner who appreciates your individuality.

2. **Finance/Employment:**

   In finance or employment, 2332 signals that your creativity and teamwork will bring success. Use your innovative ideas to foster collaboration and build harmonious work relationships.

3. **Health:**

   For health, 2332 advises balancing emotional well-being with creative outlets. Focus on your throat chakra (linked to the number 3) for communication and self-expression, alongside the sacral chakra (linked to the number 2), which governs emotional balance and relationships.

Angel Number 2442

Primary Number: 4 (Stability, structure)
Secondary Number: 2 (Harmony, relationships)
Category: Supportive

Analysis: Angel number 2442 brings a message of stability (4) and harmony (2), encouraging you to create a solid foundation in your life and relationships. This sequence emphasizes the importance of structure in maintaining balance.

1. **Love:**

   In love, 2442 suggests that building a stable and secure foundation will lead to a harmonious relationship. If you're single, this number encourages you to focus on creating stability in your personal life, which will attract a balanced partnership.

2. **Finance/Employment**:

In finance or employment, 2442 signals that a structured and organized approach will lead to success. Focus on creating stability in your work environment while fostering cooperation with colleagues.

3. **Health**:

For health, 2442 advises establishing a consistent and balanced routine to promote long-term well-being. Focus on grounding through the root chakra (linked to the number 4) while maintaining emotional harmony through the sacral chakra (linked to the number 2).

Angel Number 2552

Primary Number: 5 (Change, freedom)
Secondary Number: 2 (Harmony, relationships)
Category: Advisory

Analysis: Angel number 2552 highlights a time of change (5) and growth within relationships (2). This sequence encourages you to embrace new opportunities while maintaining balance in your connections.

1. **Love**:

In love, 2552 suggests that changes are coming, and you should remain adaptable. If you're single, this number indicates that new relationships are on the horizon. For those in relationships, it encourages embracing changes together to grow as a couple.

2. **Finance/Employment**:

In finance or employment, 2552 signals that significant changes are likely. It's a time to adapt to new career opportunities while maintaining harmony with your coworkers and partners.

3. **Health:**

For health, 2552 encourages you to embrace new routines or treatments that will promote positive change. Focus on balancing your throat chakra (linked to the number 5), which governs communication and self-expression, alongside the sacral chakra (linked to the number 2) for emotional harmony.

Angel Number 2662

Primary Number: 6 (Nurturing, responsibility)
Secondary Number: 2 (Harmony, relationships)
Category: Advisory

Analysis: Angel number 2662 emphasizes nurturing (6) relationships (2) with balance and responsibility. This sequence encourages you to care for those around you while maintaining harmony in your personal life.

1. **Love:**

In love, 2662 suggests that nurturing and responsibility are key to a successful relationship. If you're single, focus on self-care and emotional balance to attract a healthy partnership. For those in relationships, this number encourages you to nurture your connection while maintaining harmony.

2. **Finance/Employment:**

In finance or employment, 2662 signals that taking responsibility for your work and nurturing relationships with colleagues will lead to success. It's a time to focus on creating a balanced and supportive work environment.

3. **Health:**

For health, 2662 advises nurturing your body and mind while maintaining balance in your daily routines. Focus on supporting your heart chakra (linked to the number 6) for emotional healing and love, alongside the sacral chakra (linked to the number 2) for emotional harmony.

Angel Number 2772

Primary Number: 7 (Spirituality, inner wisdom)
Secondary Number: 2 (Harmony, relationships)
Category: Guiding

Analysis: Angel number 2772 encourages spiritual growth (7) alongside building harmonious relationships (2). This sequence suggests a time of introspection and spiritual development while nurturing meaningful connections.

1. **Love**:

   In love, 2772 indicates that spiritual growth will enhance your relationships. If you're single, this number encourages you to seek partners who align with your spiritual values. For those in relationships, it emphasizes the importance of growing spiritually together.

2. **Finance/Employment**:

   In finance or employment, 2772 signals that your spiritual insights and teamwork will guide you toward success. It's a time to focus on aligning your career goals with your inner wisdom and maintaining balance with your colleagues.

3. **Health**:

   For health, 2772 encourages incorporating spiritual practices like meditation into your routine to promote emotional balance. Focus on nurturing your crown chakra (linked to the number 7), which governs spiritual connection, alongside the sacral chakra (linked to the number 2) for emotional harmony.

Angel Number 2882

Primary Number: 8 (Abundance, power)
Secondary Number: 2 (Harmony, relationships)

Category: Guiding

Analysis: Angel number 2882 brings a message of abundance (8) and harmony (2). This sequence encourages you to focus on creating balance in your relationships while manifesting success and prosperity.

1. **Love:**

   In love, 2882 suggests that achieving balance in your relationships will bring emotional abundance. If you're single, this number indicates that harmony and balance will attract a fulfilling relationship. For those in relationships, it encourages working together to create a prosperous and harmonious future.

2. **Finance/Employment**:

   In finance or employment, 2882 signals that balance and cooperation will lead to material success. It's a time to focus on building harmonious partnerships that will bring financial abundance and growth.

3. **Health:**

   For health, 2882 advises creating balance in your physical and emotional well-being to promote long-term health. Focus on supporting your solar plexus chakra (linked to the number 8) for personal empowerment and abundance, alongside the sacral chakra (linked to the number 2) for emotional balance.

Angel Number 2992

Primary Number: 9 (Completion, humanitarianism)

Secondary Number: 2 (Harmony, relationships)

Category: Advisory

Analysis: Angel number 2992 emphasizes completion (9) and harmony (2), suggesting that your humanitarian efforts will bring balance and fulfillment in relationships. This sequence encourages you to focus on completing significant life goals while nurturing meaningful connections.

1. **Love:**

   In love, 2992 suggests that a chapter of your romantic life may be coming to a close, making way for new beginnings. It encourages you to focus on maintaining harmony in your relationships while embracing change and personal growth.

2. **Finance/Employment:**

   In finance or employment, 2992 signals that completing a significant project or career phase will lead to new opportunities. It's a time to focus on balancing your humanitarian goals with your financial responsibilities.

3. **Health:**

   For health, 2992 advises focusing on completing old health routines that no longer serve you and embracing new practices that promote balance and well-being. Focus on supporting your crown chakra (linked to the number 9) for spiritual fulfillment, alongside the sacral chakra (linked to the number 2) for emotional balance.

Angel Number 3113

Primary Number: 1 (New beginnings, leadership)
Secondary Number: 3 (Creativity, communication)
Category: Supportive
Analysis: Angel number 3113 encourages you to take the lead (1) in creative pursuits and self-expression (3). This sequence signifies the importance of using your creative skills to initiate new beginnings and communicate your ideas with confidence.

1. Love:

   In love, 3113 suggests that taking the initiative to communicate openly is key. If you're single, this number encourages you to express your true feelings and desires, which may lead to new romantic opportunities. For those in relationships, it's a reminder to lead with honesty and creativity to strengthen your connection.

2. Finance/Employment:

In finance or employment, 3113 emphasizes the need to take the lead in projects that allow for creativity and innovation. This is a great time to step into leadership roles or initiate new ideas that will showcase your talents and drive success in your career.

3. Health:

For health, 3113 encourages you to lead by example, especially when it comes to creating a healthy and balanced lifestyle. Embrace new habits that allow for both mental and physical well-being, and use your creativity to find enjoyable ways to stay active and healthy. Focus on your solar plexus chakra (linked to the number 3), which governs personal power and self-confidence.

Angel Number 3223

Primary Number: 2 (Harmony, relationships)

Secondary Number: 3 (Creativity, communication)

Category: Confirming

Analysis: Angel number 3223 highlights the importance of harmony (2) in relationships while fostering creativity and communication (3). This sequence encourages balancing your emotional connections with an open, creative approach.

1. Love:

In love, 3223 suggests that open communication and creative expressions of affection will bring harmony to relationships. If you're single, it's time to embrace new ways of meeting people or expressing your feelings. For those in relationships, focus on maintaining balance by communicating openly and creatively.

2. Finance/Employment:
   In finance or employment, 3223 encourages collaboration with others while bringing your creativity into the workplace. It's a good time to work on projects that allow for teamwork, where communication and innovative ideas will lead to success.

3. Health:
   For health, 3223 emphasizes the importance of balancing emotional and physical well-being through creative outlets such as art or communication. Maintaining harmony in your relationships can also contribute to your overall health. Focus on your sacral chakra (linked to the number 2), which governs emotional balance and creative expression.

Angel Number 3443

Primary Number: 3 (Creativity, expression)
Secondary Number: 4 (Stability, structure)
Category: Confirming
Analysis: Angel number 3443 emphasizes the importance of bringing structure (4) to your creative projects (3). This sequence suggests that while creativity is vital, establishing a stable foundation for your ideas is equally important.

1. Love:
   In love, 3443 encourages you to express your feelings openly but also to build a stable foundation for your relationship. If you're single, seek a partner who values both creativity and stability. In relationships, focus on maintaining open communication while ensuring a sense of security and structure.

2. Finance/Employment:
   In finance or employment, 3443 suggests that it's time to apply creativity in a structured and disciplined manner. Your innovative ideas can lead to success, but they need to be grounded in practical, well-organized plans.

3. Health:

   For health, 3443 advises balancing creativity with discipline. Establish healthy routines that allow for creative expression, such as dance, art, or music. Focus on your heart chakra (linked to the number 4), which governs emotional stability and love for yourself and others.

Angel Number 3553

Primary Number: 3 (Creativity, expression)
Secondary Number: 5 (Change, freedom)
Category: Advisory

Analysis: Angel number 3553 signals a time of creative expression (3) alongside embracing change and freedom (5). It suggests that new opportunities for personal growth may come through creative outlets.

1. Love:

   In love, 3553 encourages you to express yourself freely and openly, while also being open to change. If you're single, it's time to step out of your comfort zone and meet new people. In relationships, this number emphasizes the importance of flexibility and adapting to new dynamics.

2. Finance/Employment:

   In finance or employment, 3553 suggests that changes are on the horizon, especially those that will allow you to use your creativity. This is a time to embrace new opportunities and let go of rigid structures, as new experiences will bring growth.

3. Health:

   For health, 3553 encourages flexibility and exploration of new ways to maintain well-being. Try incorporating creative activities into your daily routine to boost your mental and physical health. Focus on your throat chakra (linked to the number 5), which governs expression and communication.

Angel Number 3663

Primary Number: 3 (Creativity, expression)

Secondary Number: 6 (Balance, nurturing)

Category: Advisory

Analysis: Angel number 3663 combines the creative and expressive energy of 3 with the nurturing and balanced nature of 6. This sequence calls for finding harmony between your creative projects and your responsibilities.

1. Love:

   In love, 3663 emphasizes the need for balance and creativity. If you're single, focus on nurturing yourself while exploring new ways to express love. In relationships, this number suggests that creative efforts to show care and affection will strengthen the bond.

2. Finance/Employment:

   In finance or employment, 3663 encourages balancing creativity with responsibility. It's time to nurture your professional goals while maintaining a focus on creativity. This combination will lead to a more fulfilling career path.

3. Health:

   For health, 3663 highlights the need to nurture yourself creatively. Engage in activities that allow you to express yourself while also maintaining balance in your daily routines. Focus on your third-eye chakra (linked to the number 6), which governs intuition and balance in your emotional and physical health.

Angel Number 3773

Primary Number: 3 (Creativity, expression)

Secondary Number: 7 (Spiritual awakening, introspection)

Category: Guiding

Analysis: Angel number 3773 emphasizes the combination of creative expression (3) with spiritual awakening and introspection (7).

This number suggests that your spiritual journey may be enhanced by exploring creative outlets.

1. Love:

   In love, 3773 encourages you to express your emotions and thoughts creatively while deepening your spiritual connection with your partner. If you're single, this number suggests that pursuing a spiritual path will bring clarity to your love life and help you attract a partner with shared values.

2. Finance/Employment:

   In finance or employment, 3773 suggests that your career path may take a more spiritual direction, possibly involving creative fields. Trust your inner wisdom as you explore new opportunities that allow you to merge your spiritual insights with your creative talents.

3. Health:

   For health, 3773 advises integrating spiritual practices such as meditation, along with creative outlets like writing or art, to maintain emotional and physical well-being. Focus on your crown chakra (linked to the number 7), which governs spiritual connection and enlightenment.

Angel Number 3883

Primary Number: 3 (Creativity, expression)

Secondary Number: 8 (Abundance, power)

Category: Guiding

Analysis: Angel number 3883 blends the energy of creativity (3) with the drive for material abundance (8). This number suggests that expressing your creativity can lead to significant success and prosperity.

1. Love:

   In love, 3883 indicates that expressing yourself creatively and confidently will attract abundance in your relationships. If you're single, this number encourages you to be bold and express your feelings. For those in relationships, focus on nurturing your connection with open communication and creativity to maintain a harmonious bond.

2. Finance/Employment:

In finance or employment, 3883 encourages you to use your creative talents to bring about financial success. This is a time to pursue creative projects with confidence, as they may lead to material prosperity and growth in your career.

3. Health:

For health, 3883 advises using creative approaches to maintain balance and vitality, such as engaging in artistic activities that bring joy and reduce stress. Focus on your solar plexus chakra (linked to the number 8), which governs personal power and physical well-being.

Angel Number 3993

Primary Number: 3 (Creativity, expression)

Secondary Number: 9 (Completion, humanitarianism)

Category: Advisory

Analysis: Angel number 3993 emphasizes the importance of creative expression (3) in completing cycles and contributing to humanitarian causes (9). This number suggests that your creative talents can have a positive impact on the world around you.

1. Love:

In love, 3993 encourages you to bring creative expression into your relationships while also considering the bigger picture of how your partnership impacts others. If you're single, it's time to complete any emotional cycles before moving on to new relationships. In a relationship, this number suggests bringing closure to old issues while focusing on expressing love creatively.

2. Finance/Employment:

In finance or employment, 3993 indicates that your creative efforts may be used for a higher purpose, such as contributing to charitable projects or humanitarian endeavors. Completing ongoing projects will bring a sense of fulfillment and open new doors for success.

3. Health:

For health, 3993 advises focusing on your well-being by engaging in activities that nourish your mind and body, such as creative hobbies. Closing old chapters in your life will also contribute to emotional healing. Focus on your heart chakra (linked to the number 9), which governs compassion, emotional healing, and balance.

Angel Number 4114

Primary Number: 4 (Stability, structure)
Secondary Number: 1 (New beginnings, independence)
Category: Supportive

Analysis: Angel number 4114 combines the stabilizing energy of 4 with the new beginnings represented by 1. This number suggests that creating structure and stability in your life will support the fresh starts you're ready to embrace.

1. **Love:**

In love, 4114 suggests that stability and independence are key for healthy relationships. If you're single, focus on building a solid foundation for yourself before entering a new relationship. For those in relationships, it emphasizes the importance of maintaining stability while encouraging each other's independence.

2. **Finance/Employment:**

In finance or employment, 4114 advises establishing a stable foundation for your career or business while taking bold steps towards new opportunities. This number encourages a balanced approach between practicality and ambition.

3. **Health:**

For health, 4114 encourages building strong and consistent health routines while embracing new practices that improve your overall well-being. Focus on your root chakra (linked to the number 4), which governs physical health, stability, and grounding.

Angel Number 4224

Primary Number: 4 (Stability, foundation)
Secondary Number: 2 (Harmony, relationships)
Category: Supportive
Analysis: Angel number 4224 focuses on building a stable foundation (4) in your relationships (2). This number suggests that finding balance and harmony within your personal connections will create stability in other areas of your life.

1. **Love:**

In love, 4224 encourages you to focus on creating a secure and harmonious relationship. If you're single, this number suggests building strong foundations of self-love and balance before seeking a partner. For those in relationships, it's a reminder to nurture your connection by maintaining stability and balance.

2. **Finance/Employment:**

In finance or employment, 4224 indicates that stable partnerships and cooperation with colleagues will lead to long-term success. Focus on creating balanced work relationships and maintaining a stable financial foundation.

3. **Health:**

   For health, 4224 advises building a stable routine that incorporates balance in all areas of your life. Pay attention to how relationships impact your well-being, and focus on maintaining harmony in your connections. Focus on your sacral chakra (linked to the number 2), which governs emotional health and balance.

Angel Number 4334

Primary Number: 4 (Stability, structure)
Secondary Number: 3 (Creativity, communication)
Category: Supportive

Analysis: Angel number 4334 emphasizes bringing structure and stability (4) to your creative endeavors and communication (3). This number encourages you to use your creativity in a disciplined and structured way to achieve long-term success.

1. **Love:**

   In love, 4334 suggests that communication is key to building a stable and lasting relationship. If you're single, this number encourages you to communicate openly and honestly to establish strong foundations for future relationships. For those in a relationship, focus on maintaining stability while expressing your feelings creatively.

2. **Finance/Employment:**

   In finance or employment, 4334 advises balancing creativity with structure. Use your creative ideas to develop practical plans that lead to success. This is a time to organize your creative projects for long-term financial growth.

3. **Health:**

   For health, 4334 encourages incorporating creative and enjoyable activities into your health routine while maintaining consistency and structure. Focus on your throat chakra (linked to the number 3), which governs communication, creativity, and expression.

Angel Number 4554

Primary Number: 4 (Stability, structure)

Secondary Number: 5 (Change, freedom)

Category: Advisory

Analysis: Angel number 4554 blends the energies of stability (4) and change (5), suggesting that embracing change within a stable framework will lead to growth and success. This number encourages finding balance between maintaining order and embracing new opportunities.

1. **Love:**

   In love, 4554 suggests that stability and change need to coexist for a healthy relationship. If you're single, this number encourages you to stay grounded while being open to new romantic opportunities. For those in relationships, it's a reminder to maintain stability while allowing room for growth and evolution within the relationship.

2. **Finance/Employment:**

   In finance or employment, 4554 indicates that changes in your career or financial situation can be beneficial if approached with a structured plan. Stay grounded while adapting to new opportunities, as this will lead to long-term stability.

3. **Health:**

   For health, 4554 encourages you to embrace new health practices or lifestyle changes while maintaining stability in your routines. Flexibility in your approach will bring long-term benefits. Focus on your solar plexus chakra (linked to the number 5), which governs personal power and adaptability.

Angel Number 4664

Primary Number: 4 (Stability, structure)

Secondary Number: 6 (Nurturing, responsibility)

Category: Advisory

Analysis: Angel number 4664 combines the energies of stability (4) with nurturing and responsibility (6), suggesting that creating a secure and structured environment is essential for nurturing yourself and others.

1. **Love:**

   In love, 4664 encourages building a stable and nurturing relationship. If you're single, this number advises focusing on creating a secure emotional foundation before seeking a partner. For those in relationships, it's a reminder to nurture your connection by providing emotional stability and care.

2. **Finance/Employment:**

   In finance or employment, 4664 advises taking a responsible and structured approach to your career or finances. Focus on creating stability while ensuring that your actions are aligned with caring for yourself and those around you.

3. **Health:**

   For health, 4664 emphasizes the importance of creating a stable routine that nurtures your physical and emotional well-being. Engage in activities that support your long-term health and foster emotional balance. Focus on your heart chakra (linked to the number 6), which governs love, care, and emotional health.

Angel Number 4774

Primary Number: 4 (Stability, structure)

Secondary Number: 7 (Spiritual awakening, introspection)

Category: Guiding

Analysis: Angel number 4774 highlights the need for a stable foundation (4) to support spiritual growth and introspection (7). This number encourages you to create a balanced and structured life that allows space for spiritual exploration.

1. **Love**:

   In love, 4774 suggests that stability and spiritual connection are key to a strong relationship. If you're single, focus on finding a partner who supports your spiritual growth. For those in relationships, this number emphasizes building a stable relationship while exploring deeper spiritual connections together.

2. **Finance/Employment**:

   In finance or employment, 4774 advises combining practicality and structure with spiritual insights. Use your inner wisdom to guide your career decisions, while staying grounded and focused on building a secure financial foundation.

3. **Health**:

   For health, 4774 encourages creating a stable routine that supports both physical and spiritual well-being. Engage in practices like meditation or yoga to maintain balance and vitality. Focus on your crown chakra (linked to the number 7), which governs spiritual awareness and enlightenment.

Angel Number 4884

Primary Number: 4 (Stability, structure)
Secondary Number: 8 (Abundance, power)
Category: Guiding

Analysis: Angel number 4884 emphasizes the importance of building a stable foundation (4) to attract abundance and success (8). This number suggests that through discipline and structured effort, you can manifest material and financial growth.

1. **Love**:

   In love, 4884 suggests that stability and abundance are key to a harmonious relationship. If you're single, this number advises building a solid emotional foundation before seeking a partner. For those in relationships, it highlights the importance of creating a stable and supportive partnership that encourages growth and abundance for both partners.

2. **Finance/Employment:**

In finance or employment, 4884 encourages you to focus on structured efforts and discipline to achieve financial success. This number signifies that hard work and careful planning will lead to material abundance and career advancement.

3. **Health:**

For health, 4884 emphasizes creating a stable and consistent routine to promote well-being and vitality. Engage in practices that support long-term health, such as exercise, balanced nutrition, and rest. Focus on your root chakra (linked to the number 4), which governs physical health and stability.

Angel Number 4994

Primary Number: 4 (Stability, structure)
Secondary Number: 9 (Completion, higher purpose)
Category: Advisory

Analysis: Angel number 4994 signifies that stability (4) is needed as you approach the completion of a major cycle or phase in your life (9). This number encourages you to stay grounded and focused as you transition into a new chapter with a higher purpose.

1. **Love:**

In love, 4994 suggests that a stable foundation is essential to completing a significant phase in your relationship. If you're single, focus on building stability in your life before seeking a relationship. For those in relationships, this number may indicate that an important chapter is coming to an end, and it's time to embrace new growth together.

2. **Finance/Employment**:

   In finance or employment, 4994 advises completing significant projects or reaching important goals with a structured approach. This number indicates that through discipline and careful planning, you can bring an important financial or career cycle to a successful conclusion.

3. **Health**:

   For health, 4994 encourages you to establish a stable health routine as you move toward completing a major life phase. Stay grounded and consistent in your efforts to improve your well-being. Focus on your third eye chakra (linked to the number 9), which governs insight and higher wisdom, helping you to align your health practices with your life's purpose.

Angel Number 5115

Primary Number: 1 (New beginnings, independence)
Secondary Number: 5 (Change, adaptability)
Category: Supportive

Analysis: Angel number 5115 suggests that new beginnings (1) are supported by change and adaptability (5). This number encourages you to embrace change while maintaining your independence and confidence. It's a sign that shifts in your life are meant to lead you towards a fresh start.

1. **Love**:

   In love, 5115 suggests that new beginnings are coming, especially if you've been through a period of change or instability. If you're single, this number signifies that embracing personal change will open doors to new romantic possibilities. For those in relationships, it highlights the need for both partners to adapt to changes while maintaining a sense of individuality.

2. **Finance/Employment:**

   In finance or employment, 5115 indicates that embracing

change will lead to new opportunities. Whether it's starting a new project or making career shifts, adaptability and taking initiative will bring long-term success. Stay open to evolving your strategies to achieve your financial goals.

3. **Health:**

For health, 5115 encourages you to adapt your routines and take initiative in your well-being. Change may be necessary to boost your health, whether it's adjusting your diet, exercise, or mental health habits. Focus on your solar plexus chakra (linked to number 5) to foster flexibility and personal empowerment during this transformative time.

Angel Number 5225

Primary Number: 2 (Harmony, relationships)
Secondary Number: 5 (Change, freedom)
Category: Confirming

Analysis: Angel number 5225 focuses on maintaining harmony (2) while navigating through changes (5). This number is a reminder to seek balance and cooperation, especially as your circumstances shift. It's a time to foster partnerships and adapt with grace.

1. **Love:**

In love, 5225 suggests that while change is inevitable, harmony and understanding in relationships are crucial. If you're single, this number encourages you to find balance within yourself before entering a new relationship. For those in relationships, it emphasizes the need to stay adaptable while maintaining emotional harmony.

2. **Finance/Employment:**

In finance or employment, 5225 advises balancing teamwork and cooperation with adaptability. This is a time when working harmoniously with others while being flexible in your approach will lead to success. Changes in your job or financial situation will require careful collaboration and adaptability.

3. **Health**:

For health, 5225 suggests finding a balance between maintaining routine and adapting to new health practices. Whether you're exploring new methods of self-care or adjusting your lifestyle, staying grounded in your relationships and emotions will enhance your overall well-being. Pay attention to your sacral chakra (linked to number 2) to maintain emotional stability during times of change.

Angel Number 5335

Primary Number: 3 (Creativity, communication)
Secondary Number: 5 (Change, freedom)
Category: Confirming

Analysis: Angel number 5335 combines the creative energy of 3 with the transformative power of 5. This number encourages you to embrace new forms of self-expression and communication while navigating life changes. It's a signal to adapt creatively and explore new paths.

1. **Love**:

In love, 5335 suggests that creative communication is key during times of change. If you're single, this number encourages you to express yourself authentically, as this will attract new romantic possibilities. For those in relationships, it highlights the importance of open dialogue and adaptability to maintain harmony during shifts.

2. **Finance/Employment**:

In finance or employment, 5335 indicates that your creativity and adaptability will lead to success. New opportunities may require innovative solutions, and embracing change will enhance your professional growth. It's a time to express your ideas and be open to evolving your career path.

3. **Health:**

   For health, 5335 encourages you to creatively approach any changes in your well-being. Whether it's exploring new fitness routines or alternative health practices, adaptability will lead to better outcomes. Focus on your throat chakra (linked to number 3) to ensure you're expressing your health needs clearly and creatively.

Angel Number 5445

Primary Number: 4 (Stability, structure)
Secondary Number: 5 (Change, adaptability)
Category: Supportive
Analysis: Angel number 5445 emphasizes the need for structure (4) while embracing change (5). This number suggests that while stability is important, flexibility is also key to adapting to life's challenges. It's a reminder to build a strong foundation while staying open to necessary adjustments.

1. **Love:**

   In love, 5445 indicates that building a stable relationship is essential, even amidst changes. If you're single, this number suggests focusing on creating stability in your life before seeking a new relationship. For those in relationships, it highlights the importance of maintaining a strong foundation while adapting to the inevitable changes that come your way.

2. **Finance/Employment:**

   In finance or employment, 5445 signals that success will come from a balance between structure and adaptability. Building a strong foundation for your career or financial ventures is essential, but so is staying open to change. Flexibility within an organized plan will lead to long-term success.

3. **Health:**

For health, 5445 encourages creating a structured routine to support your well-being while remaining adaptable to necessary changes. Establish solid habits, but don't be afraid to tweak them when needed. Focus on your root chakra (linked to number 4) to enhance your sense of security and balance during periods of change.

Angel Number 5665

Primary Number: 6 (Nurturing, responsibility)

Secondary Number: 5 (Change, freedom)

Category: Advisory

Analysis: Angel number 5665 highlights the importance of nurturing (6) while embracing change (5). This number suggests that taking care of yourself and others during times of transition is essential. It's a reminder that growth comes from both responsibility and adaptability.

1. **Love:**

In love, 5665 suggests that nurturing your relationships while adapting to changes will strengthen the bond. If you're single, this number encourages you to take responsibility for your emotional well-being before seeking a new relationship. For those in relationships, it emphasizes the need to care for one another while navigating life's changes.

2. **Finance/Employment:**

In finance or employment, 5665 advises balancing responsibility with adaptability. This number suggests that while fulfilling your duties, it's also important to be open to new opportunities and changes in your professional life. Flexibility and a nurturing approach will lead to long-term success.

3. **Health:**

For health, 5665 encourages nurturing your body and mind

while staying adaptable to new health routines. Take responsibility for your well-being, but be open to trying new approaches to enhance your health. Focus on your heart chakra (linked to number 6) to foster emotional and physical well-being during periods of change.

Angel Number 5775

Primary Number: 7 (Spiritual awakening, inner wisdom)

Secondary Number: 5 (Change, freedom)

Category: Guiding

Analysis: Angel number 5775 combines spiritual awakening (7) with change and adaptability (5). This number suggests that the changes you're experiencing will lead to a deeper spiritual understanding and personal growth. It's a time to embrace both inner wisdom and external transformation.

1. **Love:**

   In love, 5775 suggests that spiritual growth is necessary for navigating changes in relationships. If you're single, this number encourages you to focus on spiritual development before entering a new relationship. For those in relationships, it highlights the importance of adapting to changes while maintaining a spiritual connection with your partner.

2. **Finance/Employment:**

   In finance or employment, 5775 indicates that your spiritual insights will guide you through career changes. It's a time to trust your intuition and embrace shifts in your professional life. These changes will likely lead to personal and professional growth.

3. **Health:**

   For health, 5775 encourages you to embrace changes in your routines that support your spiritual and physical well-being. This number suggests that spiritual practices like meditation or mindfulness can help you adapt to new health challenges. Focus on your crown chakra (linked to number 7) to enhance your connection to spiritual guidance during times of change.

Angel Number 5885

Primary Number: 8 (Abundance, material success)
Secondary Number: 5 (Change, adaptability)
Category: Guiding

Analysis: Angel number 5885 highlights the connection between material abundance (8) and embracing change (5). This number suggests that changes in your life will lead to financial success and personal empowerment. It's a reminder to stay flexible and open to new opportunities that bring material rewards.

1. **Love:**

   In love, 5885 suggests that personal growth and material success may influence your relationships. If you're single, this number encourages you to embrace changes that will bring stability and success in future relationships. For those in relationships, it highlights the importance of balancing material pursuits with emotional adaptability.

2. **Finance/Employment:**

   In finance or employment, 5885 signals that embracing change will lead to financial abundance. Stay open to new opportunities, especially those that allow for flexibility and innovation. Your adaptability will help you achieve long-term financial success.

3. **Health:**

   For health, 5885 encourages you to focus on maintaining balance in your health practices while staying open to changes that promote well-being. This number suggests that financial stability and physical health are interconnected, and positive changes in one area can benefit the other. Focus on your root chakra (linked to number 8) to ground yourself in material and physical stability during times of change.

Angel Number 5995

Primary Number: 9 (Completion, humanitarianism)
Secondary Number: 5 (Change, freedom)
Category: Advisory

Analysis: Angel number 5995 emphasizes completion and humanitarian efforts (9) supported by change and freedom (5). This number suggests that you are nearing the end of an important phase, and the changes you're experiencing will help you fulfill your higher purpose. It's a time to embrace transformation while focusing on serving others.

1. **Love**:
   In love, 5995 suggests that a significant phase in your relationship is coming to a close, making way for new growth. If you're single, this number encourages you to focus on personal growth and completion of emotional cycles before entering a new relationship. For those in relationships, it highlights the importance of adapting to changes and completing important emotional work together.

2. **Finance/Employment**:
   In finance or employment, 5995 signals that you're approaching the completion of a major career phase. This number encourages you to embrace changes that align with your higher purpose, such as pursuing humanitarian or service-oriented work. The shifts you experience will lead to greater fulfillment in your career.

3. **Health**:
   For health, 5995 encourages you to focus on completing important health goals while adapting to new routines that promote long-term well-being. This number suggests that changes

in your health habits will lead to the completion of a significant cycle of healing. Focus on your third eye chakra (linked to number 9) to enhance your intuition and understanding of the spiritual aspects of your health journey.

Angel Number 6116

Primary Number: 1 (New beginnings, self-reliance)
Secondary Number: 6 (Nurturing, balance)
Category: Supportive

Analysis: Angel number 6116 emphasizes the need for personal initiative (1) while balancing nurturing responsibilities (6). This number encourages taking leadership in your life, particularly when it comes to creating harmony in your home and family.

1. **Love:**
   In love, 6116 suggests that balance and harmony are key to successful relationships. If you're single, this number encourages you to take the initiative in finding a relationship, while maintaining self-love and balance. For those in relationships, 6116 reminds you to nurture your partner while maintaining your independence.

2. **Finance/Employment:**
   In finance or employment, 6116 indicates that new beginnings in your career or financial situation are on the horizon, but it's essential to balance work and personal life. Focus on nurturing your professional relationships and taking responsibility for your growth.

3. **Health:**
   For health, 6116 encourages you to nurture yourself and focus on maintaining balance in your daily routines. This number suggests that new health habits will lead to better well-being. Focus on balancing the root chakra (1), which governs self-re-

liance and new beginnings, and the heart chakra (6), which influences love and emotional well-being.

Angel Number 6226

Primary Number: 2 (Harmony, relationships)
Secondary Number: 6 (Nurturing, care)
Category: Confirming
Analysis: Angel number 6226 emphasizes relationships and harmony (2), combined with nurturing and responsibility (6). This sequence encourages you to focus on creating a harmonious balance in your relationships and home life.

1. **Love:**

   In love, 6226 suggests that nurturing and harmony are essential in relationships. If you're single, this number encourages you to focus on building emotional harmony before entering a new relationship. For those in relationships, it highlights the importance of nurturing and caring for each other to maintain balance.

2. **Finance/Employment:**

   In finance or employment, 6226 indicates that cooperation and teamwork will lead to success. Focus on building harmonious relationships with colleagues and nurturing your professional connections. This is a time to balance your professional ambitions with care for others.

3. **Health:**

   For health, 6226 encourages you to focus on emotional balance and self-care. Nurturing your physical and mental well-being will lead to long-term health. Pay attention to your sacral chakra (2), which governs emotions and relationships, and your heart chakra (6), which promotes emotional healing and self-love.

Angel Number 6336

- *Primary Number:* 3 (Creativity, communication)
- *Secondary Number:* 6 (Nurturing, responsibility)
- *Category:* Confirming

Analysis: Angel number 6336 emphasizes creative self-expression (3) combined with nurturing and responsibility (6). This number encourages you to focus on expressing your creativity in ways that nurture and support others.

1. **Love:**
   In love, 6336 suggests that communication and creativity are key to maintaining a nurturing relationship. If you're single, this number encourages you to express yourself creatively and confidently as you seek new connections. For those in relationships, it highlights the importance of nurturing your partner through creative gestures of love and care.

2. **Finance/Employment:**
   In finance or employment, 6336 indicates that creative approaches to your work will lead to success, especially when combined with nurturing professional relationships. This is a time to balance your creative ambitions with responsibility and teamwork.

3. **Health:**
   For health, 6336 encourages you to focus on balancing creative self-expression with nurturing your body and mind. Engaging in creative activities that promote emotional well-being will enhance your overall health. Pay attention to your solar plexus chakra (3), which governs creativity and personal power, and your heart chakra (6), which encourages nurturing care.

Angel Number 6446

- *Primary Number:* 4 (Stability, practicality)
- *Secondary Number:* 6 (Nurturing, balance)
- *Category:* Supportive

Analysis: Angel number 6446 emphasizes stability and structure (4) combined with nurturing and care (6). This number encourages you to focus on creating a stable environment in both your home and personal life while nurturing those around you.

1. **Love:**
   In love, 6446 suggests that stability and nurturing are essential for building a strong relationship. If you're single, this number encourages you to seek relationships that offer both stability and emotional care. For those in relationships, it highlights the importance of building a strong foundation while nurturing your connection.

2. **Finance/Employment:**
   In finance or employment, 6446 indicates that creating a stable and practical foundation in your career will lead to long-term success. Nurture your professional relationships and focus on building a secure future through disciplined work.

3. **Health:**
   For health, 6446 encourages you to focus on creating structured routines that promote long-term well-being. Nurturing your body with consistent self-care will lead to stability in your health. Focus on balancing the root chakra (4), which governs stability and security, and the heart chakra (6), which promotes emotional balance and healing.

Angel Number 6556
Primary Number: 5 (Change, freedom)
Secondary Number: 6 (Nurturing, responsibility)
Category: Advisory

Analysis: Angel number 6556 emphasizes change and transformation (5) combined with nurturing and responsibility (6). This number encourages you to embrace changes in your life while remaining responsible and caring towards yourself and others.

1. **Love**:
   In love, 6556 suggests that changes are on the horizon, and it's important to nurture your relationships through these transformations. If you're single, this number encourages you to embrace new experiences while focusing on self-care. For those in relationships, it highlights the importance of adapting to change together while continuing to nurture the relationship.

2. **Finance/Employment**:
   In finance or employment, 6556 indicates that embracing changes in your career will lead to growth, especially if you maintain responsibility and care for others. Stay flexible and open to new opportunities while nurturing your professional relationships.

3. **Health**:
   For health, 6556 encourages you to embrace changes in your lifestyle that promote well-being. Nurturing your body and mind through new routines will lead to personal growth. Focus on balancing the throat chakra (5), which governs communication and adaptability, and the heart chakra (6), which encourages emotional balance and nurturing care.

Angel Number 6776

Primary Number: 7 (Spiritual growth, wisdom)
Secondary Number: 6 (Nurturing, harmony)
Category: Guiding

Analysis: Angel number 6776 combines spiritual wisdom and growth (7) with nurturing and balance (6). This number suggests that your spiritual journey is supported by a harmonious and nurturing environment.

1. **Love:**

   In love, 6776 suggests that spiritual growth and nurturing are essential for building a strong relationship. If you're single, this number encourages you to focus on spiritual growth before seeking a relationship. For those in relationships, it highlights the importance of growing spiritually together while nurturing each other.

2. **Finance/Employment:**

   In finance or employment, 6776 indicates that your spiritual insights will guide you in creating a balanced and nurturing work environment. This is a time to align your spiritual goals with your professional ambitions.

3. **Health:**

   For health, 6776 encourages you to focus on nurturing your spiritual and physical well-being. Spiritual practices like meditation and mindfulness will help you maintain harmony in your health. Focus on your crown chakra (7), which governs spiritual connection, and your heart chakra (6), which promotes emotional balance and nurturing care.

Angel Number 6886

- *Primary Number:* 8 (Abundance, power)
- *Secondary Number:* 6 (Nurturing, responsibility)

Category: Guiding

Analysis: Angel number 6886 emphasizes abundance and material success (8) combined with nurturing and responsibility (6). This number encourages you to use your material resources to nurture yourself and those around you.

1. **Love:**

   In love, 6886 suggests that material stability and nurturing are essential for building a strong relationship. If you're single, this number encourages you to focus on building a stable foundation for your future relationship. For those in relationships, it highlights the importance of balancing material success with emotional nurturing.

2. **Finance/Employment:**

   In finance or employment, 6886 indicates that financial abundance is on the horizon, especially if you maintain a nurturing and responsible approach to your work. Use your material resources to support both your career and your personal life.

3. **Health:**

   For health, 6886 encourages you to focus on balancing material success with nurturing your physical and emotional well-being. Achieving financial stability will support your health goals. Focus on your root chakra (8), which governs material stability and grounding, and your heart chakra (6), which promotes emotional balance and nurturing care.

Angel Number 6996

Primary Number: 9 (Completion, humanitarianism)

Secondary Number: 6 (Nurturing, responsibility)

Category: Advisory

Analysis: Angel number 6996 emphasizes the completion of a significant phase (9) combined with nurturing and responsibility (6). This number encourages you to focus on completing important life cycles while nurturing yourself and others.

1. **Love:**

   In love, 6996 suggests that a phase in your relationship is coming to a close, and it's important to nurture your connection through this transition. If you're single, this number encourages you to focus on completing personal growth cycles before seeking a new relationship. For those in relationships, it highlights the importance of nurturing each other as you move through changes together.

2. **Finance/Employment**:

In finance or employment, 6996 indicates that you're nearing the completion of a major career phase. This number encourages you to use your resources to support humanitarian or service-oriented work. Nurturing professional relationships will help you navigate this transition.

3. **Health**:

For health, 6996 encourages you to focus on completing important health goals while nurturing your body and mind. This number suggests that your health practices are coming full circle, leading to greater balance and well-being. Focus on your third eye chakra (9), which governs intuition and higher understanding, and your heart chakra (6), which promotes emotional balance and nurturing care.

Angel Number 7117

Primary Number: 1 (New beginnings, leadership)
Secondary Number: 7 (Spirituality, introspection)
Category: Guiding

Analysis: Angel number 7117 emphasizes new beginnings and leadership (1) combined with spiritual growth and introspection (7). This number suggests that starting fresh in life requires deep spiritual reflection and a strong sense of self-awareness.

1. **Love**:

In love, 7117 suggests that embarking on a new relationship or phase in your relationship requires deep spiritual understanding. If you're single, this number encourages you to focus on self-growth before seeking a relationship. For those in relationships, it highlights the importance of spiritual connection and introspection for growth.

2. **Finance/Employment**:

In finance or employment, 7117 indicates that new professional opportunities are ahead, but they will require introspection and alignment with your spiritual purpose. Seek roles that align with your values and support your spiritual growth.

3. **Health**:

For health, 7117 encourages you to balance new health routines with spiritual practices such as meditation or mindfulness. Focus on integrating your physical well-being with your spiritual journey. Pay attention to your root chakra (1), which governs physical vitality, and your crown chakra (7), which connects you to spiritual wisdom.

Angel Number 7227

Primary Number: 2 (Harmony, relationships)
Secondary Number: 7 (Spirituality, wisdom)
Category: Confirming

Analysis: Angel number 7227 emphasizes harmony in relationships (2) combined with spiritual growth and wisdom (7). This number encourages you to focus on building spiritually harmonious relationships and finding balance between your spiritual and personal lives.

1. **Love**:

In love, 7227 suggests that spiritual harmony is essential for deepening relationships. If you're single, focus on finding a partner who aligns with your spiritual values. For those in relationships, it highlights the importance of nurturing spiritual growth together for deeper connection.

2. **Finance/Employment**:

In finance or employment, 7227 indicates that success will come from maintaining harmony in your work relationships while seeking spiritual fulfillment in your career. Align your professional life with your spiritual purpose for greater satisfaction.

3. **Health:**

For health, 7227 encourages you to nurture both your emotional and spiritual well-being. Establish a balance between physical self-care and spiritual practices to maintain long-term health. Focus on balancing the sacral chakra (2), which governs emotional well-being, and the crown chakra (7), which connects you to spiritual growth.

Angel Number 7337

Primary Number: 3 (Creativity, communication)
Secondary Number: 7 (Spiritual growth, introspection)
Category: Confirming

Analysis: Angel number 7337 emphasizes creative expression (3) combined with spiritual growth and introspection (7). This number encourages you to explore creative endeavors that align with your spiritual path.

1. **Love:**

In love, 7337 suggests that creative communication and spiritual growth are essential for building strong relationships. If you're single, this number encourages you to express your creative side while seeking a spiritually aligned partner. For those in relationships, it highlights the importance of nurturing creativity and spirituality within the relationship.

2. **Finance/Employment:**

In finance or employment, 7337 indicates that creativity and spiritual insights will guide you to success. Focus on roles that allow for creative freedom while also fostering spiritual growth and introspection.

3. **Health**:

For health, 7337 encourages you to nurture your physical and spiritual well-being through creative self-expression. Engage in activities that promote emotional and spiritual healing. Focus on your solar plexus chakra (3), which governs creativity and self-expression, and your crown chakra (7), which enhances spiritual growth.

Angel Number 7447

Primary Number: 4 (Stability, structure)

Secondary Number: 7 (Spirituality, enlightenment)

Category: Supportive

Analysis: Angel number 7447 emphasizes the need for stability and structure (4) while fostering spiritual growth and enlightenment (7). This number encourages you to build a strong foundation for your spiritual journey.

1. **Love**:

In love, 7447 suggests that a stable foundation is essential for spiritual growth in relationships. If you're single, this number encourages you to build emotional stability before seeking a relationship. For those in relationships, it highlights the importance of creating stability while growing spiritually together.

2. **Finance/Employment**:

In finance or employment, 7447 indicates that success will come from building a stable and structured approach to your career while staying aligned with your spiritual purpose. Focus on long-term planning and personal growth in your work life.

3. **Health**:

For health, 7447 encourages you to establish a structured routine for both physical and spiritual well-being. Building a solid foundation for your spiritual practices will support your overall health. Focus on your root chakra (4), which governs stability and security, and your crown chakra (7), which connects to spiritual enlightenment.

Angel Number 7557
Primary Number: 5 (Change, freedom)
Secondary Number: 7 (Spirituality, introspection)
Category: Advisory
Analysis: Angel number 7557 emphasizes change and transformation (5) combined with spiritual growth and introspection (7). This number encourages you to embrace change while seeking spiritual guidance and wisdom.

1. **Love:**
   In love, 7557 suggests that changes in your relationship or personal life will lead to spiritual growth. If you're single, this number encourages you to embrace new opportunities while focusing on your spiritual journey. For those in relationships, it highlights the importance of adapting to change together while deepening your spiritual connection.

2. **Finance/Employment:**
   In finance or employment, 7557 indicates that changes in your career will bring opportunities for spiritual growth. Stay open to new experiences and align your work with your spiritual path to achieve fulfillment.

3. **Health:**
   For health, 7557 encourages you to embrace changes in your lifestyle that support your spiritual and physical well-being. Engage in practices that promote spiritual introspection and personal growth. Focus on balancing the throat chakra (5), which governs communication and adaptability, and the crown chakra (7), which enhances spiritual wisdom.

Angel Number 7667

Primary Number: 6 (Nurturing, responsibility)
Secondary Number: 7 (Spiritual growth, introspection)
Category: Advisory

Analysis: Angel number 7667 combines nurturing and responsibility (6) with spiritual growth and wisdom (7). This number encourages you to focus on nurturing both yourself and others while deepening your spiritual understanding.

1. **Love**:

   In love, 7667 suggests that nurturing and spiritual growth are essential for building strong relationships. If you're single, this number encourages you to focus on personal growth and self-care before entering a new relationship. For those in relationships, it highlights the importance of nurturing each other while growing spiritually together.

2. **Finance/Employment**:

   In finance or employment, 7667 indicates that nurturing your professional relationships and aligning your career with your spiritual path will lead to success. Focus on balancing your responsibilities with your spiritual growth.

3. **Health**:

   For health, 7667 encourages you to nurture both your physical and spiritual well-being. Engage in self-care practices that support your body while also promoting spiritual growth. Focus on balancing the heart chakra (6), which governs love and nurturing, and the crown chakra (7), which connects to spiritual wisdom.

Angel Number 7887

Primary Number: 8 (Abundance, authority)
Secondary Number: 7 (Spirituality, introspection)
Category: Guiding

Analysis: Angel number 7887 emphasizes abundance and material success (8) combined with spiritual growth and wisdom (7). This number encourages you to seek balance between material wealth and spiritual fulfillment.

1. **Love:**
   In love, 7887 suggests that achieving balance between material stability and spiritual connection is essential for building a strong relationship. If you're single, this number encourages you to focus on finding a partner who shares both your material and spiritual goals. For those in relationships, it highlights the importance of nurturing both material success and spiritual growth together.

2. **Finance/Employment:**
   In finance or employment, 7887 indicates that material success is within reach, but it's essential to align your career with your spiritual purpose. Use your financial resources to support your spiritual journey and personal growth.

3. **Health:**
   For health, 7887 encourages you to focus on balancing material success with your spiritual and physical well-being. Engage in practices that support both your physical health and spiritual growth. Focus on your root chakra (8), which governs material stability, and your crown chakra (7), which enhances spiritual wisdom.

Angel Number 7997

Primary Number: 9 (Completion, humanitarianism)
Secondary Number: 7 (Spiritual growth, introspection)
Category: Advisory

Analysis: Angel number 7997 emphasizes the completion of a significant phase (9) combined with spiritual growth and wisdom (7).

This number encourages you to focus on completing important life cycles while deepening your spiritual understanding.

1. **Love:**

   In love, 7997 suggests that completing a phase in your relationship or personal life will lead to spiritual growth. If you're single, this number encourages you to focus on personal growth and spiritual development before seeking a new relationship. For those in relationships, it highlights the importance of nurturing each other through the completion of important life cycles.

2. **Finance/Employment:**

   In finance or employment, 7997 indicates that you're nearing the completion of a major career phase. Focus on aligning your professional goals with your spiritual path and using your resources to support humanitarian or service-oriented work.

3. **Health:**

   For health, 7997 encourages you to focus on completing important health goals while nurturing your body and spirit. This number suggests that your health practices are coming full circle, leading to greater balance and well-being. Focus on your crown chakra (7), which connects to spiritual wisdom, and your third eye chakra (9), which governs intuition and higher understanding.

Angel Number 8118

Primary Number: 1 (New beginnings, leadership)
Secondary Number: 8 (Abundance, power)
Category: Supportive

Analysis: Angel number 8118 is a powerful blend of leadership (1) and material success (8). This number encourages taking initiative in your endeavors, as your efforts will lead to abundance and power.

1. **Love:**

   In love, 8118 suggests that embracing independence and taking the lead in your relationship can foster a stronger bond. If you're single, this number signifies that new beginnings in love are coming, potentially with someone who shares your values of growth and abundance.

2. **Finance/Employment:**

   For finance or employment, 8118 is a positive indicator of financial success. By taking initiative and leading your projects, you'll see material gains. This number encourages confidence and assertiveness in achieving financial goals.

3. **Health:**

   In health, 8118 highlights the importance of a disciplined approach to well-being. Focus on your root chakra (connected to 8), which governs stability and grounding. Implement structured routines that support long-term health and vitality.

Angel Number 8228

Primary Number: 2 (Harmony, relationships)
Secondary Number: 8 (Abundance, power)
Category: Confirming

Analysis: Angel number 8228 blends harmony in relationships (2) with material abundance (8). This number indicates that fostering cooperation and balance will bring success in various areas of life.

1. **Love:**

   In love, 8228 suggests that harmony and balance are essential to building a strong relationship. For singles, this number indicates that a harmonious partnership leading to long-term abundance is on the horizon.

2. **Finance/Employment:**

   In finance or employment, 8228 highlights that teamwork and cooperation will lead to material success. Balance your independent work with collaboration to achieve financial stability and success.

3. **Health:**

In health, 8228 encourages creating balance in your wellness routine to support long-term stability. Focus on your root chakra (8) for grounding, and sacral chakra (2) for emotional and relational harmony.

Angel Number 8338

Primary Number: 3 (Creativity, communication)
Secondary Number: 8 (Abundance, power)
Category: Confirming

Analysis: Angel number 8338 combines the creative energy of 3 with the material success of 8. This sequence encourages you to express yourself creatively while attracting abundance into your life.

1. **Love:**

In love, 8338 suggests that open communication and creativity will strengthen your relationship. If you're single, it's a sign to express your true self to attract a partner who aligns with your path to abundance.

2. **Finance/Employment:**

In finance or employment, 8338 highlights that creative projects will lead to material success. This is a time to trust your innovative ideas and use them to bring financial gains.

3. **Health:**

For health, 8338 emphasizes creativity in your approach to well-being. Focus on balancing your throat chakra (3), which governs communication, and your root chakra (8) for grounding and stability.

Angel Number 8448

Primary Number: 4 (Stability, structure)

Secondary Number: 8 (Abundance, power)

Category: Supportive

Analysis: Angel number 8448 emphasizes building stability (4) to achieve material success (8). This number encourages structured efforts and hard work, which will lead to long-term abundance.

1. **Love:**

   In love, 8448 suggests that creating a stable foundation is crucial for long-term success in relationships. If you're single, focus on building security within yourself to attract a partner who values stability and growth.

2. **Finance/Employment:**

   In finance or employment, 8448 is a positive sign of financial stability through hard work and organization. Focus on creating long-term strategies to achieve material success.

3. **Health:**

   In health, 8448 encourages a structured approach to maintaining well-being. Focus on your root chakra (8) for stability and your heart chakra (4) to nurture your emotional health.

Angel Number 8558

Primary Number: 5 (Change, freedom)

Secondary Number: 8 (Abundance, power)

Category: Advisory

Analysis: Angel number 8558 signifies that embracing change (5) will lead to material abundance (8). This number encourages being flexible and adaptable, as these qualities will help you achieve success.

1. **Love:**

   In love, 8558 suggests that embracing change and freedom within your relationship will lead to greater harmony and abundance. If you're single, this number indicates that new and exciting relationships are on the horizon.

2. **Finance/Employment:**

For finance or employment, 8558 highlights that changes in your career or financial situation will lead to abundance. Stay adaptable and open to new opportunities that bring success.

3. **Health:**

In health, 8558 encourages embracing new habits that support long-term well-being. Focus on balancing your throat chakra (5) for expressing your needs and your root chakra (8) for physical stability.

Angel Number 8668

Primary Number: 6 (Nurturing, responsibility)
Secondary Number: 8 (Abundance, power)
Category: Advisory

Analysis: Angel number 8668 highlights the importance of nurturing (6) your life's responsibilities to achieve material success (8). This sequence encourages a balance between care and ambition.

1. **Love:**

In love, 8668 suggests that nurturing and taking responsibility within the relationship will lead to long-term abundance and harmony. For singles, this number encourages focusing on self-care to attract a stable partner.

2. **Finance/Employment:**

For finance or employment, 8668 indicates that taking responsibility for your career and being nurturing towards your goals will lead to material success. Balance ambition with care for your well-being.

3. **Health:**

In health, 8668 encourages nurturing your physical and emotional well-being. Focus on balancing your third eye chakra (6) for intuition and spiritual connection and your root chakra (8) for grounding and physical stability.

Angel Number 8778

Primary Number: 7 (Spirituality, wisdom)

Secondary Number: 8 (Abundance, power)

Category: Guiding

Analysis: Angel number 8778 signifies that spiritual wisdom (7) will lead to material abundance (8). This number encourages aligning your spiritual path with your goals for success.

1. **Love:**

   In love, 8778 suggests that spiritual alignment with your partner will strengthen your relationship. If you're single, this number encourages you to seek a partner who shares your spiritual values.

2. **Finance/Employment:**

   In finance or employment, 8778 indicates that spiritual insight and wisdom will guide you toward material success. Trust your intuition when making career or financial decisions.

3. **Health:**

   For health, 8778 encourages balancing spiritual practices with your physical well-being. Focus on aligning your crown chakra (7) for spiritual connection and your root chakra (8) for grounding and vitality.

Angel Number 8998

Primary Number: 9 (Completion, humanitarianism)

Secondary Number: 8 (Abundance, power)

Category: Advisory

Analysis: Angel number 8998 combines the energy of completion and humanitarianism (9) with material success (8). This number encourages using your success to benefit others and complete important life chapters.

1. **Love:**

   In love, 8998 suggests that completing important cycles in your relationship will lead to greater harmony and abundance. If you're single, this number indicates that a relationship focused on humanitarian or shared goals may be approaching.

2. **Finance/Employment:**

   In finance or employment, 8998 highlights that your success can be used to benefit others. It's a time to complete projects and focus on how your work can contribute to a greater cause.

3. **Health:**

   For health, 8998 encourages completing cycles of healing and using your strength to help others. Focus on your crown chakra (9) for spiritual enlightenment and your root chakra (8) for physical stability.

Angel Number 9119

Primary Number: 1 (New beginnings, leadership)
Secondary Number: 9 (Completion, humanitarianism)
Category: Supportive

Analysis: Angel number 9119 combines the energy of new beginnings (1) with completion (9). It suggests that in order to move forward, you must bring closure to something significant in your life.

1. **Love:**

   In love, 9119 suggests that a new chapter is opening, but only after you let go of old wounds or a past relationship. For those in relationships, this number encourages bringing closure to old issues to make room for a fresh start together.

2. **Finance/Employment:**

   In finance or employment, 9119 signals the completion of a significant project or phase and the opportunity for a new beginning. It's a time to let go of what's no longer serving your career or business and embrace fresh opportunities.

3. **Health:**

   For health, 9119 suggests completing old health routines that no longer serve you and adopting new practices that support your well-being. Focus on maintaining your root chakra, which is linked to grounding and physical vitality.

Angel Number 9229

Primary Number: 2 (Balance, relationships)
Secondary Number: 9 (Completion, humanitarianism)
Category: Confirming
Analysis: Angel number 9229 is about bringing harmony to relationships while completing a significant cycle. It suggests balancing personal growth with compassion for others.

1. **Love:**

   In love, 9229 encourages you to focus on relationships that bring balance and harmony. If you're single, this is a good time to reflect on past relationships, learn from them, and prepare for a new beginning.

2. **Finance/Employment:**

   In finance or employment, 9229 indicates that balance and co-operation are key to completing important projects. Work in harmony with others, and focus on partnerships that can help you achieve your career goals.

3. **Health:**

   For health, 9229 reminds you to focus on balancing your emotional and physical health. This is a good time to bring closure to unhealthy habits. Focus on your sacral chakra, which governs emotional balance and relationships.

Angel Number 9339

Primary Number: 3 (Creativity, communication)
Secondary Number: 9 (Completion, humanitarianism)

Category: Confirming

Analysis: Angel number 9339 combines creativity (3) with the completion of important life chapters (9). This is a time to use your creative talents to wrap up significant projects.

1. Love:

   In love, 9339 suggests a creative approach to resolving relationship issues. If you're single, use this time to complete personal growth and prepare yourself for a meaningful relationship.

2. Finance/Employment:

   In finance or employment, 9339 indicates that your creative ideas will help you complete an important project. It's time to finish what you've started so you can move forward with new opportunities.

3. Health:

   For health, 9339 encourages you to explore creative ways to improve your well-being. This could involve trying new approaches to fitness or stress relief. Focus on maintaining your solar plexus chakra, which is linked to personal power and creativity.

Angel Number 9449

Primary Number: 4 (Stability, structure)

Secondary Number: 9 (Completion, humanitarianism)

Category: Supportive

Analysis: Angel number 9449 encourages creating a stable and structured foundation as you bring things to completion. It's a time to focus on practicality while wrapping up significant projects.

1. Love:

   In love, 9449 suggests that stability and structure are key to completing any relationship issues. If you're single, focus on creating a solid foundation in your personal life before entering a new relationship.

2. Finance/Employment:

In finance or employment, 9449 indicates that a structured approach will help you complete important tasks and achieve success. Focus on organization and practicality to reach your goals.

3. Health:

For health, 9449 encourages you to create stable routines that promote your well-being. This is a good time to bring closure to old health habits and establish new, healthier ones. Focus on your heart chakra, which is linked to emotional balance and stability.

Angel Number 9559

Primary Number: 5 (Change, freedom)

Secondary Number: 9 (Completion, humanitarianism)

Category: Advisory

Analysis: Angel number 9559 signals major changes (5) as you bring significant life chapters to a close (9). It encourages you to embrace transformation while completing important tasks.

1. Love:

In love, 9559 suggests that changes are coming in your relationships. If you're single, this number encourages you to embrace personal growth before entering a new relationship. For those in relationships, 9559 indicates that changes are necessary to bring balance and harmony.

2. Finance/Employment:

In finance or employment, 9559 suggests that significant changes are on the horizon. This is a good time to finish old projects and prepare for new opportunities that align with your goals.

3. Health:

For health, 9559 encourages you to embrace change in your routines, especially if old habits are no longer serving you. This is a time to adopt new practices that support your well-being. Focus on maintaining your throat chakra, which is linked to communication and transformation.

Angel Number 9669

Primary Number: 6 (Nurturing, responsibility)
Secondary Number: 9 (Completion, humanitarianism)
Category: Advisory
Analysis: Angel number 9669 emphasizes nurturing and caring for yourself and others (6) while completing significant life cycles (9). It's a time to focus on family, relationships, and responsibilities.

1. Love:

In love, 9669 encourages you to nurture your relationships and bring closure to past issues. If you're single, this is a time to focus on self-care and prepare yourself for new relationships by completing old emotional cycles.

2. Finance/Employment:

In finance or employment, 9669 suggests that taking responsibility and nurturing your career will lead to success. Focus on completing important tasks and fulfilling your responsibilities.

3. Health:

For health, 9669 encourages you to focus on nurturing your well-being by completing any unfinished health goals. Take care of your family's health as well. Focus on maintaining your third eye chakra, which is linked to intuition and spiritual insight.

Angel Number 9779

Primary Number: 7 (Spirituality, introspection)

Secondary Number: 9 (Completion, humanitarianism)

Category: Guiding

Analysis: Angel number 9779 emphasizes spiritual growth (7) while completing important life cycles (9). It's a time for deep introspection and focusing on your higher purpose.

1. Love:

   In love, 9779 suggests that spiritual growth is essential for completing relationship cycles. If you're single, this number encourages you to focus on your spiritual development before seeking new relationships. For those in relationships, it's time to bring closure to old issues and grow together spiritually.

2. Finance/Employment:

   In finance or employment, 9779 indicates that your spiritual insights will help you complete important projects and move forward in your career. This is a time to align your work with your higher purpose.

3. Health:

   For health, 9779 encourages you to focus on spiritual practices that promote your well-being. Meditation and mindfulness will help you complete your health goals. Focus on maintaining your crown chakra, which is linked to spiritual connection and enlightenment.

Angel Number 9889

Primary Number: 8 (Abundance, power)

Secondary Number: 9 (Completion, humanitarianism)

Category: Guiding

Analysis: Angel number 9889 signals abundance and success (8) while completing important cycles in your life (9). It's a time to use your power and resources for humanitarian causes.

1. Love:

   In love, 9889 suggests that success in relationships comes from embracing abundance and completing old emotional cycles. If you're single, focus on finding a partner who shares your values and humanitarian goals.

2. Finance/Employment:

   In finance or employment, 9889 indicates that financial success is within reach as you complete important projects. Use your abundance and leadership skills to contribute to the greater good.

3.

   Health:

   For health, 9889 encourages you to focus on abundance and completion in your well-being routines. Use your resources to take care of your health and the health of others. Focus on maintaining your root chakra, which is linked to physical vitality and grounding.

27

Basic Continuum Sequence Numbers

1234-9123
In the realm of angel numbers, continuum sequences such as 1234 or 9876 present a more intricate layer of guidance. While these numbers, like other angel numbers, follow the rule where the first digit represents the primary energy and the second digit reveals the secondary, they offer an additional layer of meaning that lies in the progression or regression of the sequence.

One unique feature of these continuum sequences is their directional flow—whether the numbers rise or fall. A rising sequence, like 1234, carries an uplifting, intensifying energy. It often signals forward movement, growth, or a boost in the message's significance. Conversely, a falling sequence, like 9876, tends to offer a more calming or easing influence, indicating that the energy may be softening or winding down. This is particularly helpful when you're undergoing transitions or shifts, offering comfort or closure as needed.

Because continuum sequences consist of four numbers, each representing its own angelic vibration, they carry a more complex, multi-layered meaning. Each digit brings its own influence, and the overall flow of the number gives context to how these energies interrelate. As a result, continuum sequences often appear when we are already well attuned to our spiritual guidance, having developed a deeper ability to decode the messages from our spirit guides.

In the following list, we will explore each continuum sequence and break down how to interpret their primary and secondary numbers, while also considering the flow of the sequence and how it might enhance or moderate the message being conveyed. This method of decoding adds another layer of richness to your spiritual journey, empowering you to receive messages in more nuanced ways.

Angel Number 1234

Primary Number: 1 (New beginnings, independence, leadership)
Secondary Number: 2 (Balance, partnership, harmony)
Category: Supportive
Analysis: Angel number 1234 represents steady growth and progression in your life. It encourages taking the first step (1), balancing your relationships (2), expressing creativity (3), and building solid foundations (4).

1. Love:

   In love, 1234 suggests the importance of creating a balanced and harmonious relationship. If you're single, it's a sign to take the initiative in seeking meaningful partnerships while ensuring emotional balance. For those in relationships, focus on maintaining balance and building trust step-by-step.

2. Finance/Employment:

   In finance or employment, 1234 signals a step-by-step approach to success. Take the lead in initiating projects (1), work in harmony with others (2), express creative solutions (3), and establish practical steps (4) to achieve long-term stability.

3. Health:

   Health-wise, 1234 urges you to build a balanced approach to your well-being. Start by initiating new habits (1), find harmony in your routines (2), and focus on creative ways (3) to enhance your health. Pay special attention to the heart chakra, which supports both physical and emotional balance.

Angel Number 2345

Primary Number: 2 (Balance, relationships, harmony)

Secondary Number: 3 (Creativity, self-expression, joy)

Category: Confirming

Analysis: Angel number 2345 signals the need for harmony in relationships and creativity, followed by embracing changes (5) that lead to freedom and growth. This number shows a progression towards greater expression and adventure.

1. Love:

   In love, 2345 indicates that balance and harmony (2) should come first, followed by open communication and joy (3). Then, be ready for change and adventure (5), which will strengthen your bond. Single? It's time to express yourself fully and embrace new experiences.

2. Finance/Employment:

   In career matters, 2345 advises finding balance in teamwork (2) and embracing creativity (3). As changes approach (5), stay adaptable and ready for new challenges that could lead to more freedom and fulfillment in your career.

3. Health:

   Health-wise, 2345 encourages balanced emotional and physical health (2), and creative approaches to wellness (3). Be open to making changes (5) in your routine, particularly those that allow more freedom and flexibility in how you care for yourself. Focus on your sacral chakra for creative and emotional balance.

Angel Number 3456

Primary Number: 3 (Creativity, joy, expansion)

Secondary Number: 4 (Stability, structure, foundations)

Category: Confirming

Analysis: Angel number 3456 encourages creative expansion (3) built on stable foundations (4). As you move forward (5), embrace change with enthusiasm, knowing that it leads to a more harmonious and balanced life (6).

1. Love:

   In relationships, 3456 suggests a need for creative expression and joy (3), while also building a strong foundation (4). Be open to changes (5) that bring more harmony and nurturing energy (6) into the relationship. If single, embrace your creativity while searching for a stable partnership.

2. Finance/Employment:

   In finance, 3456 indicates that creative ideas (3) will bring success as long as they are supported by practical steps (4). Expect changes (5) that will push you to adapt but will ultimately lead to stability and success (6).

3. Health:

   For your health, 3456 encourages using creative strategies (3) to build a solid routine (4) while adapting to any necessary changes (5). Ensure your self-care nurtures both your body and mind (6). Focus on your solar plexus and heart chakras to maintain joy and harmony in your physical and emotional health.

Angel Number 4567

Primary Number: 4 (Stability, practicality, structure)

Secondary Number: 5 (Change, adaptability, freedom)

Category: Supportive

Angel number 4567 highlights a transition from stability (4) into embracing changes (5), which lead to personal growth (6) and spiritual development (7). It's a call to balance the practical with the spiritual.

1. Love:

   In love, 4567 suggests first creating stability (4) before embracing changes (5) that allow for more harmony (6) and spiritual connection (7). For singles, focus on grounding yourself before allowing change to enter your romantic life.

2. Finance/Employment:

   In finance, 4567 encourages practical steps (4) to navigate upcoming changes (5). Stay adaptable and look for ways to grow (6) while embracing spiritual and personal development (7) in your career journey.

3. Health:

   Health-wise, 4567 asks you to establish a stable routine (4), make changes (5) where needed, and focus on nurturing your mind and body (6). Spiritual practices (7) should become an integral part of your healing process, and balancing your root and crown chakras will provide holistic well-being.

Angel Number 5678

Primary Number: 5 (Change, freedom, adaptability)

Secondary Number: 6 (Harmony, love, nurturing)

Category: Advisory

Analysis: Angel number 5678 speaks of major life changes (5) leading to greater harmony (6), followed by spiritual growth (7) and material success (8). This is a number of transformation, where changes result in growth and abundance.

1. Love:

   In love, 5678 suggests embracing changes (5) that lead to more harmony and nurturing (6) in your relationship. It also points to a period of spiritual growth (7) and emotional abundance (8). If single, expect changes that will lead to a more balanced and fulfilling relationship.

2. Finance/Employment:

   In your career, 5678 indicates that change is coming (5), which will lead to harmony and fulfillment (6). Spiritual growth (7) in your career will guide you to success and material abundance (8).

3. Health:

   In terms of health, 5678 asks you to be adaptable to changes (5) while nurturing yourself (6). Focus on spiritual practices (7) that lead to emotional well-being and material success (8). Strengthening your sacral and third-eye chakras will aid in navigating these transitions.

Angel Number 6789

Primary Number: 6 (Harmony, nurturing, responsibility)
Secondary Number: 7 (Spirituality, wisdom, introspection)
Category: Advisory
Analysis: Angel number 6789 represents a sequence of growth, where nurturing (6) leads to spiritual awakening (7), followed by material success (8) and a phase of completion (9).

1. Love:

   In love, 6789 encourages focusing on nurturing relationships (6), deepening spiritual connection (7), achieving emotional abundance (8), and letting go of any cycles that no longer serve you (9). If single, focus on healing and growing spiritually before entering a new relationship.

2. Finance/Employment:

   In finance, 6789 suggests nurturing your career (6), followed by spiritual growth (7), which leads to material abundance (8) and the completion of important projects (9). Be ready to close chapters and move forward.

3. Health:

   For health, 6789 asks you to nurture your well-being (6), focusing on spiritual practices (7) that lead to abundance (8) and completion (9) of health routines that are no longer serving you. Focus on the heart and crown chakras for healing and guidance.

Angel Number 7891

Primary Number: 7 (Spiritual awakening, inner wisdom)
Secondary Number: 8 (Abundance, power, success)
Category: Guiding

Analysis: Angel number 7891 suggests a spiritual awakening (7) that leads to material success (8), followed by new beginnings (1) in the form of independence or leadership.

1. Love:
   In love, 7891 indicates a time of spiritual growth (7) that brings emotional abundance (8). It also signals a new beginning (1) in your relationship. If single, expect a spiritual awakening that prepares you for a fresh romantic start.
2. Finance/Employment:
   In your career, 7891 signals that spiritual growth (7) will lead to material success (8) and the start of a new venture (1). Trust your inner wisdom as you enter this phase of abundance and leadership.
3. Health:
   For health, 7891 encourages you to focus on spiritual healing (7) that leads to greater abundance in your well-being (8) and marks a new beginning (1). Balance your crown and solar plexus chakras to enhance this process.

Angel Number 8912

Primary Number: 8 (Abundance, power, success)
Secondary Number: 9 (Completion, humanitarianism)
Category: Guiding

Analysis: Angel number 8912 signals the completion of important life cycles (9), followed by a period of material abundance (8) and new beginnings (1), balanced with harmony and cooperation (2).

1. Love:

   In love, 8912 encourages completing old cycles (9), followed by a time of emotional and material abundance (8). A fresh start (1) awaits you, supported by a focus on harmony and balance (2). Singles will find success in relationships after completing emotional healing.

2. Finance/Employment:

   In career matters, 8912 indicates the successful completion (9) of major projects, leading to abundance (8) and new opportunities (1). Work in cooperation with others (2) to achieve balance and success.

3. Health:

   For health, 8912 advises completing long-standing health routines (9) in favor of new, more balanced habits (1). This number suggests that abundance (8) in your health will come from nurturing and balanced approaches (2). Focus on your root and heart chakras.

Angel Number 9123

Primary Number: 9 (Completion, humanitarianism)
Secondary Number: 1 (New beginnings, independence)
Category: Advisory
Analysis: Angel number 9123 represents the completion of important cycles (9) followed by a new beginning (1), balanced by creative expression (3) and partnership harmony (2).

1. Love:

   In love, 9123 suggests completing emotional cycles (9) and entering a new relationship phase (1), followed by nurturing harmony and balance (2). Singles may see the end of an old chapter and the beginning of a new, fulfilling relationship.

2. Finance/Employment:

In career, 9123 indicates that completing major tasks (9) will lead to new opportunities (1), with a focus on balance and creativity (2, 3). This is a great time to take the lead in new projects that require cooperation and creative problem-solving.

3. Health:

For health, 9123 advises completing health routines that no longer serve you (9) and embracing new, healthier habits (1). Balancing your approach to emotional and physical well-being (2, 3) will lead to harmony. Pay attention to the crown and sacral chakras for guidance.

28

The Angel Number 0

One number that frequently slips under the radar is the number 0. It's easy to dismiss it as nothingness or a lack of value, but in the spiritual realm, 0 holds profound significance. This number, often overlooked, is indeed a cosmic gift, brimming with potential and endless possibilities.

As an angel number 0 is not just a symbol of nothingness. It's a profound reminder of the infinite potential that lies within and around us. It's an invitation to start anew, to open ourselves to higher dimensions, and to embrace the boundless possibilities that life offers. So, next time you encounter this powerful number, pause and reflect on its deep and mystical significance. Remember, in the universe's grand tapestry, even what seems like nothing can hold everything.

When '0' appears alongside other numbers, it invites us to consider a deeper, more universal perspective. For instance, if you frequently encounter numbers like 103 or 402, pay attention to how '0' influences the overall meaning. In numerology, '0' represents the concept of infinity, wholeness, and the beginning point. It's a symbol of potential and a reminder that the spiritual journey is a continuous loop with no end.

Consider '0' as a magnifying glass, intensifying the vibrations of the numbers it accompanies. In 103, '0' amplifies the attributes of '1' (new beginnings, leadership) and '3' (creativity, communication), suggesting a journey of creative leadership that's ever-evolving. In 402, '0' enhances '4' (stability, determination) and '2' (duality, harmony), pointing towards a path of balanced and steadfast progress.

When you see angel numbers with '0', think about the broader implications of this inclusion. It's a call from the universe to acknowledge your role in the endless cycle of life, to recognize the continuous flow of energy and opportunities that come your way. '0' is a reminder that in every ending there is a beginning, in every void there's a space for creation. It beckons you to look at your situation with an understanding of the cyclical nature of the universe and to find comfort in the ongoing journey of growth and evolution. So, next time '0' appears in your angel numbers, take it as a cue to widen your perspective. See it as an encouragement to embrace the infinite possibilities, to start anew with a holistic view, and to realize that every moment is an opportunity to begin again on your spiritual path.

EPILOGUE

Reflecting upon the journey this book has guided you through, I harbor a profound hope. It is a hope that, by reaching the conclusion, you find yourself not just holding a collection of pages but standing at the precipice of a newfound understanding—both of the self and of the ancient numerical wisdom that threads through the fabric of our existence. The intention was never solely to educate but to illuminate paths within you that lead to deeper introspection, a better grasp of the choices that define your journey, and an enhanced perception of the intricate world that cradles us all.

I envisage this book not as an endpoint but as a beacon, lighting the way for what I believe to be the ultimate goal: the awakening of lightworkers. This vision paints a picture of unity, of souls coming together with a shared purpose to nurture and protect the new Earth that is our home. But the aspirations stretch further, aiming to prepare the ground for new souls ready to embrace a 5D Earth from their first breath. In this envisioned world, communication transcends the barriers that once seemed insurmountable. The dialogue between the spirit world and us becomes a fluid, continuous exchange, where those who have crossed over are not lost to us but remain present in a transformed essence, their energy mingling with ours despite the physical divide of dimensions.

In this new Earth, the limitations and labels that once constrained us dissolve. There's no room for fear in expressing or utilizing psychic abilities; instead, there's an encouragement, a societal enhancement, urging everyone to weave these capabilities into the fabric of daily life. It's a vision of a world unbound by the fears and restrictions that once stifled our spiritual potential and collective evolution.

What fuels this vision is not a solitary dream but a collective aspiration—a shared desire for a future where our connections to each other and the source of all existence are not hindered by physicality or societal constructs. It's a future where the direct line to the higher dimensions, our spirit guides, and even the source itself is open and actively engaged by all. This book, then, is more than a manual; it's a call to arms for the lightworkers among us, an invitation to step into the light and work together to realise this collective vision. It's a hope that these words not only resonate with you but spark a flame that lights the way for others, heralding the dawn of a new era where we all live in harmony with the higher dimensions, unencumbered by the physical and spiritual limitations that once defined our existence.

As this book ends, I want to express my gratitude for your journey and the invaluable contribution your radiant consciousness has made to our collective awakening.

If you found insight, comfort, or inspiration in these pages, I would be truly grateful if you could take a moment to leave a review. By leaving a review, you're not only sharing your thoughts but also helping to guide others towards their own spiritual awakening. Your words may inspire someone else to find the answers they seek. Together, let's contribute to the collective awakening and light the path for others on their journey.

Thank you, beautiful soul.

Love and Light

Ahmira

Sirian B & Mantis Hybrid Starseed

References

Grabovoi, G.P. (2003). *Restoration of the Human Organism through Concentration on Numbers.* Moscow: Grigori Grabovoi DOO.

Judith, A. (1987). *Wheels of Life: A User's Guide to the Chakra System.* St. Paul, MN: Llewellyn Publications.

Lawlor, R. (1982). *Sacred Geometry: Philosophy and Practice.* Thames & Hudson.

Marciniak, B. (1992). *Bringers of the Dawn: Teachings from the Pleiadians.* Bear & Company.

Parker, J., & Parker, D. (2001). *The New Complete Astrologer.* Dorling Kindersley.

Royal, L., & Priest, K. (1992). *The Prism of Lyra: An Exploration of Human Galactic Heritage.* Granite Publishing.

Tesla, N. (1900). *The Problem of Increasing Human Energy.* Century Magazine, June issue. Retrieved from various digital archives.

von Däniken, E. (1968). *Chariots of the Gods? Unsolved Mysteries of the Past.* Putnam.

Zohar, D. (1990). *The Quantum Self: Human Nature and Consciousness Defined by the New Physics.* New York, NY: William Morrow and Company.

Designs and Editing are from Olga Gerogianni

Please contact : olga.awaken888@gmail.com

for any enquiries

www.olgaawaken.com

www.ingramcontent.com/pod-product-compliance
Lightning Source LLC
Chambersburg PA
CBHW051432050726
47593CB00005B/1751